Rethinking International Trade

Rethinking International Trade

Paul R. Krugman

The MIT Press
Cambridge, Massachusetts
London, England

Second Printing, 1990

© 1990 Massachusetts Institute of Technology

This book was set in Palatino by Asco Trade Typesetting Ltd., Hong Kong and printed and bound by Halliday Lithograph in the United States of America.

Library of Congress Cataloging-in-Publication Data

Krugman, Paul R.
    Rethinking international trade / Paul R. Krugman.
        p.   cm.
    Bibliography: p.
    Includes index.
    ISBN 0-262-11148-9
    1. International trade—Congresses.   2. Competition, International—Congresses.
I. Title.
HF 1372.K78   1990   HF
382—dc20   1379
                     . K79   / 67581
                      1990
                                                            89-34673
                                                            CIP

Contents

Preface

This book collects papers written over a ten-year period. It is by no means a complete collected works: like many of my colleagues in this age of word processors and international conferences, I write too much, not all of it different. What this volume tries to do, instead, is offer a limited selection of papers that represent my main contribution to what for want of a better term I call the "new trade theory."

New trade theory is an approach to international trade that emphasizes precisely the features of the international economy that traditional trade theory leaves out: increasing returns and imperfect competition. The new approach emerged quite quickly in the late 1970s and represents a fundamental change in the way we think about international trade. Although I have worked in a number of other areas in international economics, from exchange rate determination to international debt, it is the research on new approaches to international trade that I regard as the main justification for my professional existence.

No one does research in a vacuum. I first began to think about imperfect competition and trade as a result of a short course given by Robert Solow; I was encouraged to take the risk of moving into this research area by my one-time teacher and now colleague Rudiger Dornbusch. In the early period when I found little acceptance for my ideas, crucial moral support came from Carlos Díaz-Alejandro. This is not to say that there was anything like a struggle between a stubborn old guard and the new idea: in fact, critical professional support was provided by the grand master of traditional theory, Jagdish Bhagwati (another of my former teachers). My longtime collaborator Elhanan Helpman, in addition to being a great innovative international economic theorist himself, has provided me with an example of professional integrity and intellectual discipline that I have badly needed.

Most of the work collected here was done under the auspices of two great Cambridge institutions. MIT's Department of Economics has some of the best faculty and unquestionably the best students in the world. The National Bureau of Economic Research has provided financial support and, more important, a kind of invisible college that has been invaluable in many ways.

The greatest thanks go, of course, to my family—to my parents and to my wife, Robin Bergman, who makes it all worthwhile.

Rethinking International Trade

Introduction

The past ten years have seen a remarkable change, a sort of quiet revolution, in the theory of international trade. As late as 1980 the study of international trade was widely regarded in the economics profession as a deeply conservative area marked by a reverence for intellectual tradition rare in the generally brash environment of North American economics. Beginning in the late 1970s, however, an initially small group of theorists began to develop a new approach to international trade, reopening the most basic questions in the field: Why is there international trade? What determines the international pattern of specialization? What are the effects of protectionism? What is the optimal trade policy? In each case the new theory has challenged the traditional wisdom.

The papers collected in this volume represent part of my own contribution to the new theory of international trade. This is not my first book-length venture in the area. Together with Elhanan Helpman of Tel-Aviv University I have written a pair of monographs on international trade: *Market Structure and Foreign Trade* (1985) and *Trade Policy and Market Structure* (1989). I have also edited a volume of informal essays in the field: *Strategic Trade Policy and the New International Economics* (1986). This collection supplements the other books, providing a more personal if less methodical tour of the new concepts that have emerged so rapidly over the past decade.

What Is the New Trade Theory?

If one had to provide a concrete example of what the new trade theory is about, it might be this: conventional trade theory views world trade as taking place entirely in goods like wheat; new trade theory sees it as being largely in goods like aircraft. Since a good part of world trade *is* in goods like wheat, and since even trade in aircraft is subject to some of the same influences that bear on trade in wheat, traditional theory has by no means been disposed of completely. Yet the new theory introduces a whole set of new possibilities and concerns.

Begin with the most basic question: Why is there international trade? The traditional theory answers, Because countries are different. Canada exports wheat to Japan because Canada has so much more arable land per capita, and as a result in the absence of trade wheat would be much cheaper in Canada. The differences between countries that drive trade may lie in resources, technology, or even in tastes, but in any case, traditional theory takes it as axiomatic that countries trade in order to take advantage of their differences.

The new theory acknowledges that differences between countries are one reason for trade, but it adds another: Countries may trade because there are inherent advantages to specialization. The economies of scale in aircraft manufacture are so large that the world market can accommodate at best only a few efficient-scale producers and thus only a few centers of production. Even if Japan and the United States were identical, it is likely that only one country would be producing (say) wide-bodied jet aircraft, and as a result there must be trade in order to allow the centers of production to serve the world market. Of course, the United States and Japan are not identical, but the new theory says that much trade, especially between similar countries, represents specialization to take advantage of increasing returns rather than to capitalize on inherent differences between the countries.

What determines the international pattern of specialization? In traditional theory the answer emerges from the explanation of trade itself: Countries produce goods that would have been relatively cheap in the absence of trade. Comparative advantage may arise from a variety of sources, but in any case the attributes of a country determine what it produces.

In the new theory an important element of arbitrariness is added to this story. Why are aircraft manufactured in Seattle? It is hard to argue that there is some unique attribute of the city's location that fully explains this. The point is, instead, that the logic of increasing returns mandates that aircraft production be concentrated *somewhere*, and Seattle just happens to be where the roulette wheel came to a stop. In many of the new models of trade, the actual location of production is to some degree indeterminate. Yet what the example of Seattle suggests, and what is explicit in some of the models, is a crucial role for history: Because Seattle (or Detroit or Silicon Valley) was where an industry initially got established, increasing returns keep the industry there.

What are the effects of protection? In traditional trade models a tariff or import quota raises the price of a good for both domestic producers and domestic consumers, reduces imports, and generally, except in some well-understood cases, is a bad thing. In new trade theory the result could be either much worse or much better. Let all countries protect domestic aircraft industries, and the result will be a fragmented world market in which losses arise not only from failure to specialize in accord with comparative advantage but also from inefficient scale production. On the other hand, an individual country that protects its aircraft industry might conceivably increase the scale of that industry sufficiently to reap a net benefit, possibly even lower prices to domestic consumers.

Finally, what is the optimal trade policy? Traditional theory is the usual basis for advocating free trade, one of the most strongly held positions in the economics profession (although actually even in traditional theory a second-best case can be made for protection as a corrective for domestic market failures). The new trade theory suggests a more complex view. The potential gains from trade are even larger in a world of increasing returns, and thus, in a way, the case for free trade is all the stronger. On the other hand, the aircraft example clearly suggests that an individual country acting alone may have reasons not to adopt free trade. New trade models show that it is *possible* (not certain) that such tools as export subsidies, temporary tariffs, and so on, may shift world specialization in a way favorable to the protecting nation.

The Problem of Market Structure

The brief description of the differences between old and new trade theory given above sounds very simple, and one may wonder why it took so long for the new theory to emerge. The main answer is that while trade based on increasing returns is easy to talk about in a general sense, it is difficult to model formally. Since economics as practiced in the English-speaking world is strongly oriented toward mathematical models, any economic argument that has not been expressed in that form tends to remain invisible. While many economists no doubt understood that increasing returns could explain international trade even in the absence of comparative advantage, before 1980 there were no clean and simple models making the point. As a result this idea was often simply left out of textbooks and trade courses, and even good trade theorists often seemed unaware of the possibility. It is always difficult to recapture the state of mind of a profession before a major change in thinking, but I can report from experience with early presentations of some of the papers here that in the late 1970s the role of scale economies in trade was neither well understood nor readily accepted.

The principal obstacle to formal modeling of increasing returns in trade before the late 1970s was the problem of market structure. In general, increasing returns are inconsistent with perfect competition, and economists in general and trade theorists in particular have usually relied on the assumption of perfect competition to make their models tractable. Perfect competition requires, in particular, that price equal marginal cost, yet in an environment of increasing returns, marginal cost pricing would lead to universal losses. The only exception is where the increasing returns are wholly external to firms, that is, where costs fall with the size of the industry but not with the size of the firms that comprise it. External economies are, however, theoretically awkward and empirically elusive. Although a small literature on trade in the presence of external scale economies existed before the great change in the field, it was a literature with little influence.

What made the difference was the revolution in industrial organization theory during the 1970s. Once upon a time the field of industrial organization was largely atheoretical—a matter of case studies and summary regressions. During the 1970s, however, economists began to offer a variety of explicit models of behavior in imperfectly competitive markets, in what eventually became an explosion of theory. At a certain point the idea of applying these models to international trade was bound to occur to somebody, and by the late 1970s several people were independently working on models of trade that drew for the first time on industrial organization concepts.

Surprisingly, it proved possible to develop models of trade in the presence of increasing returns and imperfect competition that were not only illuminating but also simple and elegant. The long dominance of Ricardo over Smith—of comparative advantage over increasing returns—was largely due to the belief that the alternative was necessarily a mess. In effect, the theory of international trade followed the perceived line of least mathematical resistance. Once it was clear that papers on noncomparative-advantage trade could be just as tight and clean as papers in the traditional mold, the field was ripe for rapid transformation.

Somewhat surprisingly, a side product of the emergence of models that combine industrial organization and trade theory has been a mild resurgence of interest in external economies. This is partly because some models with increasing returns give rise to effects that closely resemble external economies, for example, when there are increasing returns in the production of intermediate goods. More important, perhaps, is that once the role of increasing returns was legitimized as a concern of trade theory, all forms of increasing returns were given greater respect. It is also true that some of the modeling tricks used to make industrial organization models tractable turn out to work on external economies too.

Themes of the New Trade Theory

The papers collected in this book are organized into four parts reflecting four themes that have emerged in the new literature on international trade.

The Causes of International Trade

The original purpose of the new trade theory was to offer an alternative answer to the most basic question of international economics: the reason for international trade. Chapter 1 presents the view in its starkest form: this is a model in which trade arises entirely because of increasing returns, in a world of initially identical countries. In chapter 2 this view is elaborated upon in a model that can accommodate transport costs and differences in demand patterns among countries. The main additional insight from this chapter is the "home market effect," the tendency of countries to export goods for which they have a relatively large domestic market. This insight turned out to play a significant role in the analysis of trade policy.

Not too surprisingly, few of my colleagues were eager to drop well-studied models of comparative advantage in favor of an approach that could not make any allowance for comparative advantage at all, nor were they eager to adopt the new approach unless it could be demonstrated that it made a difference. Chapter 3 represents an effort to overcome both sources of resistance. It offers a model in which both comparative advantage and increasing returns give rise to trade and in which the relative importance of the two motives can be measured by a pair of parameters. It shows how the pattern and volume of trade is altered by the presence of scale economies. More important in terms of selling the new theory, I was able to show how the effects of trade on the distribution of income depended crucially on the motives for trade.

One might have thought that once comparative advantage and economies of scale were included, one had a complete accounting of the possible reasons for international trade. However, in a surprising paper James Brander (1981) pointed out that oligopolistic firms might well sell into each others' markets even in the absence of both comparative advantage and increasing returns. Brander's original model depended on the assumption of zero transport costs and thus was dismissed by some economists as a trivial case. What he and I attempted to do in chapter 4 was show that the case was by no means trivial but rather a true alternative to both comparative advantage and increasing returns for explaining trade.

Chapter 5 is a survey that ties together themes not only from my own work but from the work of the other economists who developed the new trade theory. It also presents in a brief form some of the key lines of thought from my first monograph with Elhanan Helpman (Helpman and Krugman 1985), a work that tried, among other things, to go beyond the special assumptions of the monopolistic competition models and find the deeper underlying structure.

The Role of History

Part II of the collection contains three papers in a line of work that is still relatively undeveloped. As suggested earlier in this introduction, in the presence of increasing returns—perhaps especially when these increasing returns take the form of external economies—history matters. A pattern of specialization can be established as a result of accident or some initial difference in countries' resources, then get locked in by the cumulative advantages that go with large scale.

Chapter 6 applies this idea to the perennial question of why some countries are richer than others. It was written at a time when the agitation for a New International Economic Order was still at its height, and the purpose of the paper was to show what kind of model was necessary to make sense of the then widely popular doctrine of uneven development. Fashions in politics come and go, but the model is still, I believe, useful as a sharp-edged presentation of the idea that a small initial disparity in industrialization can lead to growing inequality over time.

Chapter 7 shows how learning by doing can lock in a pattern of international specialization and how temporary shocks, including temporary protection, can have permanent effects on who produces what. This chapter is also almost unique in the volume, and indeed in the whole literature, in linking long-run specialization and trade to short-run monetary and exchange rate developments.

Chapter 8 links monetary economics to the new trade theory in a different way. It points out that the special role of a few currencies as international media of exchange is unquestionably the result of increasing returns, and it follows this line of argument to show that the international monetary system has the characteristic features that the new trade theory tells us to expect: arbitrary specialization (in this case selection of one currency as vehicle), multiple possible equilibria, and a key role for history.

Technology and Trade

There is a natural alliance between the new trade theory, with its emphasis on increasing returns and imperfect competition, and the view that technological change is a key factor driving international specialization. The two views are not necessarily linked: conventional trade theory can say many useful things about the *effects* of technological change (though little about its causes), and many of the new models focus on garden-variety static scale economies. Nonetheless, technological development is normally an increasing returns process carried out in imperfectly competitive industries, and the most important sources of increasing returns in practice probably lie in dynamic economies of learning and R&D.

Chapters 9 and 10 are actually conventional trade models that borrow techniques and images from the new trade theory to examine the effects of technology on trade. The first is a product cycle model that examines the effects of continuous product innovation; the second a model that is similar in spirit but focuses on process innovation instead. In each case the key question is whether a country needs to keep running in order to stay in the same place. That is, in a dynamic world does a country that fails to innovate suffer an absolute as well as a relative decline in its standard of living? The answer in both cases is a qualified yes.

Chapter 11 ties the analysis of technology and trade to the new trade theory; it shows how the increasing returns inherent in innovation lead to imperfect competition and, conversely, how temporary monopoly is a necessary incentive for technological change.

Trade Policy

To many people the bottom line of any economic theory must be its implications for policy. I am not sure this is the case: in the long run contributing to understanding may be more important than offering an immediate guide for action. Still, a good deal of the excitement around the new trade theory has been generated by the possibility that it may offer new arguments against free trade.

Chapters 12 and 13 focus on one issue that has assumed a great deal of practical prominence in U.S. trade disputes with Japan: the idea that a protected domestic market is actually an export promotion device and that such export promotion can be a successful beggar-thy-neighbor strategy. Chapter 12 sets out the theory; chapter 13, coauthored with Richard Baldwin, is an application to the case of international competition in semiconductors.

Finally, chapter 14 is an attempt to take stock of the role of imperfect competition in trade theory. While it was originally intended as a general survey for industrial organization theorists, it focuses largely on the policy issues.

I

Rethinking the Causes of International Trade

1 Increasing Returns, Monopolistic Competition, and International Trade

1.1 Introduction

It has been widely recognized that economies of scale provide an alternative to differences in technology or factor endowments as an explanation of international specialization and trade. The role of economies of large-scale production is a major subtheme in the work of Ohlin (1933), while some authors, especially Balassa (1967) and Kravis (1971), have argued that scale economies play a crucial role in explaining the postwar growth in trade among the industrial countries. Nonetheless, increasing returns as a cause of trade has received relatively little attention from formal trade theory. The main reason for this neglect seems to be that it has appeared difficult to deal with the implications of increasing returns for market structure.

This chapter develops a simple formal model in which trade is caused by economies of scale instead of differences in factor endowments or technology. The approach differs from that of most other formal treatments of trade under increasing returns, which assume that scale economies are external to firms, so that markets remain perfectly competitive.[1] Instead, scale economies are here assumed to be internal to firms, with the market structure that emerges being one of Chamberlinian monopolistic competition.[2] The formal treatment of monopolistic competition is borrowed with slight modifications from recent work by Dixit and Stiglitz (1977). A Chamberlinian formulation of the problem turns out to have several advantages. First, it yields a very simple model; the analysis of increasing returns and trade is hardly more complicated than the two good Ricardian model. Second, the model is free from the multiple equilibria that are the rule when economies are external to firms, and that can detract from the main point.

Originally published in the *Journal of International Economics* 9, 4 (November 1979): 469–479.

Finally, the model's picture of trade in a large number of differentiated products fits in well with the empirical literature on "intraindustry" trade (e.g., Grubel and Lloyd 1975).

The chapter is organized as follows: Section 1.2 develops the basic modified Dixit-Stiglitz model of monopolistic competition for a closed economy. Section 1.3 then examines the effects of opening trade as well as the essentially equivalent effects of population growth and factor mobility. Finally, section 1.4 summarizes the results and suggests some conclusions.

1.2 Monopolistic Competition in a Closed Economy

This section develops the basic model of monopolistic competition with which I will work in the next sections. The model is a simplified version of the model developed by Dixit and Stiglitz. Instead of trying to develop a general model, this paper will assume particular forms for utility and cost functions. The functional forms chosen give the model a simplified structure which makes the analysis easier.

Consider, then, an economy with only one scarce factor of production, labor. The economy is assumed able to produce any of a large number of goods, with the goods indexed by i. We order the goods so that those actually produced range from 1 to n, where n is also assumed to be a large number, although small relative to the number of potential products.

All residents are assumed to share the same utility function, into which all goods enter symmetrically.

$$U = \sum_{i=1}^{n} v(c_i), \qquad v' > 0, \qquad v'' < 0, \tag{1}$$

where c_i is the consumption of the ith good.

It will be useful to define a variable, ε, where

$$\varepsilon_i = -\frac{v'}{v'' c_i}, \tag{2}$$

and where we assume $\partial \varepsilon_i / \partial c_i < 0$. The variable ε_i will turn out to be the elasticity of demand facing an individual producer; the reasons for assuming that is is decreasing in c_i will become apparent later.

All goods are also assumed to be produced with the same cost function. The labor used in producing each good is a linear function of output,

$$l_i = \alpha + \beta x_i, \qquad \alpha, \beta > 0, \tag{3}$$

where l_i is labor used in producing good i, x_i is the output of good i, and α

is a fixed cost. In other words, there are decreasing average costs and constant marginal costs.

Production of a good must equal the sum of individual consumptions of the good. If we identify individuals with workers, production must equal the consumption of a representative individual times the labor force:

$$x_i = Lc_i. \tag{4}$$

Finally, we assume full employment, so that the total labor force L must be exhausted by employment in production of individual goods:

$$L = \sum_{i=1}^{n} l_i = \sum_{i=1}^{n} [\alpha + \beta x_i]. \tag{5}$$

Now there are three variables we want to determine: the price of each good relative to wages, p_i/w; the output of each good, x_i; and the number of goods produced, n. The symmetry of the problem will ensure that all goods actually produced will be produced in the same quantity and at the same price, so that we can use the shorthand notation

$$\left. \begin{array}{l} p = p_i \\ x = x_i \end{array} \right\}, \qquad \text{for all } i. \tag{6}$$

We can proceed in three stages. First, we analyze the demand curve facing an individual firm; then we derive the pricing policy of firms and relate profitability to output; finally, we use an analysis of profitability and entry to determine the number of firms.

To analyze the demand curve facing the firm producing some particular product, consider the behavior of a representative individual. He will maximize his utility (1) subject to a budget constraint. The first-order conditions from that maximization problem have the form

$$v'(c_i) = \lambda p_i, \qquad i = 1, \dots, n, \tag{7}$$

where λ is the shadow price on the budget constraint, which can be interpreted as the marginal utility of income.

We can substitute the relationship between individual consumption and output into (7) to turn it into an expression for the demand facing an individual firm,

$$p_i = \lambda^{-1} v'\left(\frac{x_i}{L}\right). \tag{8}$$

If the number of goods produced is large, each firm's pricing policy will have a negligible effect on the marginal utility of income, so that it can take

λ as fixed. In that case the elasticity of demand facing the ith firm will, as already noted, be $\varepsilon_i = -v'/v''c_i$.

Now let us consider profit-maximizing pricing behavior. Each individual firm, being small relative to the economy, can ignore the effects of its decisions on the decisions of other firms. Thus, the ith firm will choose its price to maximize its profits.

$$\Pi_i = p_i x_i - (\alpha + \beta x_i)w. \tag{9}$$

The profit-maximizing price will depend on marginal cost and on the elasticity of demand:

$$p_i = \frac{\varepsilon}{\varepsilon - 1}\beta w \tag{10}$$

or $p/w = \beta\varepsilon/(\varepsilon - 1)$.

Now this does not determine the price, since the elasticity of demand depends on output; thus, to find the profit-maximizing price we would have to derive profit-maximizing output as well. It will be easier, however, to determine output and prices by combining (10) with the condition that profits be zero in equilibrium.

Profits will be driven to zero by entry of new firms. The process is illustrated in figure 1.1. The horizontal axis measures output of a representative firm: the vertical axis revenue and cost expressed in wage units. Total cost is shown by TC, while OR and OR' represent revenue functions. Suppose that given the initial number of firms, the revenue function facing each firm is given by OR. The firm will then choose its output so as to set marginal revenue equal to marginal cost, at A. At that point, since price (average revenue) exceeds average cost, firms will make profits. But this will lead entrepreneurs to start new firms. As they do so, the marginal utility of income will rise and the revenue function will shrink in. Eventually equilibrium will be reached at a point such as B, where it is true both that marginal revenue equals marginal cost and that average revenue equals average cost. This is, of course, Chamberlin's famous tangency solution (Chamberlin 1962).

To characterize this equilibrium more carefully, we need to show how the price and output of a representative firm can be derived from cost and utility functions. In figure 1.2 the horizontal axis shows *per capita* consumption of a representative good, while the vertical axis shows the price of a representative good in wage units. We have one relationship between c and p/w in the pricing condition (10), which is shown as the curve PP. Price lies everywhere above marginal cost and increases with c because, by assumption, the elasticity of demand falls with c.

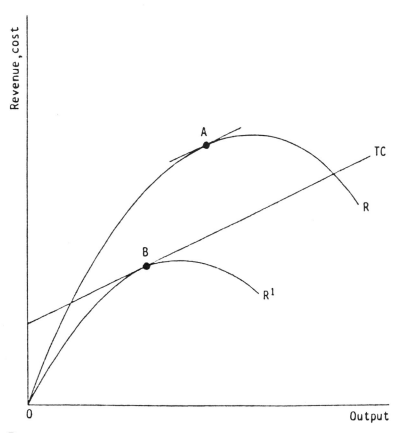

Figure 1.1

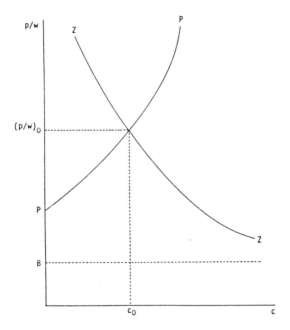

Figure 1.2

A second relationship between p/w and c can be derived from the condition of zero profits in equilibrium. From (9), we have

$$0 = px - (\alpha + \beta x)w, \tag{11}$$

which can be rewritten

$$\frac{p}{w} = \beta + \frac{\alpha}{x} = \beta + \frac{\alpha}{Lc}. \tag{12}$$

This is a rectangular hyperbola above the line $p/w = \beta$, and is shown in figure 1.2 as ZZ.

The intersection of the PP and ZZ schedules determines individual consumption of each good and the price of each good. From the consumption of each good we have output per firm, since $x = Lc$. And the assumption of full employment lets us determine the number of goods produced:

$$n = \frac{L}{\alpha + \beta x}. \tag{13}$$

We now have a complete description of equilibrium in the economy. It is indeterminate *which* n goods are produced, but it is also unimportant, since the goods enter into utility and cost symmetrically. We can now use the model to analyze the related questions of the effects of growth, trade, and factor mobility.

1.3   Growth, Trade, and Factor Mobility

The model developed in the last section was a one-factor model, but one in which there were economies of scale in the use of that factor, so that in a real sense the division of labor was limited by the extent of the market. In this section we consider three ways in which the extent of the market might increase: growth in the labor force, trade, and migration.

Effects of Labor Force Growth

Suppose that an economy of the kind analyzed in the last section were to experience an increase in its labor force. What effect would this have? We can analyze some of the effects by examining figure 1.3. The PP and ZZ schedules have the same definitions as in figure 1.2; before the increase in the labor force equilibrium is at A. By referring back to equations (10) and (11) we can see that an increase in L has no effect on PP but that it causes ZZ to shift left. The new equilibrium is at B: c falls, and so does p/w. We can show, however, that both the output of each good and the number of

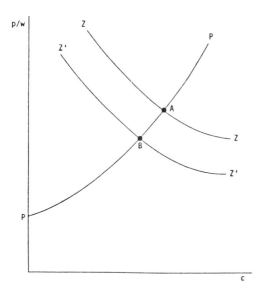

Figure 1.3

goods produced rise. By rearranging (12), we have

$$x = \frac{\alpha}{p/w - \beta},$$
(14)

which shows that output must rise; since $n = L/(\alpha + \beta Lc)$, a rise in L and a fall in c imply a rise in n.

Notice that these results depend on the fact that the PP curve slopes upward, which in turn depends on the assumption that the elasticity of demand falls with c. This assumption, which might alternatively be stated as an assumption that the elasticity of demand rises when the price of a good is increased, seems plausible. In any case, it seems to be necessary if this model is to yield reasonable results, and I make the assumption without apology.

We can also consider the welfare implications of growth. Comparisons of overall welfare would be illegitimate, but we can look at the welfare of representative individuals. This rises for two reasons: there is a rise in the "real wage" w/p, and there is also a gain from increased choice, as the number of available products increases.

I have considered the case of growth at some length, even though our principal concern is with trade, because the results of the analysis of growth will be useful next, when we turn to the analysis of trade.

Effects of Trade

Suppose there exist two economies of the kind analyzed in section 1.2, and that they are initially unable to trade. To make the point most strongly, assume that the countries have identical tastes and technologies. (Since this is a one-factor model, we have already ruled out differences in factor endowments.) In a conventional model, there would be no reason for trade to occur between these economies, and no potential gains from trade. In this model, however, there will be both trade and gains from trade.

To see this, suppose that trade is opened between these two economies at zero transportation cost. Symmetry will ensure that wage rates in the two countries will be equal and that the price of any good produced in either country will be the same. The effect will be the same as if *each* country had experienced an increase in its labor force. As in the case of growth in a closed economy, there will be an increase both in the scale of production and in the range of goods available for consumption. Welfare in both countries will increase, both because of higher w/p and because of increased choice.

The direction of trade—which country exports which goods—is indeterminate; all that we can say is that each good will be produced only in one country, because there is (in this model) no reason for firms to compete for markets. The *volume* of trade, however, is determinate. Each individual will be maximizing his utility function, which may be written

$$U = \sum_{i=1}^{n} v(c_i) + \sum_{i=n+1}^{n+n^*} v(c_i), \tag{15}$$

where goods $1, \ldots, n$ are produced in the home country and $n + 1, \ldots,$ $n + n^*$ in the foreign country. The number of goods produced in each country will be proportional to the labor forces:

$$n = \frac{L}{\alpha + \beta x},$$

$$n^* = \frac{L^*}{\alpha + \beta x}. \tag{16}$$

Since all goods will have the same price, expenditures on each country's goods will be proportional to the country's force. The share of imports in home country expenditures, for instance, will be $L^*/(L + L^*)$; the values of imports of each country will be national income times the import share, i.e.,

$$M = \frac{wL \cdot L^*}{L + L^*}$$

$$= \frac{wLL^*}{L + L^*} \tag{17}$$

$$= M^*.$$

Trade is balanced, as it must be, since each individual agent's budget constraint is satisfied. The volume of trade as a fraction of world income is maximizied when the economies are of equal size.

We might note that the result that the volume of trade is determinate but the direction of trade is not is very similar to the well-known argument of Linder (1961). This suggests an affinity between this model and Linder's views, although Linder does not explicitly mention economies of scale.

The important point to be gained from this analysis is that economies of scale can be shown to give rise to trade and to gains from trade even when there are no international differences in tastes, technology, or factor endowments.

Effects of Factor Mobility[3]

An interesting extension of the model results when we allow for movement of labor between countries or regions. There is a parallel here with Heckscher-Ohlin theory. Mundell (1957) has shown that in a Heckscher-Ohlin world trade and factor mobility would be substitutes for another and that factor movements would be induced by impediments to trade such as tariffs or transportation costs. The same kinds of results emerge from this model.

To see this, suppose that there are two regions of the kind we have been discussing and that they have the same tastes and technologies. There is room for mutual gains from trade, because the combined market would allow both greater variety of goods and a greater scale of production. The same gains could be obtained without trade, however, if the population of one region were to migrate to the other. In this model, trade and growth in the labor force are essentially equivalent.

If there are impediments to trade, there will be an incentive for workers to move to the region that already has the larger labor force. This is clearest if we consider the extreme case where no trade in goods is possible but labor is perfectly mobile. Then the more populous region will offer both a greater real wage w/p and a greater variety of goods, inducing immigration. In equilibrium all workers will have concentrated in one region or the other. Which region ends up with the population depends on initial conditions; in the presence of increasing returns history matters.

Before proceeding further we should ask what aspect of reality, if any, is captured by the story we have just told. In the presence of increasing returns factor mobility appears to produce a process of agglomeration. If we had considered a many-region model the population would still have tended to accumulate in only one region, which we may as well label a city; for this analysis seems to make most sense as an account of the growth of metropolitan areas. The theory of urban growth suggested by this model is of the "city lights" variety: people migrate to the city in part because of the greater variety of consumption goods it offers.

Let us return now to the two-region case to make a final point. We have seen that which region ends up with the population depends on the initial distribution of population. As long as labor productivity is the same in both regions, though, there is no difference in welfare between the two possible outcomes. If there is any difference in the conditions of production between the two regions, however, it does matter which gets the population—and the process of migration can lead to the wrong outcome.

Consider, for example, a case in which both fixed and variable labor costs are higher in one region. Then it is clearly desirable that all labor should move to the other region. But if the inferior region starts with a large enough share of the population, migration may move in the wrong direction.

To summarize: in the model of this paper, as in some more conventional trade models, factor mobility can substitute for trade. If there are impediments to trade, labor will concentrate in a single region; which region depends on the initial distribution of population. Finally, the process of agglomeration may lead population to concentrate in the wrong place.

1.4 Summary and Conclusions

This chapter adapts a Chamberlinian approach to the analysis of trade under conditions of increasing returns to scale. It shows that trade need not be a result of international differences in technology or factor endowments. Instead, trade may simply be a way of extending the market and allowing exploitation of scale economies, with the effects of trade being similar to those of labor force growth and regional agglomeration. This is a view of trade that appears to be useful in understanding trade among the industrial countries.

What is surprising about this analysis is that it is extremely simple. While the role of economies of scale in causing trade has been known for some time, it has been underemphasized in formal trade theory (and in textbooks). This chapter shows that a clear, rigorous, and, one hopes, persuasive model of trade under conditions of increasing returns can be constructed. Perhaps this will help give economies of scale a more prominent place in trade theory.

2 Scale Economies, Product Differentiation, and the Pattern of Trade

For some time now there has been considerable skepticism about the ability of comparative cost theory to explain the actual pattern of international trade. Neither the extensive trade among the industrial countries nor the prevalence in this trade of two-way exchanges of differentiated products make much sense in terms of standard theory. As a result many people have concluded that a new framework for analyzing trade is needed.[1] The main elements of such a framework—economies of scale, the possibility of product differentiation, and imperfect competition—have been discussed by such authors as Bela Balassa, Herbert Grubel (1967, 1970), and Irving Kravis and have been "in the air" for many years. In this chapter I present a simple formal analysis that incorporates these elements and show how it can be used to shed light on some issues that cannot be handled in more conventional models. These include, in particular, the causes of trade between economies with similar factor endowments and the role of a large domestic market in encouraging exports.

The basic model of this chapter is one in which there are economies of scale in production and in which firms can costlessly differentiate their products. In this model, which is derived from recent work by Avinash Dixit and Joseph Stiglitz, equilibrium takes the form of Chamberlinian monopolistic competition: Each firm has some monopoly power, but entry drives monopoly profits to zero. When two imperfectly competitive economies of this kind are allowed to trade, increasing returns produce trade and gains from trade even if the economies have identical tastes, technology, and factor endowments. This basic model of trade is presented in section 2.1. It is closely related to a model I have developed elsewhere; in this paper a somewhat more restrictive formulation of demand is used to make the analysis in later sections easier.

Originally published in *American Economic* Review 70 (1980): 950–959.

The rest of the chapter is concerned with two extensions of the basic model. In section 2.2, I examine the effect of transportation costs, and show that countries with larger domestic markets will, other things equal, have higher wage rates. Section 2.3 then deals with "home market" effects on trade patterns. It provides a formal justification for the commonly made argument that countries will tend to export those goods for which they have relatively large domestic markets.

This chapter makes no pretense of generality. The models presented rely on extremely restrictive assumptions about cost and utility. Nonetheless, it is to be hoped that the paper provides some useful insights into those aspects of international trade which simply cannot be treated in our usual models.

2.1 The Basic Model

Assumptions of the Model

There are assumed to be a large number of potential goods, all of which enter symmetrically into demand. Specifically, we assume that all individuals in the economy have the same utility functions.

$$U = \sum_i c_i^\theta, \qquad 0 < \theta < 1, \tag{1}$$

where c_i is consumption of the ith good. The number of goods actually produced, n, will be assumed to be large, although smaller than the potential range of products.[2]

There will be assumed to be only one factor of production, labor. All goods will be produced with the same cost function:

$$l_i = \alpha + \beta x_i \qquad \alpha, \beta > 0, \quad i = 1, \dots, n, \tag{2}$$

where l_i is labor used in producing the ith good and x_i is output of that good. In other words, I assume a fixed cost and constant marginal cost. Average cost declines at all levels of output, although at a diminishing rate.

Output of each good must equal the sum of individual consumptions. If we can identify individuals with workers, output must equal consumption of a representative individual times the labor force:

$$x_i = Lc_i, \qquad i = 1, \dots, n. \tag{3}$$

We also assume full employment, so that the total labor force must just be exhausted by labor used in production:

$$L = \sum_{i=1}^{n} (\alpha + \beta x_i). \tag{4}$$

Finally, we assume that firms maximize profits but that there is free entry and exit of firms, so that in equilibrium profits will always be zero.

Equilibrium in a Closed Economy

We can now proceed to analyze equilibrium in a closed economy described by the assumptions just laid out. The analysis proceeds in three stages. First I analyze consumer behavior to derive demand functions. Then profit-maximizing behavior by firms is derived, treating the number of firms as given. Finally, the assumption of free entry is used to determine the equilibrium number of firms.

The reason that a Chamberlinian approach is useful here is that, in spite of imperfect competition, the equilibrium of the model is determinate in all essential respects because the special nature of demand rules out strategic interdependence among firms. Because firms can costlessly differentiate their products, and all products enter symmetrically into demand, two firms will never want to produce the same product; each good will be produced by only one firm. At the same time, if the number of goods produced is large, the effect of the price of any one good on the demand for any other will be negligible. The result is that each firm can ignore the effect of its actions on other firms' behavior, eliminating the indeterminacies of oligopoly.

Consider, then, an individual maximizing (1) subject to a budget constraint. The first-order conditions from that maximum problem have the form

$$\theta c_i^{\theta-1} = \lambda p_i, \qquad i = 1, \dots, n, \tag{5}$$

where p_i is the price of the ith good and λ is the shadow price on the budget constraint, that is, the marginal utility of income. Since all individuals are alike, (5) can be rearranged to show the demand curve for the ith good, which we have already argued is the demand curve facing the single firm producing that good:

$$p_i = \theta \lambda^{-1} \left(\frac{x_i}{L} \right)^{\theta-1} \qquad i = 1, \dots, n. \tag{6}$$

Provided that there are a large number of goods being produced, the pricing decision of any one firm will have a negligible effect on the marginal utility of income. In that case, (6) implies that each firm faces a demand curve with an elasticity of $1/(1 - \theta)$, and the profit-maximizing price is therefore

$$p_i = \theta^{-1} \beta w \qquad i = 1, \ldots, n \tag{7}$$

where w is the wage rate and prices and wages can be defined in terms of any (common!) unit. Note that since θ, β, and w are the same for all firms, prices are the same for all goods and we can adopt the shorthand $p = p_i$ for all i.

The price p is independent of output given the special assumptions about cost and utility (which is the reason for making these particular assumptions). To determine profitability, however, we need to look at output. Profits of the firm producing good i are

$$\pi_i = p x_i - \{\alpha + \beta x_i\} w, \qquad i = 1, \ldots, n. \tag{8}$$

If profits are positive, new firms will enter, causing the marginal utility of income to rise and profits to fall until profits are driven to zero. In equilibrium, then, $\pi = 0$, implying for the output of a representative firm:

$$x_i = \frac{\alpha}{p/w - \beta} - \frac{\alpha\theta}{\beta(1 - \theta)}, \qquad i = 1, \ldots, n. \tag{9}$$

Thus output per firm is determined by the zero-profit condition. Again, since α, β, and θ are the same for all firms, we can use the shorthand $x = x_i$ for all i.

Finally, we can determine the number of goods produced by using the condition of full employment. From (4) and (9), we have

$$n = \frac{L}{\alpha + \beta x} = \frac{L(1 - \theta)}{\alpha}. \tag{10}$$

Effects of Trade

Now suppose that two countries of the kind just analyzed open trade with one another at zero transportation cost. To make the point most clearly, suppose that the countries have the same tastes and technologies; since we are in a one-factor world there cannot be any differences in factor endowments. What will happen?

In this model there are none of the conventional reasons for trade; but there will nevertheless be both trade and gains from trade. Trade will occur because, in the presence of increasing returns, each good (i.e., each differentiated product) will be produced in only one country—for the same reasons that each good is produced by only one firm. Gains from trade will occur because the world economy will produce a greater diversity of goods than would either country alone, offering each individual a wider range of choice.

We can easily characterize the world economy's equilibrium. The symmetry of the situation ensures that the two countries will have the same wage rate and that the price of any good produced in either country will be the same. The number of goods produced in each country can be determined from the full-employment condition

$$n = \frac{L(1 - \theta)}{\alpha},$$

$$n^* = \frac{L^*(1 - \theta)}{\alpha},$$

(11)

where L^* is the labor force of the second country and n^* the number of goods produced there.

Individuals will still maximize the utility function (1), but they will now distribute their expenditure over both the n goods produced in the home country and the n^* goods produced in the foreign country. Because of the extended range of choice, welfare will increase even though the "real wage" w/p (i.e., the wage rate in terms of a representative good) remains unchanged. Also, the symmetry of the problem allows us to determine trade flows. It is apparent that individuals in the home country will spend a fraction $n^*/(n + n^*)$ of their income on foreign goods, while foreigners spend $n/(n + n^*)$ of their income on home country products. Thus the value of home country imports measured in wage units is $Ln^*/(n + n^*) = LL^*/(L + L^*)$. This equals the value of foreign country imports, confirming that with equal wage rates in the two countries we will have balance-of-payments equilibrium.

Notice, however, that while the *volume* of trade is determinate, the *direction* of trade—which country produces which goods—is not. This indeterminacy seems to be a general characteristic of models in which trade is a consequence of economies of scale. One of the convenient features of the models considered in this paper is that nothing important hinges on who produces what within a group of differentiated products. There is an indeterminacy, but it doesn't matter. This result might not hold up in less special models.

Finally, I should note a peculiar feature of the effects of trade in this model. Both before and after trade, equation (9) holds; that is, there is no effect of trade on the scale of production, and the gains from trade come solely through increased product diversity. This is an unsatisfactory result. In another paper I have developed a slightly different model in which trade leads to an increase in scale of production as well as an increase in diversity.[3] That model is, however, more dificult to work with, so that it seems worth sacrificing some realism to gain tractability here.

2.2 Transport Costs

In this section I extend the model to allow for some transportation costs. This is not in itself an especially interesting extension although the main result—that the larger country will, other things being equal, have the higher wage rate—is somewhat surprising. The main purpose of the extension is, however, to lay the groundwork for the analysis of home market effects in the next section. (These effects can obviously occur only if there are transportation costs.) I begin by describing the behavior of individual agents, then analyze the equilibrium.

Individual Behavior

Consider a world consisting of two countries of the type analyzed in section 2.1, able to trade but only at a cost. Transportation costs will be assumed to be of the "iceberg" type, that is, only a fraction g of any good shipped arrives, with $1 - g$ lost in transit. This is a major simplifying assumption, as will be seen below.

An individual in the home country will have a choice over n products produced at home and n^* products produced abroad. The price of a domestic product will be the same as that received by the producer, p. Foreign products will cost more than the producer's price; if foreign firms charge p^*, home country consumers will have to pay the c.i.f. price $\hat{p}^* = p^*/g$. Similarly foreign buyers of domestic products will pay $\hat{p} = p/g$.

Since the prices to consumers of goods of different countries will in general not be the same, consumption of each imported good will differ from consumption of each domestic good. Home country residents, for example, in maximizing utility will consume $(p/\hat{p}^*)^{1/(1-\theta)}$ units of a representative imported good for each unit of a representative domestic good they consume.

To determine world equilibrium, however, it is not enough to look at consumption; we must also take into account the quantities of goods used up in transit. If a domestic resident consumes one unit of a foreign good, his combined direct and indirect demand is for $1/g$ units. For determining total demand, then, we need to know the ratio of total demand by domestic residents for each foreign product to demand for each domestic product. Letting σ denote this ratio and σ^* the corresponding ratio for the other country, we can show that

$$\sigma = \left(\frac{p}{p^*}\right)^{1/(1-\theta)} g^{\theta/(1-\theta)},$$

$$\sigma^* = \left(\frac{p}{p^*}\right)^{-1/(1-\theta)} g^{\theta/(1-\theta)}. \tag{12}$$

The overall demand pattern of each individual can then be derived from the requirement that his spending just equal his wage; that is, in the home country we must have $(np + \sigma n^* p^*)d = w$, where d is the consumption of a representative domestic good; and similarly in the foreign country.

This behavior of individuals can now be used to analyze the behavior of firms. The important point to notice is that the elasticity of *export* demand facing any given firm is $1/(1 - \theta)$, which is the same as the elasticity of *domestic* demand. Thus transportation costs have no effect on firms' pricing policy; and the analysis of section 2.1 can be carried out as before, showing that transportation costs also have no effect on the number of firms or output per firm in either country.

Writing out these conditions again, we have

$$p = \frac{w\beta}{\theta}, \qquad p^* = \frac{w^*\beta}{\theta},$$

$$n = \frac{L(1 - \theta)}{\alpha}, \qquad n^* = \frac{L^*(1 - \theta)}{\alpha}. \tag{13}$$

The only way in which introducing transportation costs modifies the results of section 2.1 is in allowing the possibility that wages may not be equal in the two countries; the number and size of firms are not affected. This strong result depends on the assumed form of the transport costs, which shows at the same time how useful and how special the assumed form is.

Determination of Equilibrium

The model we have been working with has a very strong structure—so strong that transport costs have no effect either on the numbers of goods

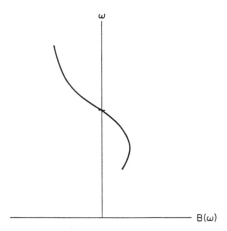

Figure 2.1

produced in the countries, n and n^*, or on the prices relative to wages, p/w and p^*/w^*. The only variable that can be affected is the relative wage rate $w/w^* = \omega$, which no longer need be equal to one.

We can determine ω by looking at any one of three equivalent market-clearing conditions: equality of demand and supply for home country labor, equality of demand and supply for foreign country labor, and balance-of-payments equilibrium. It will be easiest to work in terms of the balance of payments. If we combine (12) with the other equations of the model, it can be shown that the home country's balance of payments, measured in *wage units* of the *other* country, is

$$B = \frac{\sigma^* n\omega}{\sigma^* n + n^*} L^* - \frac{\sigma n^*}{n + \sigma n^*} \omega L$$

$$= \omega L L^* \left[\frac{\sigma^*}{\sigma^* L + L^*} - \frac{\sigma}{L + \sigma L^*} \right].$$

(14)

Since σ and σ^* are both functions of $p/p^* = \omega$, the condition $B = 0$ can be used to determine the relative wage. The function $B(\omega)$ is illustrated in figure 2.1. The relative wage $\bar{\omega}$ is that relative wage at which the expression in brackets in (4) is zero and at which trade is therefore balanced. Since σ is an increasing function of ω and σ^* a decreasing function of ω, $B(\omega)$ will be negative (positive) if and only if ω is greater (less) than $\bar{\omega}$, which shows that $\bar{\omega}$ is the unique equilibrium relative wage.

We can use this result to establish a simple proposition: *that the larger country, other things being equal, will have the higher wage.* To see this, suppose that we were to compute $B(\omega)$ for $\omega = 1$. In that case we have $\sigma = \sigma^* < 1$. The expression for the balance of payments reduces to

$$B = LL^* \left[\frac{1}{\sigma L + L^*} - \frac{1}{L + \sigma L^*} \right]. \tag{14'}$$

But (14') will be positive if $L > L^*$, negative if $L < L^*$. This means that the equilibrium relative wage ω must be greater than one if $L > L^*$, less than one if $L < L^*$.

This is an interesting result. In a world characterized by economies of scale, one would expect workers to be better off in larger economies, because of the larger size of the local market. In this model, however, there is a secondary benefit in the form of better terms of trade with workers in the rest of the world. This does, on reflection, make intuitive sense. If production costs were the same in both countries, it would always be more profitable to produce near the larger market, thus minimizing transportation costs. To keep labor employed in both countries, this advantage must be offset by a wage differential.

2.3   "Home Market" Effects on the Pattern of Trade

In a world characterized both by increasing returns and by transportation costs, there will obviously be an incentive to concentrate production of a good near its largest market, even if there is some demand for the good elsewhere. The reason is simply that by concentrating production in one place one can realize the scale economies, while by locating near the larger market, one minimizes transportation costs. This point—which is more often emphasized in location theory than in trade theory—is the basis for the common argument that countries will tend to export those kinds of products for which they have relatively large domestic demand. Notice that this argument is wholly dependent on increasing returns; in a world of diminishing returns, strong domestic demand for a good will tend to make it an import rather than an export. But the point does not come through clearly in models where increasing returns take the form of external economies (see W. M. Corden). One of the main contributions of the approach developed in this paper is that by using this approach the home market effect can be given a simple formal justification.

I will begin by extending the basic closed economy model to one in which there are two industries (with many differentiated products within each industry). It will then be shown for a simple case that when two countries of this kind trade, each will be a net exporter in the industry for whose products it has the relatively larger demand. Finally, some extensions and generalizations will be discussed.

A Two-Industry Economy

As in section 2.1, we begin by analyzing a closed economy. Assume that there are two classes of products, *alpha* and *beta*, with many potential products within each class. A tilde will distinguish *beta* products from *alpha* products; for example, consumption of products in the first class will be represented us $c_1, \ldots, c_n$, while consumption of products in second are $\tilde{c}_1, \ldots, \tilde{c}_n$.

Demand for the two classes of products will be assumed to arise from the presence of two groups in the population.[4] There will be one group with L members, which derives utility only from consumption of *alpha* products; and another group with $\tilde{L}$ members, deriving utility only from *beta* products. The utility functions of representative members of the two classes may by written

$$U = \sum_i c_i^\theta; \quad \tilde{U} = \sum_j \tilde{c}_j^\theta, \qquad 0 < \theta < 1. \tag{15}$$

For simplicity assume that not only the form of the utility function but the parameter θ is the same for both groups.

On the cost side, the two kinds of products will be assumed to have identical cost functions:

$$l_i = \alpha + \beta x_i, \qquad i = 1, \ldots, n,$$
$$\tilde{l}_j = \alpha + \beta \tilde{x}_j, \qquad j = 1, \ldots, \tilde{n}, \tag{16}$$

where l_i, $\tilde{l}_j$ are labor used in production on typical goods in each class and x_i, $\tilde{x}_j$ are total output of the goods.

The demand conditions now depend on the population shares. By analogy with (3), we have

$$x_i = L c_i, \qquad i = 1, \ldots, n,$$
$$\tilde{x}_j = \tilde{L} \tilde{c}_j, \qquad j = 1, \ldots, \tilde{n}. \tag{17}$$

The full-employment condition, however, applies to the economy as a whole:

$$\sum_{i=1}^{n} l_i + \sum_{j=1}^{\tilde{n}} \tilde{l}_j = L + \tilde{L}. \tag{18}$$

Finally, we continue to assume free entry, driving profits to zero. Now it is immediately apparent that the economy described by equations (15)–(18) is very similar to the economy described in equations (1)–(4). The price and output of a representative good—of either class—and the total number of products $n + \tilde{n}$ are determined just as if all goods belonged to a single industry. The only modification we must make to the results of section 2.1 is that we must divide the total production into two industries. A simple way of doing this is to note that the sales of each industry must equal the income of the appropriate group in the population:

$$npx = wL.$$
$$\tilde{n}\tilde{p}\tilde{x} = \tilde{w}\tilde{L}. \tag{19}$$

But wages of the two groups must be equal, as must the prices and outputs of any products of either industry. So this reduces to the result $n/\tilde{n} = L/\tilde{L}$: the shares of the industries in the value of output equal the shares of the two demographic groups in the population.

This extended model clearly differs only trivially from the model developed in section 2.1 when the economy is taken to be closed. When two such economies are allowed to trade, however, the extension allows some interesting results.

Demand and the Trade Pattern: A Simple Case

We can begin by considering a particular case of trade between a pair of two-industry countries in which the role of the domestic market appears particularly clearly. Suppose that there are two countries of the type just described and that they can trade with transport costs of the type analyzed in section 2.2.

In the home country, some fraction f of the population will be consumers of *alpha* products. The crucial simplification I will make is to assume that the other country is a *mirror image* of the home country. The labor forces will be assumed to be equal, so that

$$L + \tilde{L} = L^* + \tilde{L}^* = \bar{L}. \tag{20}$$

But in the foreign country the population shares will be reversed, so that we have

$$L = f\bar{L}; \qquad L^* = (1 - f)\bar{L}. \tag{21}$$

If f is greater than one-half, then the home country has the larger domestic market for the *alpha* industry's products; and conversely. In this case there is a very simple home market proposition: *that the home country will be a net exporter of the first industry's products if f > 0.5.* This proposition turns out to be true.

The first step in showing this is to notice that this is a wholly symmetrical world, so that wage rates will be equal, as will the output and prices of all goods. (The case was constructed for that purpose.) It follows that the ratio of demand for each imported product to the demand for each domestic product is the same in both countries.

$$\sigma = \sigma^* = g^{\theta/(1-\theta)} < 1. \tag{22}$$

Next we want to determine the pattern of production. The expenditure on goods in an industry is the sum of domestic residents' and foreigners' expenditures on the goods, so we can write the expressions

$$npx = \frac{n}{n + \sigma n^*} wL + \frac{\sigma n}{\sigma n + n^*} wL^*,$$

$$n^*px = \frac{\sigma n^*}{n + \sigma n^*} wL + \frac{n^*}{\sigma n + n^*} wL^*, \tag{23}$$

where the price p of each product and the output x are the same in the two countries. We can use (23) to determine the relative number of products produced in each country, n/n^*.

To see this, suppose *provisionally* that some products in the *alpha* industry are produced in both countries; that is, $n > 0$, $n^* > 0$. We can the divide the equations (23) through by n and n^*, respectively, and rearrange to get

$$\frac{I.}{L^*} = \frac{n + \sigma n^*}{\sigma n + n^*} \tag{24}$$

which can be rearranged to give

$$\frac{n}{n^*} = \frac{L/L^* - \sigma}{1 - \sigma L/L^*} \tag{25}$$

Figure 2.2 shows the relationship (25). If $L/L^* = 1$, so does n/n^*; that is, if the demand patterns of the two countries are the same, their production patterns will also be the same, as we would expect. And as the relative size of either country's home market rises for *alpha* goods, so does its domestic production, as long as L/L^* lies in the range $\sigma < L/L^* < 1/\sigma$.

Outside that range, (25) appears to give absurd results. Recall, however, that the derivation of (24) was made on the provisional assumption that n

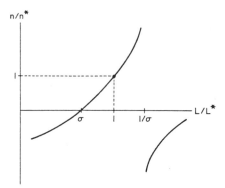

Figure 2.2

and n^* were both nonzero. Clearly, if L/L^* lies outside the range from σ to $1/\sigma$, this assumption is not valid. What the figure suggests is that if L/L^* is less than σ, $n = 0$; the home country specialized entirely in *beta* products, producing no *alpha* products (while the foreign country produces only *alpha* products). Conversely, if L/L^* is greater than $1/\sigma$, $n^* = 0$, and we have the opposite pattern of specialization.

We can easily demonstrate that this solution is in fact an equilibrium. Suppose that the home country produced no *alpha* products and that a firm attempted to start production of a single product. This firm's profit-maximizing f.o.b. price would be the same as that of the foreign firm's. But its sales would be less, in the ratio

$$\frac{\sigma^{-1}L + \sigma L^*}{L + L^*} < 1.$$

Thus such a firm could not compete.

This gives us our first result on the effect of the home market. It says that if the two countries have sufficiently dissimilar tastes, each will specialize in the industry for which it has the larger home market. Obviously, also, each will be a net exporter of the class of goods in which it specializes. Thus the idea that the pattern of exports is determined by the home market is quite nicely confirmed.

We also get some illuminating results on the conditions under which specialization will be incomplete. Incomplete specialization and two-way trade within the two classes of products will occur if the relative size of the domestic markets for *alpha* goods lies in the range from σ to $1/\sigma$, where $\sigma = g^{\theta/(1-\theta)}$. But g measures transportation costs, while $\theta/(1 - \theta)$ is, in equilibrium, the ratio of variable to fixed costs;[5] that is, it is an index of the importance of scale economies. So we have shown that the possibility of incomplete specialization is greater, the greater are transport costs and the less important are economies of scale.

A final result we can take from this special case concerns the pattern of trade when specialization is incomplete. In this case each country will both import and export products in *both* classes (though not the same products). But it remains true that, if one country has the larger home market for *alpha* producers, it will be a *net* exporter in the *alpha* class and a net importer in the other. To see this, note that we can write the home country's trade balance in *alpha* products as

$$
\begin{aligned}
B_\alpha &= \frac{\sigma n}{\sigma n + n^*} wL^* - \frac{\sigma n^*}{n + \sigma n^*} wL \\
&= wL^* \left[\frac{\sigma n}{\sigma n + n^*} - \frac{\sigma n^*}{n + \sigma n^*} \frac{L}{L^*} \right] \\
&= \frac{\sigma wL^*}{\sigma n + n^*} [n - n^*],
\end{aligned}
\tag{26}
$$

where we used (24) to eliminate the relative labor supplies. This says that the sign of the trade balance depends on whether the number of *alpha* products produced in the home country is more or less than the number produced abroad. But we have already seen that n/n^* is an increasing function of L/L^* in the relevant range. So the country with the larger home market for the *alpha*-type products will be a net exporter of those goods, even if specialization is not complete.

Generalizations and Extensions

The analysis we have just gone through shows that there is some justification for the idea that countries export what they have home markets for. The results were arrived at, however, only for a special case designed to make matters at simple as possible. Our next question must be the extent to which these results generalize.

One way in which generalization might be pursued is by abandoning the "mirror image" assumption: we can let the countries have arbitrary populations ard demand patterns while retaining all the other assumptions of the model. It can be shown that in that case, although the derivations become more complicated, the basic home market result is unchanged. Each country will be a net exporter in the industry for whose goods it has a relatively larger demand. The difference is that wages will in general not be equal; in particular, smaller countries with absolutely smaller markets for both kinds of goods will have to compensate for this disadvantage with lower wages.

Another, perhaps more interesting, generalization would be to abandon the assumed symmetry between the industries. Again, we would like to be able to make sense of some arguments made by practical men. For example, is it true that large countries will have an advantage in the production and export of goods whose production is characterized by sizable economies of scale? This explanation is sometimes given for the United States' position as an exporter of aircraft.

A general analysis of the effects of asymmetry between industries would run to too great a length. We can learn something, however, by considering another special case. Suppose that the *alpha* production is the same as in our last analysis but that the production of *beta* goods is characterized by *constant* returns to scale and perfect competition. For simplicity, also assume that *beta* goods can be transported costlessly.

It is immediately apparent that in this case the possibility of trade in *beta* products will ensure that wage rates are equal. But this in turn means that we can apply the analysis of the preceding subsection to the *alpha* industry. Whichever country has the larger market for the products of that industry will be a net exporter of *alpha* products and a net importer of *beta* products. In particular: if two countries have the same composition of demand, the larger country will be a net exporter of the products whose production involves economies of scale.

The analysis in this section has obviously been suggestive rather than conclusive. It relies heavily on very special assumptions and on the analysis of special cases. Nonetheless, the analysis does seem to confirm the idea that in the presence of increasing returns, countries will tend to export the goods for which they have large domestic markets. And the implications for the pattern of trade are similar to those suggested by Steffan Linder, Grubel (1970), and others.

Notes

1. A paper that points out the difficulties in explaining the actual pattern of world trade in a comparative cost framework is the study of Gary Hufbauer and John Chilas.

2. To be fully rigorous, we would have to use the concept of a continuum of potential products.

3. To get an increase in scale, we must assume that the demand facing each individual firm becomes more elastic as the number of firms increases, whereas in this model the elasticity of demand remains unchanged. Increasing elasticity of demand when the variety of products grows seems plausible, since the more finely differentiated are the products, the better substitutes they are likely to be for one another. Thus an increase in scale as well as diversity is probably the "normal" case. The constant elasticity case, however, is much easier to work with, which is my reason for using it in this chapter.

4. An alternative would be to have all people alike, with a taste for both kinds of goods. The results are similar. In fact, if each industry receives a fixed share of expenditure, they will be identical.

5. One can see this by rearranging equation (9) to get $\beta x/\alpha = \theta/(1 - \theta)$.

3 Intraindustry Specialization and the Gains from Trade

Over the years many empirical students of international trade have argued that trade among the industrial countries cannot adequately be explained by conventional theories of comparative advantage. One might summarize this empirical critique by pointing to three aspects of world trade that seem to contradict received theory. First, much of world trade is between countries with similar factor endowments. Second, a large part of trade is intraindustry in character—that is, it consists of two-way trade in similar products. Finally, much of the expansion of trade in the postwar period has taken place without sizable reallocation of resources or income-distribution effects. This last point is particularly noticeable in the cases of the EEC and the North American automobile pact.

The purpose of this paper is to formalize one possible explanation of these seeming paradoxes. The explanation is not a new one: It is essentially the same as that put forward by Balassa (1967), Grubel (1970), and Kravis (1971), among others. What this paper does is put the argument in terms of a formal model, a step that may be of some help in clarifying and disseminating ideas that have been "in the air" for some time.

Briefly, the argument of these empirical workers, a very clear exposition of which is given by Kravis (1971), runs as follows. The conventional forces of comparative advantage operate on *groups* of products ("industries") and thus give rise to *interindustry* specialization and trade. Economies of scale in production, however, lead each country to produce only a subset of the products within each group, so that there is also *intraindustry* specialization and trade. This provides a simple explanation of two of our empirical ostensible paradoxes. Countries with similar factor endowments will still trade because of scale economies, and their trade will be largely intraindustry

Originally published in the *Journal of Political Economy* 89, 5 (1981): 959–974. © 1981 by The University of Chicago.

in character. The third seeming paradox—the apparent painlessness of some trade liberalization—can also be resolved if we argue that income-distribution effects are outweighed by the gains from a larger market when countries are sufficiently similar.

While this is a simple and straightforward explanation, it is not so easy to formalize. Scale economies are crucial to the argument and they are notoriously awkward to handle in general equilibrium models. In this chapter I follow an earlier paper (Krugman 1979) and use the device of Chamberlinian monopolistic competition. As in the earlier paper, this proves to be a very convenient approach, yielding a simple and tractable model. The structure of this model and the determination of this model's equilibrium in a closed economy are set forth in section 3.1. Section 3.2 shows how the pattern of trade between two countries is determined in the model, developing the basic relationship between differences in factor endowments and the extent of intraindustry trade. Section 3.3 then examines the effects of trade on income distribution and shows how the extent of intraindustry trade determines whether scarce factors of production gain or lose from trade. Finally, section 3.4 summarizes the results and discusses some implications for theory and policy.

It must be emphasized that the model presented here is in no sense a general one. In addition to making strong assumptions about functional forms of cost and utility functions, I impose a great deal of symmetry on the model to simplify the analysis and give a natural meaning to the concept of "similarity" in factor proportions. Thus the results of the analysis are at best suggestive. Nonetheless, they seem intuitively plausible and also seem to have something to do with actual experience.

3.1   The Model in a Closed Economy

Intraindustry trade depends on the existence of unexhausted economies of scale in production. The main problem in modeling this kind of trade is how to handle these scale economies, which must lead to a breakdown of perfect competition (unless they are wholly external to firms). In this chapter, as in an earlier paper (Krugman 1979), I will use the device of Chamberlinian monopolistic competition, basing the model on recent work by Dixit and Stiglitz (1977). An "industry" will consist of a large number of firms, all producing somewhat differentiated products, all operating on the downward-sloping parts of their average cost curves. There will be two-way international trade within an industry because firms in different countries will produce different differentiated products. What prevents countries from producing a complete range of products domestically is the existence of fixed costs in production; thus scale economies are the basic cause of intraindustry trade.

We should note at the outset that the concept of an industry used in this chapter is a somewhat special one. One might want to define an industry either as a group of products that are close substitutes on the supply side or as a group of products that are close substitutes on the demand side. In the model of this chapter, I assume that there are two groups of products that fit both definitions. Products within each group are closer substitutes than products in different groups, while factors of production are assumed mobile among products within each group yet immobile between groups. This conventent coincidence of the two possible concepts of an industry may or may not be empirically reasonable; it is certainly not theoretically necessary and should be regarded as one among many special assumptions.

Another conceptual difficulty concerns the notion of a "product." In the formulation below, all products seem to look alike, since they enter symmetrically into both cost and utility functions. This may seem to involve an illegitimate comparison of physical quantities of different goods. I show in the appendix, however, that the formulation of many "identical" products can be interpreted as a restriction on the parameters of a model in which products really do differ.

Let us begin, then, with a two-industry model of a closed economy. Each industry consists of a large number of products, all of which enter symmetrically into demand, with the two industries—industry 1 and industry 2—themselves playing symmetric roles. All individuals will have the convenient utility function

$$U = \ln\left(\sum_{i=1}^{N_1} c_{1,i}^{\theta}\right)^{1/\theta} + \ln\left(\sum_{j=1}^{N_2} c_{2,j}^{\theta}\right)^{1/\theta}, \qquad 0 < \theta < 1, \tag{1}$$

where $c_{1,i}$ is consumption of the ith product of industry 1; $c_{2,j}$ is consumption of the jth product of industry 2; and N_1 and N_2 are the (large) numbers of potential products in each industry. Not all potential products will necessarily be produced, and we will in fact assume that the actual numbers of products produced—n_1 and n_2—while large, fall short of N_1 and N_2.

The utility function (1) has several useful properties. First, it ensures that half of income will always be spent on industry 1's products. Second, if the number of products in each industry is large, it implies that every producer faces a demand curve with elasticity $1/(1 - \theta)$. Finally, (1) will allow us to represent the gains and losses from trade in a particularly simple way.

On the demand side, then, an industry is assumed to consist of a number of products that are *imperfect* substitutes for one another. On the supply side, however, they will be assumed to be *perfect* substitutes. There will be only two factors of production, type 1 labor and type 2 labor, each of which is wholly specific to an industry but nonspecific among products within an industry. Thus type 1 labor will be used only in industry 1, type 2 only in industry 2. Within each industry the labor required to produce a particular product will consist of a fixed setup cost and a constant variable cost:

$$l_{1,i} = \alpha + \beta x_{1,i}, \qquad i = 1, \ldots, n_1,$$

$$l_{2,j} = \alpha + \beta x_{2,j}, \qquad j = 1, \ldots, n_2, \tag{2}$$

where $l_{1,i}$ is labor used in producing the ith product of industry, 1; $x_{1,i}$ is the output of that product; and so on. To go from these required labor inputs to nominal costs, we must multiply by the wage rates of the two types of labor, w_1 and w_2.

To close the model, we begin by noting that output of each product, x, is the sum of individual consumptions of the product. At the same time, total employment in each industry is the sum of employment in producing all the individual products. Assuming full employment, we have

$$\left. \begin{array}{l} \displaystyle\sum_{i=1}^{n_1} l_{1,i} = L_1 = 2 - z \\[2em] \displaystyle\sum_{j=1}^{n_2} l_{2,j} = L_2 = z \end{array} \right\} 0 < z < 1. \tag{3}$$

Thus the total labor force is set equal to 2, with the parameter z measuring factor proportions. As we will see below, z will assume crucial significance in determining the importance of intraindustry trade and the effect of trade on income distribution.

We are now prepared to examine the determination of equilibrium in this model. This involves determining how many products are actually produced in each industry, the output of each product, the prices of products, and the relative wages of the two kinds of labor. We should note at the outset that it is indeterminate *which* products are produced—but it is also unimportant.

Our first step is to determine the pricing policy of firms. We assume that producers can always costlessly differentiate their products. This means that each product will be produced by only one firm. If there are many products, the elasticity of demand for each product will, as already noted, be $1/(1 - \theta)$. (This is proved in the appendix.) Thus each firm will face a demand curve of constant elasticity. We then have the familiar result that the profit-maximizing price will be marginal cost plus a constant percentage markup:

$$p_1 = \theta^{-1}\beta w_1,$$
$$p_2 = \theta^{-1}\beta w_2,$$

(4)

where p_1 and p_2 are the prices of any products in industry 1 and 2, respectively, which are actually produced.

Given the pricing policy of firms, actual profits depend on sales:

$$\pi_1 = p_1 x_1 - (\alpha + \beta x_1)w_1,$$
$$\pi_2 = p_2 x_2 - (\alpha + \beta x_2)w_2,$$

(5)

where x_1 and x_2 are sales of representative firms in the two industries.

But in this model there will be free entry of firms, driving each industry to Chamberlin's "tangency solution" where profits are zero. Thus we can use the condition of zero profits in equilibrium to determine the equilibrium size and number of firms. Setting $\pi_1 = \pi_2 = 0$ and using (4) and (5), we have

$$x_1 = x_2 = \frac{\alpha}{\beta} \cdot \frac{\theta}{1 - \theta}$$

(6)

for the size of firms. The number of firms can then be determined from the full-employment condition:

$$n_1 = \frac{2 - z}{\alpha + \beta x_1},$$

(7)

$$n_2 = \frac{z}{\alpha + \beta x_2}.$$

The final step in determining equilibrium is to determine relative wages. This can be done very simply by noting that the industries receive equal shares of expenditure and that, since profits are zero in equilibrium, these receipts go entirely to the wages of the industry-specific labor forces. So $w_1 L_1 = w_2 L_2$, implying

$$\frac{w_1}{w_2} = \frac{z}{2 - z}.$$

(8)

We now have a completely worked out equilibrium for a two-sector, monopolistically competitive economy. It is indeterminate which of the range of potential products within each industry are actually produced, but since all products appear symmetrically, this is of no welfare significance. The character of the economy is determined by the two parameters z and θ. The value of z determines relative wages: If z is low, type 2 labor will receive much higher wages than type 1 labor. The value of θ measures the degree of substitutability among products within an industry. The lower is θ, the more differentiated are products and the industry. The lower is θ, the more differentiated are products and the more important are unexploited scale economies. From (4) we have $\theta = \beta w_1 / p_1 = \beta w_2 / p_2$. But βw_1 and βw_2 are the marginal costs of production, while in equilibrium price equals average cost. Thus θ is the ratio of marginal to average cost (which is also the elasticity of cost with respect to output).

3.2 Factor Proportions and the Pattern of Trade

In the last section we saw how equilibrium can be determined in a simple closed-economy model with scale economies and differentiated products. We can now examine what happens when two such economies trade. What we are principally concerned with is the proposition, advanced in the introduction, that countries with similar factor endowments will engage in intraindustry trade while countries with very different endowments will engage in Heckscher-Ohlin trade.

As a first step we need a working measure of the extent of intraindustry trade. The empirical literature on intraindustry trade (e.g., Hufbauer and Chilas 1974; Grubel and Lloyd 1975) generally concentrates on an index of trade overlap, that is,

$$I = 1 - \left(\sum_k \left| X_k - M_k \right| \right) \Big/ \left[\sum_k (X_k + M_k) \right], \tag{9}$$

where X_k is a country's exports in industry k and M_k is imports in that industry. This index has the property that, if trade is balanced industry by industry, it equals one, while if there is complete international specialization so that every industry is either an export or import industry, it equals zero. As we will see, this index fits in quite well with the model of this chapter.

The other concept we need to make operational is that of similarity in factor endowments. In general, this is not well defined. What I will do in this paper, however, is consider a special case in which the concept does have a natural meaning without trying to arrive at a general definition.

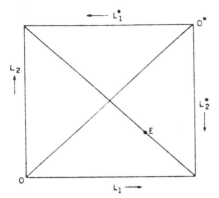

Figure 3.1

Let us suppose, then, that there are two countries, the home country and the foreign country. The home country will be just as described in Section 3.9. The foreign country will be identical except for one thing: the relative sizes of the two industries' labor forces will be reversed. That is, the foreign country will be a mirror image of the home country. If we use a star on a variable to indicate that it refers to the foreign country, we have

$$L_1 = 2 - z, \qquad L_2 = z,$$
$$L_1^* = z, \qquad L_2^* = 2 - z. \tag{10}$$

Obviously, given this pattern of endowments, we can regard z as an index of similarity in factor proportions. If $z = 1$, the countries have identical endowments. As z gets smaller, the factor proportions become increasingly different.

The mirror-image assumption can be given a geometric interpretation. In figure 3.1, an Edgeworth box is used to represent the international distribution of productive resources. The origin O is used to measure home country endowments, O^* to measure foreign endowments. The two diagonals of the box can then be given economic interpretations: OO^* is a line along which factor proportions are equal in the two countries, while the other diagonal is a line along which the countries are of equal economic size. The mirror-image assumption is saying that the endowment point E lies on this diagonal. The parameter z then determines the position of E; as z goes from 0 to 1, E moves from the corner to the center of the box.

Suppose, now, that these countries are able to trade at zero transportation cost. As before, we can determine pricing behavior, the size and number of firms, and relative wages. In addition we can determine the volume and pattern of trade.

The first point to note is that the elasticity of demand for any particular product is still $1/(1 - \theta)$. This gives us price equations exactly the same as before:

$$p_1 = \theta^{-1}\beta w_1,$$

$$p_2 = \theta^{-1}\beta w_2,$$

$$p_1^* = \theta^{-1}\beta w_1^*,$$

$$p_2^* = \theta^{-1}\beta w_2^*.$$

(11)

Now, however, the symmetry of the setup insures that all wages will be equal, both across industries and internationally:

$$w_1 = w_1^* = w_2 = w_2^*.$$

(12)

The zero-profit condition will determine the equilibrium size of firm, x, which will be the same for both industries in both countries:

$$x = \frac{\alpha\theta}{\beta(1 - \theta)}.$$

(13)

Finally, full employment determines the number of firms in each industry in each country:

$$n_1 = n_2^* = \frac{2 - z}{\alpha + \beta x},$$

$$n_2 = n_1^* = \frac{z}{\alpha + \beta x}.$$

(14)

What these results show is that trade will lead to factor price equalization while leaving the pattern of production unchanged. Our remaining task is to determine the volume and pattern of trade. We can do this by noting two points. First, everyone will devote equal shares of expenditure to the two industries. Second, everyone will spend an equal amount on each of the products within an industry. This means that the share of all individuals' income falling on, say, industry 1 products produced in the foreign country is $\frac{1}{2} \cdot [n_1^*/(n_1 + n_1^*)]$—that is, the industry share in expenditure times that country's share of the industry. But the number of products is proportional to the labor force. Thus, if we let Y be the home country's income (equal to the foreign country's), X_1 be exports of industry 1 products, X_2 be exports of industry 2 products, M_1 be imports of industry 1 products, and M_2 be imports of industry 2 products, we have

$$X_1 = \tfrac{1}{2}Y \cdot \left(\frac{2-z}{2}\right),$$

$$X_2 = \tfrac{1}{2}Y \cdot \left(\frac{z}{2}\right),$$

$$M_1 = \tfrac{1}{2}Y \cdot \left(\frac{z}{2}\right), \tag{15}$$

$$M_2 = \tfrac{1}{2}Y \cdot \left(\frac{2-z}{2}\right).$$

Now, the relations (15) have two important implications. First, consider the volume of trade. Total home country exports are $X_1 + X_2 = \tfrac{1}{2}Y$. Thus the ratio of trade to income is independent of z, the index of similarity in factor proportions. This can be regarded as an answer to the first ostensible empirical paradox mentioned in the introduction—the large volume of trade among similar countries. In this model, similar countries will trade just as much as dissimilar countries.

The second seeming empirical paradox was the prevalence, in trade among similar countries, of two-way trade in similar products. If we substitute (15) into our expression for intraindustry trade (9), we get a simple, striking result:

$$I = z. \tag{16}$$

The index of intraindustry trade equals the index of similarity in factor proportions.

These results may appear to depend crucially on the assumptions of this model, but in qualitative terms they can survive a good deal of generalization. The persistence of trade between countries with similar factor endowments will occur in almost any model with economies of scale. The relationship between similarity of countries and the extent of intraindustry trade can be shown to hold, for an appropriate definition of similarity, in a much more general model and has also been noted in a quite different context by Ethier (1979). Insofar as these insights are concerned, the virtue of this model is not in the difference of its conclusions but in the clarity with which they emerge.

Where the special assumptions of this model become particularly useful, however, is in attempting to deal with the welfare consequences of trade. These consequences are considered in the next section.

3.3 Gains and Losses from Trade

In this section we must again begin by delineating a concept that I have been using loosely. This is the idea of the "seriousness" of distribution problems. What we need is a clear way of formulating the notion that distribution problems from opening trade will not be serious, if countries are sufficiently similar in factor proportions that the trade which results is primarily intraindustry trade.

The criterion I will use to define nonserious distribution problems is the following: Distribution problems arising from trade will be held not to be serious if *both factors gain from trade*. This, of course, begs some questions, since there may be difficulties in getting groups to accept a relative decline in income even if they are absolutely better off. But this criterion is fairly reasonable and turns out to give suggestive results.

To find out whether factors gain from trade, we need to know how utility depends on the variables of the model. Suppose an individual receives a wage w and has the utility function (1). He will then spend $w/2$ on the products of each industry and divide his expenditure equally among the products within an industry. Thus his utility will depend on his wage, the prices of representative products in each industry, and the number of products available:

$$
\begin{aligned}
U &= \ln\left[n_1\left(\frac{w}{2n_1 p_1}\right)^\theta\right]^{1/\theta} + \ln\left[n_2\left(\frac{w}{2n_2 p_2}\right)^\theta\right]^{1/\theta} \\
&= -2\ln 2 + \ln\frac{w}{p_1} + \ln\frac{w}{p_2} + \frac{1-\theta}{\theta}\ln n_1 + \frac{1-\theta}{\theta}\ln n_2.
\end{aligned}
\tag{17}
$$

The function (17) has the convenient property that all the effects enter additively. Utility depends on real wages in terms of representative products and on diversity.

To analyze the effects of trade on welfare, it is useful to introduce some more notation:

U_1, U_2 = utility of workers in industries 1 and 2,

w_{11}, w_{12} = real wage of industry 1 workers in terms of products of industries 1 and 2,

w_{21}, w_{22} = real wage of industry 2 workers in terms of products of industries 1 and 2.

Then we can substitute into (17) to get (suppressing the constant term):

$$U_1 = \ln w_{11} + \ln w_{12} + \frac{1-\theta}{\theta} \ln n_1 + \frac{1-\theta}{\theta} \ln n_2,$$

$$(18)$$

$$U_2 = \ln w_{21} + \ln w_{22} + \frac{1-\theta}{\theta} \ln n_1 + \frac{1-\theta}{\theta} \ln n_2.$$

We are now in a position to measure the welfare effects of trade. Suppose we start from a position of autarky, as in section 3.1, then move to free trade, as in section 3.2. There will then be two kinds of effects. First, there will be a distribution effect as factor prices are equalized. As one can easily verify, labor's real wage remains the same in terms of the products of its own industry while rising or falling in terms of the other industry's products, depending on whether the factor is abundant or scarce. Thus, in the home country this effect benefits labor in industry 1 and hurts labor in industry 2.

The second effect comes from the increase in the size of the market, which makes a greater variety of products available. This works to everyone's benefit.

Since both effects work in its favor, the abundant factor must be made better off. This leaves us with the problem of determining the change in utility of the scarce factor—industry 2 labor in the home country and the symmetrically placed industry 1 labor in the foreign country.

Let a prime on a variable indicate its free-trade value while unmarked variables refer to autarky. Then, as we move from the autarky solution in section 3.1 to the free-trade solution in section 3.2, the change in U_2 is

$$U_2' - U_2 = \ln \frac{w_{21}'}{w_{21}} + \frac{1-\theta}{\theta} \ln \frac{n_1'}{n_1} + \frac{1-\theta}{\theta} \ln \frac{n_2'}{n_2}$$

$$(19)$$

$$= \ln \frac{z}{2-z} + \frac{1-\theta}{\theta} \ln \frac{2}{2-z} + \frac{1-\theta}{\theta} \ln \frac{2}{z},$$

where the first term is negative and represents the distribution loss; the remaining terms are positive and represent the gains from being part of a larger market. The question is under what conditions these terms will outweigh the first terms.

By collecting terms, we can rewrite (19) as

$$U_2' - U_2 = \frac{2\theta - 1}{\theta} \ln z - \frac{1}{\theta} \ln 2 - z + \frac{2-2\theta}{\theta} \ln 2.$$

$$(20)$$

This gives us one immediate result: If $\theta < 0.5$, the scarce factor necessarily gains from trade, since the first term will be positive and the third term will

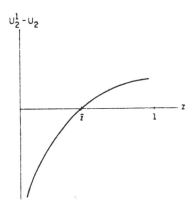

Figure 3.2

outweigh the second. Recall that θ is a measure of the substitutability of products within an industry. What this result then says is that *if products are sufficiently differentiated, both factors gain from trade.*

If $\theta > 0.5$, whether both factors gain depends on the extent to which trade is intraindustry in character, which in turn depends on how similar the countries are in factor proportions. When $\theta > 0.5$, the function (20) has three properties: (1) as z approaches 1, $U_2' - U_2$ goes to $[(2 - 2\theta)/\theta]$ ln $2 > 0$; (2) as z goes to zero, $U_2' - U_2$ goes to minus infinity; and (3) $U_2' - U_2$ is strictly increasing in z_1. Thus, if we were to graph (20), it would look like figure 3.2. There is a critical value of z, $\bar{z}$, for which $U_2' - U_2 = 0$. If $z > \bar{z}$, both factors gain; if $z < \bar{z}$, the scarce factor loses. But z is our measure of similarity in factor proportions. Thus what we have shown is that *if countries have sufficiently similar factor endowments, both factors gain from trade.*

What is particularly nice about this result is that we have already seen that there is a one-for-one relationship between similarity of factor endowments and intraindustry trade. So this result can be taken as a vindication of the arguments of such authors as Kravis (1971) and Hufbauer and Chilas (1974) that intraindustry trade poses fewer adjustment problems than interindustry trade.

We should note, however, that the critical value of interindustry trade depends on the substitutability of products. The function (20) is decreasing in θ: $\partial(U_2' - U_2)/\partial\theta = \theta^{-2}$ ln $z(2 - z) < 0$. So an increase in θ will shift the function down. This will increase $\bar{z}$. *The less differentiated are products, the more similar countries must be if both factors are to gain from trade.* In the limit, as θ goes to 1, so does $\bar{z}$.

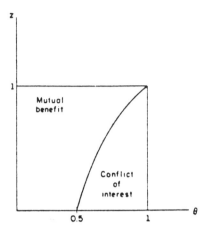

Figure 3.3

The results of this section are summarized in figure 3.3. On the axes are the two parameters θ and z, both capable of taking on values between zero and one. What we have shown is that the qualitative effects of trade depend on where we are in the unit square. In the southeastern part of the square—labeled "conflict of interest"—either scale economies are unimportant or countries are very different in factor endowments, and scarce factors lose from trade. In the other region—"mutual benefit"—the gains from intraindustry specialization outweigh the conventional distributional effects, and everyone gains from trade.

3.4 Summary and Conclusions

This chapter began with three "paradoxes" about international trade. Since they do not seem paradoxical in the light of this model, perhaps we should state them as "stylized facts": (1) Much of world trade is between countries with similar factor endowments. (2) The trade between similar countries is largely intraindustry in character; that is, it consists of two-way trade in similar products. (3) The growth of intraindustry trade has not posed serious income-distribution problems.

This chapter offers a simple model that formalizes one possible explanation of these stylized facts. According to this view, the variety of products produced in any one country is limited by the existence of scale economies in production. Thus similar countries have an incentive to trade; their trade will typically be in products produced with similar factor proportions; and this trade will not involve the income-distribution effects characteristic of more conventional trade.

In addition to helping make sense of some puzzling empirical results, this chapter is, I hope, of some interest from the standpoint of pure theory. The model dispenses with the two most fundamental assumptions of standard trade theory: perfect competition and constant returns to scale. Instead, I have dealt in this chapter with a world in which economies of scale are pervasive and all firms have monopoly power. While the model depends on extremely restrictive assumptions, it does show that it is possible for trade theory to make at least some progress into this virtually unexplored territory.

Appendix

The Concept of a Product

In the formulation in section 3.1, an industry was assumed to consist of many products with the "same" cost function and entering in the "same" way into utility. This may seem to involve a comparison of apples and oranges. However, it can be justified as a restriction on the parameters of a more general model.

Consider the utility and cost functions for a one-industry model (the generalization to two industries is obvious):

$$U = \left[\sum_{i=1}^{N} (\delta_i C_i)^\theta \right]^{1/\theta}, 0 < \theta < 1, \tag{A1}$$

$$l_i = \alpha_i + \beta_i X_i, \qquad i = 1, \ldots, n. \tag{A2}$$

Here we allow goods to enter with different weights into utility and to have different cost functions; thus no assumption is made about comparability of units. Given certain restrictions on parameters, however, it is possible to choose units so that a formulation where all products appear identical is valid. Let us suppose first that $\alpha_i = \alpha$ for all i. The measurement of this cost is independent of the choice of units, so this is a meaningful assumption. Let us also assume $\beta_i/\delta_i = \beta$ for all i. This again does not depend on units of measurement; measuring product 27 in batches of 10 instead of individual units will increase both β_{27} and δ_{27} by a factor of 10 and leave the ratio unchanged.

If the assumptions about parameters are granted—and they are special assumptions, not general properties—we can justify the model in the text by a choice of units. Let $\hat{C}_i = \delta_i C_i$ for all i. Then the utility and cost functions become

$$U = \left(\sum_{i=1}^{N} \hat{C}_i^{\theta} \right)^{1/\theta} \tag{A3}$$

$$l_i = \alpha + \beta \hat{X}_i, \qquad i = 1, \ldots, n. \tag{A4}$$

Elasticity of Demand for Individual Products

The analysis in section 3.1 depends on the result that the elasticity of demand for any particular product is $1/(1 - \theta)$. This appendix gives a demonstration of this.

Consider an individual maximizing his utility function (1) subject to a budget constraint. The first-order conditions from that maximization will have the form

$$p_{1,i} = \frac{c_{1,i}^{-(1-\theta)}}{\lambda \Sigma_k c_{1,k}^{\theta}}, \qquad i = 1, \ldots, n_1,$$

$$p_{2,j} = \frac{c_{2,j}^{-(1-\theta)}}{\lambda \Sigma_m c_{2,m}^{\theta}}, \qquad j = 1, \ldots, n_2,$$

where λ is the shadow price on the budget constraint, that is, the marginal utility of income.

If there are many products, however, the firm producing a particular product can take the denominators of these expressions as given. Thus each individual's demand for a particular product, and therefore also market demand, will have elasticity $1/(1 - \theta)$.

Note

This research was supported by a grant from the National Science Foundation. An earlier version of this chapter, "International Trade and Income Distribution: A Reconsideration," was presented at the NBER Summer Institute in International Studies, Cambridge, Massachusetts, July 1979.

4

A "Reciprocal Dumping" Model of International Trade

with James Brander

4.1 Introduction

The phenomenon of "dumping" in international trade can be explained by the standard theory of monopolistic price discrimination.[1] If a profit-maximizing firm believes it faces a higher elasticity of demand abroad than at home, and it is able to discriminate between foreign and domestic markets, then it will charge a lower price abroad than at home. Such an explanation seems to rely on "accidental" differences in country demands. In this paper, however, we show how dumping arises for systematic reasons associated with oligopolistic behavior.

Brander (1981) develops a model in which the rivalry of oligopolistic firms serves as an indepenednt cause of international trade and leads to two-way trade in identical products.[2] In this chapter we build on Brander (1981) to argue that the oligopolistic rivalry between firms naturally gives rise to "reciprocal dumping": each firm dumps into other firms' home markets.

We generalize Brander (1981) in that reciprocal dumping is shown to be robust to a fairly general specification of firms' behavior and market demand. The crucial element is what Helpman (1982) refers to as a 'segmented markets' perception: each firm perceives each country as a separate market and makes distinct quantity decisions for each.

Reciprocal dumping is rather striking in that there is pure waste in the form of unnecessary transport costs.[3] Without free entry, welfare may improve as trade opens up and reciprocal dumping occurs, but it is also possible that welfare may decline. One wonders, therefore, if such a model might not provide a rationale for trade restriction. With free entry, the

Originally published in the *Journal of International Economics* 15 (1983): 313–321. © North-Holland Publishing Company.

contrary seems to be true. We derive the fairly strong result that with free entry both before and after trade, the opening of trade (and the resultant reciprocal dumping) is definitely welfare improving for the Cournot case. The procompetitive effect of having more firms and a larger overall market dominates the loss due to transport costs in this second-best, imperfectly competitive world.

Section 4.2 develops a simple model of Cournot duopoly and trade that shows how reciprocal dumping can occur and presents the associated welfare analysis. Section 4.3 describes the free-entry, zero-profit equilibrium and derives the result that trade is welfare improving in this case. Section 4.4 contains concluding remarks.

4.2   The Basic Model

Assume there are two identical countries, one "domestic" and one "foreign," and that each country has one firm producing commodity Z. There are transport costs incurred in exporting goods from one country to the other. The main idea is that each firm regards each country as a separate market and therefore chooses the profit-maximizing quantity for each country separately. Each firm has a Cournot perception: it assumes the other firm will hold output fixed in each country.

The domestic firm produces output x for domestic consumption and output x^* for foreign consumption. Marginal cost is a constant, c, and transport costs of the "iceberg" type that the marginal cost of export is c/g, when $0 \leq g \leq 1$. Similarly, the foreign firm produces output y for export to the domestic country and output y^* for its own market, and faces a symmetric cost structure. Using p and p^* to denote domestic and foreign price, domestic and foreign profits can be written, respectively, as

$$\pi = xp(Z) + x^*p^*(Z^*) - c\left(x + \frac{x^*}{g}\right) - F, \tag{1}$$

$$\pi^* = yp(Z) + y^*p^*(Z^*) - c\left(\frac{y}{g} + y^*\right) - F^*. \tag{2}$$

where asterisks generally denote variables associated with the foreign country and F denotes fixed costs. A little inspection reveals that the profit-maximizing choice of x is independent of x^* and similarly for y and y^*: each country can be considered separately.[4] By symmetry we need consider only the domestic country.

Each firm maximizes profit with respect to its own output, which yields the first-order conditions:

$$\pi_x = xp' + p - c = 0, \tag{3}$$

$$\pi_y^* = yp' + p - \frac{c}{g} = 0, \tag{4}$$

where primes or subscripts denote derivatives. These are "best-reply" functions in implicit form. Their solution is the trade equilibrium. Using the variable σ to denote y/Z, the foreign share in the domestic market, and letting $\varepsilon = -p/Zp'$, the elasticity of domestic demand, these implicit best-reply functions can be rewritten as

$$p = \frac{c\varepsilon}{\varepsilon + \sigma - 1}, \tag{3'}$$

$$p = \frac{c\varepsilon}{g(\varepsilon - \sigma)}. \tag{4'}$$

Equations (3') and (4') are two equations that can be solved for p and σ. The solutions are

$$p = \frac{c\varepsilon(1 + g)}{g(2\varepsilon - 1)}, \tag{5}$$

$$\sigma = \frac{\varepsilon(g - 1) + 1}{1 + g}. \tag{6}$$

These solutions are an equilibrium only if second-order conditions are satisfied:

$$\pi_{xx} = xp' + 2p' < 0, \qquad \pi_{yy}^* = yp'' + 2p' < 0. \tag{7}$$

We also impose the following conditions:

$$\pi_{xy} = xp'' + p' < 0, \qquad \pi_{yx}^* = yp'' + p' = 0. \tag{8}$$

Conditions (8) mean that own marginal revenue declines when the other firm increases its output, which seems a very reasonable requirement. They are equivalent to reaction functions (or best-reply functions), being downward sloping. They imply stability and, if they hold globally, uniqueness of the equilibrium. It is not inconceivable that (8) might be violated by possible demand structures, but such cases would have to be considered unusual. In any case, pathological examples of noncooperative models are

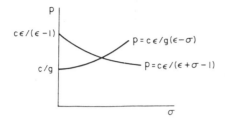

Figure 4.1

well understood (see, e.g., Seade 1980; Friedman 1977), and we have nothing new to say about such problems here. Accordingly, we assume (7) and (8) are satisfied.[5]

Positive solutions to (5) and (6) imply the two-way trade arises in this context. A positive solution will arise if $\varepsilon < 1/(1 - g)$ at the equilibrium, since this implies that price exceeds the marginal cost of exports ($p > c/g$) and that $\sigma > 0$. Subject to this condition, and given (7) and (8), a unique stable two-way trade equilibrium holds for arbitrary demand. (Brander 1981 considered the case of linear demand only.) It can be easily shown[6] that, at equilibrium, each firm has a smaller market share of its export market than of its domestic market. Therefore, perceived marginal revenue is higher in the export market. The effective marginal cost of delivering an exported unit is higher than for a unit of domestic sales, because of transport costs, but this is consistent with the higher marginal revenue. Thus, perceived marginal revenue can equal marginal cost in both markets at positive output levels. This is true for firms in both countries, which thus gives rise to two-way trade. Moreover, each firm has a a smaller markup over cost in its export market than at home: The f.o.b. price for exports is below the domestic price, and therefore there is reciprocal dumping.

The case of constant elasticity demand, $p = AZ^{-1/\varepsilon}$, is a useful special case which is illustrated in figure 4.1. For profit maximization by the domestic firm (condition (3')), p is decreasing in σ, while condition (4') for the foreign firm has price increasing in σ. The intercepts on the price axis are, respectively, $c\varepsilon/(\varepsilon - 1)$ and c/g. Thus, provided $c\varepsilon/(\varepsilon - 1) > c/g$ [or $\varepsilon < 1/(1 - g)$], the intersection must be at a positive foreign market share. This condition has a natural economic interpretation, since $c\varepsilon/(\varepsilon - 1)$ is the price that would prevail if there were no trade, which c/g is the marginal cost of exports. What the condition says is that reciprocal dumping will occur if monopoly markups in its absence were to exceed transport costs.

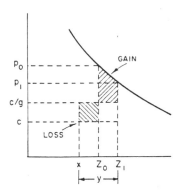

Figure 4.2

Clearly, the reciprocal dumping solution is not Pareto efficient. Some monopoly distortion persists even after trade, and there are socially pointless transportation costs incurred in cross-hauling. What is less clear is whether, given a second-best world of imperfect competition, free trade is superior to autarky. This is a question with an uncertain answer, because there are two effects. On the one hand, allowing trade in this model leads to waste in transport, tending to reduce welfare. On the other hand, international competition leads to lower prices, reducing the monopoly distortion.

If demand is assumed to arise from a utility function that can be approximated by the form $U = u(Z) + K$, where K represents consumption of a numeraire competitive good, then the welfare effects of trade can be measured by standard surplus measures.

Figure 4.2 illustrates the point that there are conflicting effects on welfare. In the figure Z_0 is the pretrade output of the monopolized good, p_0 is the pretrade price, and c is marginal cost. After trade, consumption rises to Z_1 and price falls to p_1. But output for domestic consumption falls to x, with imports y. As the figure shows, there is a gain from the 'consumption creation' $Z_1 - Z_0$ but a loss from the 'production diversion' $Z_0 - x$.

There are two special cases in which the welfare effect is clear. First, if transport costs are negligible, cross-hauling, though pointless, is also costless, and the procompetitive effect insures that there will be gains from trade.

At the other extreme, if transport costs are just at the prohibitive level, then decline slightly so that trade takes place, such trade is welfare reducing. This is easily shown as follows. Overall welfare is given by

$$W = 2[u(Z) - cZ - ty] - F - F^*,\tag{9}$$

where we now use t to denote per unit transport costs instead of the iceberg notation. The 2 arises because there are two symmetric countries. A slight change in t alters welfare as indicated:

$$\frac{dW}{dt} = 2\left[\frac{(p - c)dZ}{dt} - t\frac{dy}{dt - y}\right].\tag{10}$$

Starting at the prohibitive level, $p = c + t$ and $y = 0$; therefore since

$$\frac{dZ}{dt} = \frac{dx}{dt} + \frac{dy}{dt},$$

equation (10) reduces to:

$$dW/dt = 2(p - c)dx/dt = 2t\,dx/dt > 0.\tag{11}$$

   A slight fall in transport costs tends to make x fall[7] (as imports y come in), implying that dW/dt is positive. Therefore, a slight fall in t from the prohibitive level would reduce welfare. The intuition runs along the following lines. A decrease in transport costs has three effects. First, costs fall for the current level of imports, which is a gain. Second, consumption rises; so, for each extra unit consumed, there is a net gain equal to price minus the marginal cost of imports. Finally, there is a loss due to the replacement of domestic production with high cost imports. For near prohibitive levels of transport costs the first two effects are negligible, leaving only the loss.

4.3   Welfare Effects under Free Entry

The Cournot duopoloy model of section 4.2 is quite specific. However, the existence result is robust to a wide variety of generalizations. One important generalization is to the free entry case. Moreover, this case has strong welfare properties. Maintaining the assumptions and notation of section 4.2, except that there will now be n firms in each country in equilibrium, the after-trade price and foreign market share ny/Z, are given by

$$p = \frac{c\varepsilon n(1 + g)}{g(2n\varepsilon - 1)},\tag{12}$$

$$\sigma = \frac{n\varepsilon(g - 1) + 1}{1 + g},\tag{13}$$

where n is the number of firms that sets profits equal to zero for each firm i.

We now prove that, under free entry, trade improves welfare. Consider a pretrade free entry equilibrium.[8] In the domestic industry each firm maximizes profit so that the following first-order condition is satisfied:

$$x_i p' + p - c = 0. \tag{14}$$

Also each firm earns zero profit:

$$\pi_i = x_i p - c x_i - F = 0. \tag{15}$$

After trade opens, price changes, and the direction of price movement determines whether consumer surplus rises or falls, and therefore determines the direction of welfare movement since profits remain at zero by free entry. If price falls, welfare rises. The main step in the argument, then, is that price must fall with the opening of trade.

This is most easily seen by contradiction. From (14), $x_i = -(p - c)/p'$, so:

$$\frac{dx_i}{dp} = \frac{-p' + (p - c)p'' \, dZ/dp}{(p')^2} \tag{16}$$

$$= \frac{-p' + x_i p''}{(p')^2}, \tag{17}$$

since $dZ/dp = 1/p'$ and $(p - c) = -p'x_i$. But (17) is strictly positive by (8), which means that x_i must rise if p rises. Also, x_i must stay constant if p remains constant, so as to satisfy (14). However, profits are now given by

$$\pi_i = (p - c)x_i - F + \left(p^* - \frac{c}{g}\right)x_i^*. \tag{18}$$

If price and quantity both rise or remain constant, then $(p - c)x_i - F$ is nonnegative by (15), and $(p^* - c/g)x_i^*$ is strictly positive since $p^* > c/g$ if trade is to take place. Therefore π_i must be strictly positive, which is a contradiction. Price must fall and welfare must rise.

The structural source of welfare improvement is that firms move down their average cost curves. Although x_i falls, $x_i + x_i^*$ must exceed the original production levels and average cost must fall. Profits remain at zero and consumer surplus rises.

4.4   Concluding Remarks

This chapter has shown that oligopolistic interaction between firms can cause trade in the absence of any of the usual motivations for trade; neither cost difference nor economies of scale are necessary. The model provides possible explanations for two phenomena not well explained by standard neoclassical trade theory: intraindustry trade and dumping. We refer to such trade as "reciprocal dumping." The welfare effects of such trade are interesting. If firms earn positive profits, the opening of trade will increase welfare if transport costs are low. On the other hand, if transport costs are high, opening trade may actually cause welfare to decline because the procompetitive effect is dominated by the increased waste due to transport costs. However, in the free entry Cournot model, opening trade certainly increases welfare.

Reciprocal dumping is much more general than the Cournot model. One direction of generalization (either with or without free entry) is to a generalized conjectural variation model, of which the Cournot model is a special case. The essential element of the conjectural variation model is that each firm has a nonzero expectation concerning the response of other firms to its own output. Letting λ denote the expected change in industry output as own output changes, so that $\lambda = 1$ is the Cournot case, and letting foreign and domestic numbers of firms be n^* and n, respectively, yields $\sigma = (nn^* \varepsilon(g - 1) + n^*\lambda)/\lambda(n^* + ng)$ for the case of symmetric linear conjectural variations. This is positive for some range of transport costs. As long as $\lambda > 0$, so that firms believe that their behavior can affect price, the possibility of reciprocal dumping arises.[9] In general, the conjectures need not be symmetric and, for that matter, they need not be linear. An easily developed special case is the Stackelberg leader-follower model in which each firm is, for example, a leader in its home market and a follower abroad.[10]

If price is the strategy variable, reciprocal dumping does not arise in the homogeneous product case. However, a slight amount of product differentiation will restore the reciprocal dumping result, in which case the intraindustry trade motives described here augment the usual product differentiation motives for intraindustry trade. The important element is just that firms have a segmented markets perception. Given this perception, the possibility of the kind of two-way trade described here is relatively robust.

Finally, we should briefly note another application of our basic analysis. Throughout this paper we have assumed that firms must produce in their home country. Given the assumed equality of production costs, however, firms clearly have an incentive to save transport costs by producing near the markets, if they can. But if we allow them to do this, each firm will produce in both countries—and we will have moved from a model of reciprocal dumping in trade to a model of two-way direct foreign investment.

Notes

We would like to thank an anonymous referee for very helpful comments. J. Brander wishes to gratefully acknowledge financial support from a Social Science and Humanities Research Council of Canada postdoctoral fellowship.

1. For an exposition of dumping as monopolistic price discrimination, see Caves and Jones (1977, pp, 152–154).

2. Two-way trade in similar (but not necessarily identical) products is often referred to as intraindustry trade. Standard references on the importance of intraindustry trade are Balassa (1966) and Grubel and Lloyd (1975). Alternative explanatory models include Krugman (1979) and Lancaster (1980).

3. The "basing point" pricing literature of the 1930s and 1940s was concerned largely with the waste due to cross-hauling in spatial markets. Of special interest is a paper by Smithies (1942) which contains a model of spatial imperfect competition in which cross-hauling arises. It is a short step to extend this model to an international setting. Smithies' model differs from ours in that he stakes price as the strategy variable, but the basic insight that imperfect competition can cause cross-hauling is central to both.

4. This separation is a very convenient simplification that arises from the assumption of constant marginal cost. It is not essential to the results.

5. Conditions (7) and (8) taken together imply, if they hold globally, that $\pi_{xx}\pi_{yy}^* - \pi_{xy}\pi_{yx}^* > 0$ globally, which in turn implies that reaction functions cross only once and that they do so such that the equilibrium is stable. Allowing violation of (8) and the possibility of multiple equilibria clearly does not upset the result that a two-way trade equilibrium exists. It would however, complicate welfare analysis in the usual way: one could not be sure which equilibrium would obtain, so welfare comparisons of different regimes would usually be ambiguous.

6. Expression (3) implies that $\varepsilon > (1 - \sigma)$, while (4) implies that $\varepsilon > \sigma$. Adding these it follows that $\varepsilon > 1/2$ at equilibrium. It is then clear from (6) that $\sigma < 1/2$ if $g < 1$. ($\sigma = 1/2$ if $g = 1$.)

7. The fact that x does fall is easily shown by totally differentiating (3) and (4), and using (7) and (8).

8. Demonstrating existence and uniqueness of free entry Cournot equilibrium is a general problem to which we have nothing to add. Clearly, there may be "integer" problems in small-numbers cases. The interested reader might consult Friedman (1977) and the references cited there.

9. If $\lambda = 0$, the first-order conditions become $p = c$ for domestic firms and $p = c/g$ for foreigners. Clearly, these cannot both hold. There is a corner solution at $p = c$ and $\sigma = 0$ where the Kuhn-Tucker condition $y(p - c/g) = 0$ holds. Ignoring the lower bound at $y = 0$ leads to the nonsense result that foreign firms would want to produce negative output in the domestic market, which is why the expression

for σ approaches $-\infty$ as λ approaches 0. σ should of course be bounded below at 0.

10. Brander and Spencer (1981) examine the implications for tariff policy of a market structure in which the foreign firm is an entry-deterring or potentially Stackelberg leader in both markets.

5

Increasing Returns and the Theory of International Trade

Since the beginnings of analytical economics, the concept of comparative advantage has been the starting point for virtually all theoretical discussion of international trade. Comparative advantage is a marvelous insight: simple yet profound, indisputable yet still (more than ever?) misunderstood by most people, lending itself both to theoretical elaboration and practical policy analysis. What international economist, finding himself in yet another confused debate about U.S. "competitiveness," has not wondered whether anything useful has been said since Ricardo?

Yet it has long been clear that comparative advantage—which I will here interpret loosely to mean a view that countries trade in order to take advantage of their differences—is not the only possible explanation of international specialization and exchange. As Ricardo doubtless knew, and as modern theorists from Ohlin on have reemphasized, countries may also trade because there are inherent advantages in specialization, arising from the existence of economies of scale. At a logical level a theory of trade based on increasing returns is as fundamental as one based on comparative advantage; at a practical level it is reasonable to argue that economies of scale, if perhaps not as important as national differences as a motive for trade, are at least of the same order of magnitude.

Increasing returns as an explanation of trade has, however, until recently received only a tiny fraction of the theoretical attention lavished upon comparative advantage. Again, the reasons are not hard to find. Where the concept of trade based on comparative advantage has opened up broad avenues of research, the attempt to formalize trade based on increasing returns seemed until recently to lead to an impenetrable jungle of complexity. Economics understandably and inevitably follows the line of least

Originally published in *Advances in Economic Theory, Fifth World Congress,* edited by Truman F. Bewley. © Cambridge University Press 1987.

mathematical resistance, and so until ten years ago the role of scale economies was at best a point to be mentioned in passing within most discussions of international trade.

During the last decade, however, several paths through the wilderness have been found. The new literature on increasing returns and trade does not yet have the generality and unity of traditional trade theory, and it may never be tied up in quite as neat a package. We can, however, now provide a far more systematic account of the role of increasing returns in international trade—and of the way this role interacts with that of comparative advantage—than would have seemd possible not long ago. The purpose of this chapter is to review the new concepts that have made this progress possible.

The central problem in theoretical analysis of economies of scale has always been, of course, the problem of market structure. Unexhausted scale economies are inconsistent with the standard competitive model; the problem of introducing them into trade theory is thus one of finding departures from that model that are both tractable and capable of accommodating increasing returns. Progress in recent years has been based on three such departures, and this chapter deals with each type of market structure in turn.

The first departure from the standard competitive model is the oldest. This is the Marshallian approach, in which increasing returns are assumed to be wholly external to the firm, allowing perfect competition to remain. Marshallian analyses of increasing returns and trade go back to the early postwar period. The early literature on the Marshallian approach, however, seemed discouraging in that even with the simplest assumptions it seemed to lead to a welter of multiple equilibria. Only in the last few years has it become clear that under certain circumstances it is possible to bring order to this complexity.

The second departure is a more recent creation. Less than ten years ago, several trade theorists independently applied formal models of Chamberlinian monopolistic competition to trade. The Chamberlinian approach has proved extremely fruitful, providing a simple tool for thinking about a variety of issues in international economics.

Finally, the Cournot approach to oligopoly has begun to be widely used in international trade theory. Much of this use is in normative analyses of trade policy, which are not the subject of this chapter, but some positive analysis of trade has also been based on this approach.

The plan of this chapter, then, is to discuss in succession recent developments in trade theory based on Marshallian, Chamberlinian, and Cournot approaches to the problem of market structure. A final section concludes with some issues for future research.

The limitations of the chapter should be made clear at the outset. The work discussed here is theoretical work aimed at understanding the causes and effects of trade, rather than at providing guidance to trade policy. That is, I am concerned here with why trade happens and what difference it makes, not with what we should do about it. Nor will I attempt to discuss the major implications that imperfect competition may have for the analysis of trade policy (see Dixit 1987 for a discussion of these implications), or empirical work, which in any case has so far been quite scarce in this area.

5.1   The Marshallian Approach

In a sense, the Marshallian approach to the analysis of trade under increasing returns goes back to Frank Graham's famous argument for protection (Graham 1923). Explicit general-equilibrium analysis of trade in the presence of external economies began with Matthews (1949) and was continued in a number of papers, including Kemp and Negishi (1970), Melvin (1969), Chacholiades (1978), and Panagariya (1981). For the most part, however, this literature was not successful in bringing increasing returns into trade theory in a way that generated useful insights or attracted additional research. In particular, the literature did not seem to offer the possibility of a fruitful marriage of increasing returns and comparative advantage as explanations of trade. Ironically, this failure may been been in part because of an excessive loyalty to the *techniques* of conventional models—production possibility curves, offer curves, and so forth. As it turns out, it is possible to have models in which comparative advantage and Marshallian economies interact in a clear way, but the development of such models depends crucially on the introduction of new techniques.

The key innovation here was the work of Ethier (1979, 1982a), who showed that the analysis of trade in the presence of Marshallian external economies is greatly clarified if we work from the allocation of resources to production and trade rather than the other way around. This may seen like a minor change, but it leads to a thorough revamping of modeling strategy. As we will see, a synthesis of Marshallian increasing returns and comparative advantage comes easily only if we focus on factor prices and the factor content of trade, rather than on goods prices and goods trade.

In this section, then, we will focus on the new version of the Marshallian approach, distinguished from the older approach by the way it works from resource allocation to trade. In addition to its direct usefulness, we will see that this approach provides us with techniques and insights that are directly relevant to the Chamberlinian approach as well.

The Simplest Model

There is a family resemblance between the simplest model of trade based on increasing returns and the basic Ricardian model. In both cases a fundamental principle of international trade can be derived from studying an imaginary world of two countries, two goods, and one factor of production. If the increasing returns model has not had anything like the same influence, it is because there seem to be too many things that can happen. The task of the theorist is to find restrictions that narrow the set of possibilities in an interesting way.

Suppose then, following the formulation of Ethier (1982a), that the world consists of two countries, each with only one factor of production: labor. To strip the problem down to bare essentials, we assume that the two countries possess identical technology with which to produce two goods. One of these goods—call it Chips—is produced at constant returns at the level of the firm but is subject to positive external economies so that at the level of the industry there are increasing returns. These external economies are assumed to be country-specific; it is each country's domestic industry rather than the world industry as a whole that is subject to increasing returns. The other good—call it Fish—is produced at constant returns to scale at the level of both the firm and the industry. We will assume that both Fish and Chips can be traded costlessly.

Now it is immediately apparent that even though both countries start with the same technological possibilities, the existence of economies of scale makes it inevitable that there will be international specialization. To see this, suppose that both countries were to produce both goods. The fact that both were producing Fish would imply equal wage rates. But this would mean that whichever country had the larger Chips industry would have lower cost in that industry; this would presumably lead that industry's relative size to increase still further, reinforcing the cost advantage; and we will have a cumulative process of differentiation between the countries that continues until at least one of the countries has specialized. And as long as one country has specialized, we will have international trade. So the model tells us the increasing returns will, as expected, lead to specialization and trade.

The problem, of course, is that while the outcome must involve specialization and trade, this still allows a number of possible equilibria. A little thought will suggest that there are three different kinds of equilibrium that can result. First, one country might produce both Chips and Fish while the other produces only Fish. Second, both countries might specialize, one in Chips and one in Fish. Third, one country might specialize in Chips while the other produces both goods. Since it is also possible that either country may take on either role, we have as many as six possible equilibria even in this simplest model.

To sort out this complexity, it is useful to begin by noticing that our first kind of equilibrium, where both countries produce Fish, is quite different from the other two in its implications for factor prices and welfare. As long as both countries end up producing the constant-returns good, they will have equal wages, something that will not be true in the other types of equilibrium. Because the countries will have equal wages, it does not matter to their welfare which country the good is produced in. Suppose that we could assure ourselves that the international equilibrium was in fact going to be of this type, where common production of a constant-returns good ensures equal wage rates. Then we might still have two equilibria, in that either country could produce Chips, but these equilibria would have a good deal in common. In each, the world output of Chips would be concentrated in a single country; and the volume both of that output and the world output of Fish would be the same across the two equilibria. Further, welfare —not only for the world as a whole but for each individual—would be the same regardless of which country ends up with the Chips industry. Thus the indeterminacy of the model, while not eliminated, would be sharply circumscribed.

Welfare in this case does not depend on which country produces Chips; how does it compare with autarky? A further appealing feature of the equal-wage equilibrium is that it yields a very simple condition for gains from trade. This is that each country gains from trade provided that the scale of the world Chips industry after trade is larger than the scale of the national industry before trade. The reason is that this implies a lower unit labor cost and therefore a lower price in terms of the (common) wage rate. The important points to notice about this criterion are (first) that it does not depend on which country actually produces Chips, and (second) that it is a very mild condition, likely to be satisfied. Thus we have in a quite simple way captured the idea that it is to everyone's advantage to be part of larger market.

The relative simplicity of the analysis when wage rates are equalized might lead us to ask whether there is some common ground between this case and the case of factor price equalization in the Heckscher-Ohlin model.

Figure 5.1

In fact there is a common aspect, pinpointed in Helpman and Krugman (1985). In both the Heckscher-Ohlin and external economy models, factor price equalization is a symptom of a deeper aspect of the trading equilibrium, namely that "trade reproduces the integrated economy." By this we mean that the output and resource allocation of the world economy as a whole are the same as they would have been if all factors of production had been located in a single country. Or to put it another way, equalization of factor prices occurs when the fact that the world's productive factors are geographically dispersed turns out not to matter.

Once we realize that wage equalization amounts to saying that the integrated economy is reproduced, a technique for analyzing the prospects for wage equalization readily follows. First, construct the integrated economy—that is, from tastes, technology, and factor endowments calculate what the allocation of labor between the Fish and Chips industries would have been if labor had been able to move freely between the two countries. Now, in order to reproduce the integrated economy, the trading world must be able to achieve the same scale of Chips production. Because external economies are assumed to be country specific, this means that the world Chips industry of the integrated economy must now fit into one of the national economies with some room to spare.

The implications of this condition are illustrated in figures 5.1 and 5.2. In each diagram the line OO^* represents the world endowment of labor. The division of that endowment between the two countries can be represented by a point on that line. Also in each figure the distance $OQ = Q'O^*$ represents the labor force devoted to Chips production in the integrated economy. The difference between the figures is that in figure 5.1 the Chips industry is assumed to employ less than half the world's labor force, while in figure 5.2 it is assumed to employ more than half.

It is now straightforward to see what is necessary to allow reproduction of the integrated economy. In figure 5.1, splitting the world to the left of Q allows the Chips industry to fit into Foreign at integrated economy scale; splitting it between Q and Q' allows it to fit into either; splitting it to the right of Q' allows it to fit into Home. Thus there is always a trading equilibrium in which wages are equalized. In figure 5.2, if the two countries are too nearly equal in size—the endowment lies in $Q'Q$—the integrated equilibrium cannot be reproduced, but otherwise it can.

Figure 5.2

What this analysis shows is that an equal-wage equilibrium in which both countries produce Fish is not unlikely to exist. Indeed, such an equilibrium always exists unless the share of the world labor force devoted to Chips exceeds one-half, and even then it will frequently exist. So concentrating on the equal-wage case does not mean focusing on a rare event.

Unfortunately, the fact that an equal-wage equilibrium exists need not mean that it is the only equilibrium. Suppose, for example, that Foreign is substantially smaller than Home, so that the endowment point in figure 5.1 lies to the right of Q'. Then there is an equal-wage equilibrium with the Chips industry concentrated in Home, but there might also be an equilibrium in which Foreign specializes in Chips and has higher wages. We can only rule this out if figure 5.1 is the relevant figure and the endowment division lies between Q and Q'—in effect, if the increasing returns sector is not too large and the countries are not too unequal in size.

An equal-wage equilibrium in which trade reproduces the integrated economy, then, is not the only possible outcome even in this simplest model. It is however a plausible outcome and one that yields appealingly simple results. Thus there is some justification for stressing this sort of outcome. Further, the idea of reproducing the integrated economy through trade provides a natural way to integrate the analysis of scale economies with that of comparative advantage, as we will see shortly.

Before proceeding to the next section, however, we need to ask what has happened to the traditional argument that increasing returns sectors are desirable property and that the possibility that they will contract as a result of trade is a source of doubt about the gains from trade. The answer is, of course, that this argument depends on the integrated economy *not* being reproduced, so that wages end up unequal. Suppose that figure 5.2 is the relevant diagram and that the countries have equal labor forces. Then wages cannot be equal; we will clearly have one country that specializes in Chips and has a higher wage than the other country, which might lose from trade and in any case will not be happy about the outcome. One can argue about whether this situation is more or less realistic than an equal-wage equilibrium; I would argue that it is less realistic, but that the main reason for focusing on the case of factor price equalization, here as elsewhere, is, of course, that it is so much simpler to work with.

Increasing Returns and Comparative Advantage

The model presented above is one in which increasing returns is the only source of trade and gains from trade. This is, of course, an extreme and unrealistic case, just as is the Heckscher-Ohlin model in which differences in relative factor endowments are the only source. What we would like is a model in which both types of motive are able to operate.

There is a considerable literature on what happens in the 2 × 2 model when one sector is subject to increasing returns. Contributions to that literature include in particular Kemp and Negishi (1970), Melvin (1969), and Panagariya (1981).

Our discussion of a one-factor model suggests, however, that 2 × 2 may not be the most productive or even the easiest model to study. The simplifying device we found useful there was a focus on trading equilibria that reproduce a hypothetical integrated economy. We also noted that factor price equalization in constant returns models is also equivalent to reproducing the integrated economy through trade. This makes it natural to look for assumptions that allow reproduction of an integrated economy when there are both increasing returns and differences in national factor endowments.

Suppose that there are some goods produced with country-specific external economies and that there are others produced with constant returns. Suppose also that there are two or more factors of production. Then a little thought will show that in order to reproduce the integrated economy we must be able to do the following: We must be able to distribute the integrated economy's industrial output among countries, *using the integrated economy techniques of production*, in such a way as to employ fully each country's factors of production; and when we do this each industry subject to country-specific external economies must be concentrated in a single country.

It is immediately apparent that we are very unlikely to be able to distribute industries so as to fully employ all factors of production in each country, unless there are at least as many industries to distribute as there are factors. Furthermore increasing returns sectors are not really "fungible"; because they must be concentrated in a single country, they can be reallocated among countries only in a discrete fashion. So to reproduce the integrated economy we need to have as many constant returns sectors as there are factors of production. The minimal model with this property is 2 × 3: two factors of production and three goods, only one of which is produced subject to increasing returns.

Imagine, then, that we have a world in which there are at least as many constant-returns industries as there are are factors, plus some increasing returns industries, and that trade reproduces the integrated economy. Then, of course, we have factor price equalization. What else can we say about trade?

The first thing we can say is that there will be specialization due to economies of scale: Every increasing returns sector will be concentrated in a single country. Thus, even if every country had the same factor endowment, there would still be specialization and trade due to scale economies. As in the case of the one-factor model, this specialization will in general have an arbitrary component: Each increasing returns industry must be concentrated in a single country, but which country it is concentrated in may be indeterminate.

Despite this indeterminacy, in an average sense there will be a relationship between factor endowments and the pattern of production and trade. A country with a high relative endowment of capital must on average produce a capital-intensive mix of goods, although it may produce some relatively labor-intensive ones. That is, the factor content of a country's production must match its factor endowment. On the other hand, if countries spend their income in the same way, all countries will consume the same mix of goods and thus the same mix of factor services embodied in those goods. It follows that countries will be net exporters of the services of factors in which they are abundantly endowed, and thus that in an average sense the factor proportions theory of trade will hold.

The next question is that of gains from trade. Clearly there are now two sources of potential gains from trade: specialization to take advantage of differences in relative factor endowments and specialization to take achieve larger scale of production. The usual analysis of gains from trade, with its discussion of the enlargement of each nation's consumption possibilities, does not carry over easily into an increasing returns world where the pattern of production and trade may well be indeterminate. We have just argued, however, that factor prices and the pattern of trade in factor services will still be determinate if we have factor price equalization, so we might suppose that the issue of gains from trade might also be resolvable if we focus on factors rather than goods. And this is in fact the case.

What we can establish is the following: After trade a country will be able to afford its pretrade consumption provided that the world scale of production of increasing returns goods is larger than that country's national scale of production before trade. (The scale need not be larger in all industries; roughly what is needed is that on average world industries be larger than

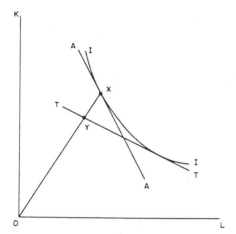

Figure 5.3

pretrade national industries would have been. For an exact statement, see Helpman and Krugman 1985.) Thus our criterion for gains from trade in the simplest model has now become a sufficient—not necessary—condition for gains in a more elaborate model. The reason it is only a sufficient condition is, of course, that there are now additional gains from comparative advantage that will occur even if scale gains should somehow fail to materialize.

To understand this condition, consider a country that uses two inputs, capital and labor. Let us first imagine that all industries operate under constant returns. In figure 5.3 we show the unit isoquant for some industry as *II*. The line *AA* represents pretrade factor prices. Thus *OX* is the vector of pretrade inputs per unit of the good. Now suppose trade is opened and that factor prices are equalized across countries. Then the new factor prices will be different from before, say, *TT*. This change in factor prices is immediately a source of gains from trade. The reason is as follows. Before trade, the economy used *OX* to produce each unit of the good. After trade, however, the income of a smaller vector of resources, *OY*, is now sufficient to buy one unit of the good. Because this must be true for every good, the economy can now earn enough to purchase its pretrade consumption and still have resources to spare.

Suppose now that some goods are produced with economies of scale. Provided that the scale of an industry after trade is larger than in the country before trade, the effect will be—as in figure 5.4—to shift the unit isoquant inward. This will add to the gains from trade. If there were no

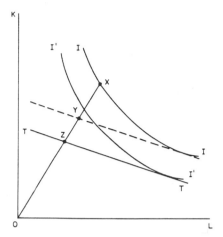

Figure 5.4

scale change, OY resources would be needed to purchase a unit of the output; so $OX-OY$ can be thought of as the comparative advantage component of the gains from trade. Scale effects, however, will generally shift the isoquant inward (not necessarily for our country, but for the country where the good is produced, which is all that matters). The result will be to lower the resources needed to purchase the good still further, to OZ, so that $OY-OZ$ can be thought of as the scale economy component of the gains from trade.

Obviously, if scale effects run the wrong way (so that isoquants shift outward) the effect will be to offset the comparative advantage gains and perhaps produce losses from trade. However, because the scale comparison is one of national scale before trade with world scale after trade, there is a strong presumption that scale effects will generally be a source of gains over and above those from comparative advantage.

The External Economy Approach: Summary

Recent work has shown that when the Marshallian external economy approach to increasing returns is looked at in the right way with the right assumptions, a clear and appealing story about trade emerges. The essential requirements to get this story are the willingness to assume that a trading world reproduces the aggregate outcomes of a hypothetical perfectly integrated economy—with factor price equalization as one of the consequences; and a willingness to focus on net trade in factor services rather than on trade in goods, which is typically indeterminate. Given these concessions, we are able to describe a world economy in which both factor proportions and scale economies contribute to international trade, and in which both are sources of gains from trade. In particular,

1. Although there is typically some indeterminacy in the precise pattern of trade, factor proportions theory continues to hold in an average sense. Countries will be net exporters of the services of factors with which they are abundantly endowed.

2. At the same time, the trading economy will be characterized by geographical concentration of each industry subject to country-specific increasing returns. This concentration will be an independent source of trade and would require trade even if factor endowments were identical.

3. The opportunity to exchange factor services at prices different from those that would prevail in the absence of trade will lead to gains from trade for all countries.

4. These gains will be supplemented by additional gains if the world scale of production in increasing returns industries—wherever they may be located—exceeds the national scale that would prevail in the absence of trade.

5.2   The Chamberlinian Approach

The 1970s were marked by substantial progress in the theoretical modeling of imperfect competition. Among the approaches developed by industrial organization theorists was a revival of Chamberlin's "large group" analysis of competition between similar firms producing differentiated products. This analysis, once put in the form of fully specified general equilibrium models, could be applied in a straightforward way to international trade, where it has proved a flexible tool of analysis.

The basic Chamberlinian idea is that one can think of at least some industries as being characterized by a process of entry in which new firms are able to differentiate their products from existing firms. Each firm will then retain some monopoly power—that is, will face a downward-sloping demand curve. Given economies of scale, however, this is not inconsistent with a situation in which entry drives economic profits to zero. Thus Chamberlin's vision was of an industry consisting of many little monopolists who have crowded the field sufficiently to eliminate any monopoly profits.

The limitation that prevented much use of this approach in international trade theory before the 1970s was the absence of any rigorous treatment of the process of product differentiation. In the 1970s, however, two approaches to this problem were developed. The first, identified with the work of Dixit and Stiglitz (1977) and Spence (1976), imposed the assumption that each consumer has a taste for many different varieties of a product. Product differentiation then simply takes the form of producing a variety not yet being produced. The alternative approach, developed by Lancaster (1979), posited a primary demand not for varieties per se but for attributes of varieties, with consumers differing in their preferred mix of attributes. Product differentiation in this case takes the form of offering a variety having attributes that differ from those of varieties already available.

For some purposes the differences between these approaches are important. For international trade theory, however, it does not much matter which approach is used. The important point is that both approaches end with an equilibrium in which a number of differentiated products are produced by firms that possess monopoly power but earn no monopoly profits. This is all we need to develop a remarkably simple model of international trade.

The Basic Model

Chamberlinian trade models that are essentially very similar can be found in papers by Dixit and Norman (1980), Ethier (1982b), Helpman (1981), Krugman (1979, 1981), and Lancaster (1980). A synthesis approach is given in Helpman and Krugman (1985), and I follow that approach here.

Consider a world consisting of two countries, Home and Foreign, endowed with two factors of production, capital and labor, and using the same technology to produce two goods, Food and Manufactures. Food is simply a homogeneous product produced under constant returns to scale. Manufactures, however, is a differentiated product, consisting of many potential varieties, each produced under conditions of increasing returns. We assume that the specification of tastes and technology in the Manufactures sector is such that it ends up being monopolistically competitive; beyond this the details do not matter.

As in our analysis of the Marshallian approach, the trick in analyzing this model is to start by constructing a reference point, the "integrated economy." That is, given tastes and technology, we find the equilibrium of a hypothetical closed economy endowed which the total world supplies of capital and labor. The key information we need from this calculation is the allocation of resources to each industry and relative factor prices. This

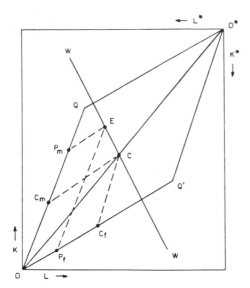

Figure 5.5

information is shown in figure 5.5. The sides of the box represent the total world supplies of capital and labor. The vector $OQ = O^*Q'$ is the allocation of resources to Manufactures production in the integrated economy; $QO^* = Q'O$ is the allocation of resources to Food; the slope of WW is relative factor prices. As drawn, Manufactures is more capital-intensive than Food, but this is not important.

The next step is to ask whether a trading economy will reproduce this integrated economy. Let us measure Home's endowment starting from O, and Foreign's endowment starting from O^*. Then the division of the world into countries can be represented by a point in the box, such as E. If we assume that the varieties of Manufactures are so numerous that we can ignore integer constraints, then it is immediately apparent that trade reproduces the integrated economy as long as the endowment point lies inside the parallelogram OQO^*Q'.

Once we have ascertained that the integrated economy's resource allocation is reproduced, we can determine the resource allocation within each country by completing parallelograms. If the endowment is E, then Home must devote resources OP_m to Manufactures and OP_f to Food; the balance of the integrated economy's production of each good must be produced in Foreign. Because there are economies of scale in production of Manufactures, each country will produce different varieties of manufactured goods; which country produces which varieties is indeterminate but also unimportant.

We have now determined the pattern of production; to determine consumption and trade we now make use of factor prices. The line WW has a slope equal to relative factor prices and thus can be seen as a line along which the shares of Home and Foreign in world income are constant. This means in particular that resources OC receive the same share of world income as OE, and thus that OC/OO^* is the Home country's share of world income. Let us now add the assumption of identical spending patterns, and we know that each country will consume embodied factor services in the same proportion as the world supplies. It follows that OC is also Home consumption of factor services and thus that EC is net trade in factor services. As in the Marshallian case analyzed above, the precise pattern of trade is indeterminate, but the factor content of trade reflects factor endowments.

We can say more, however. Since OC is Home consumption of factor services, it must consume OC_m of these services embodied in Manufactures and OC_f embodied in Food. This tells us that Home must be a net exporter of Manufactures and a net importer of Food.

Home is a net exporter of Manufactures; however, we have already noted that each country will be producing a different set of varieties. Because each country is assumed to demand all varieties, this means that Home will still demand some varieties produced in Foreign. The result will be a pattern of trade looking like that illustrated in figure 5.6. Home will

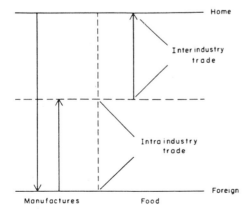

Figure 5.6

import Food and be a net exporter of Manufactures but it will also import Manufactures, so that there will be "intraindustry" trade. This intraindustry trade is essentially caused by scale economies; if there were no scale economies, each country would be able to produce all varieties of Manufactures itself. Because intraindustry trade arises from scale economies rather than differences between countries, it does not vanish as countries become more similar; indeed, it is apparent that if we shift E toward C then the volume of intraindustry trade will rise both absolutely and relatively to interindustry trade. In the limit, if countries have identical relative factor endowments, they will still trade, but all their trade will be intraindustry trade based on scale economies.

The interesting point about this analysis of the trade pattern under monopolistic competition, as it has emerged from a number of years of clarifying analysis, is how little it seems to depend on the details. At a minor level, the differences between alternative formulations of product differentiation clearly make no difference. More important, in a broad sense the analysis is essentially the same as the one we have seen emerging from the assumption that economies of scale are external to firms. The precise pattern of trade is indeterminate, but factor proportions continue to determine trade in an average sense; scale economies lead to concentration of production and to a persistence of trade even when countries have identical factor endowments. As we will argue in a moment, the analysis of gains from trade is also quite similar.

What this suggests is that it is mistake to lay too much stress on the Chamberlinian assumption per se. The models in this literature make extensive use of product differentiation and are often related to the empirical phenomenon of intraindustry trade, but the issues should be seen as broader. The importance of increasing returns in trade does not stand or fall on the validity of particular interpretations of product differentiation or of two-way trade within statistical classifications.

Applications and Extensions

Once we move away from the central issue of trade pattern, the conclusions of the Chamberlinian approach become a bit more dependent on particular assumptions. Several areas have, however, yielded results that either look fairly general or are of particular interest. We consider four such areas: the gains from trade, trade and income distribution, intermediate goods, and transport costs.

Gains from Trade

At first sight it might seem that the analysis of gains from trade in the external economies approach would carry over directly to the Chamberlinian approach as well. In fact, however, the translation is not direct, for two related reasons. First, the relevant scale variable is not the scale of the industry but the scale of production of individual firms, and with entry the effects of trade on this scale are not immediately obvious. Second, trade may lead to extra gains due to an increase in the variety of products available.

What we can certainly say is that a country will gain from trade if, after trade, both the number of available varieties and the scale of production of each variety are at least as large as before trade. Further, there is a strong presumption that the diversity of products will be larger after trade than before. The problem is one of pinning down what happens to scale.

Here the nature of product differentiation does make a difference. What happens to the scale of production depends (for homothetic production functions—otherwise still more complications arise) on what happens to the elasticity of demand for individual varieties. With Dixit-Stiglitz preferences, this elasticity is constant; trade offers greater variety but not greater scale (Dixit and Norman 1980; Krugman 1980, 1981). With Lancaster preferences, trade is likely, though not certain, to lead to more elastic demand, forcing firms to move further down their average cost curves, so that the advantages of a larger market are reflected both in greater diversity and lower average cost (Helpman 1981).

Again, however, we should not make too much of the details. Both increased scale of production and increased diversity of available products can be seen as gains from scale, broadly defined. This insight is given a more concrete form by Helpman and Krugman (1985), where it is shown that under some assumptions both scale and diversity will move monotonically with gross industry output. This leads to the following criterion for gains from trade: trade is beneficial if the world output of Manufactures is larger than our national output would have been in the absence of trade. The similarity to the criterion for the external economy case should be obvious.

Trade and Income Distribution

We have argued for a presumption that scale economies lead to additional gains from trade above and beyond those resulting from comparative advantage. This seems to be only a quantitative difference. However, it can lead to a qualitative difference in the effects of trade on particular groups within countries. Constant-returns trade models predict very strong income-distribution effects from changes in relative prices, so that even though trade is beneficial in the aggregate, individuals who draw their income mostly from factors that are relatively scarce end up worse off as a result of trade. Once we add gains from larger scale, however, it seems possible that everyone may gain from trade.

What makes this an interesting possibility is that it suggests that the effects of trade may depend on its character. If trade is mostly Heckscher-Ohlin in motivation—which we would expect if countries are quite different in relative factor endowments and there are weak economies of scale—then the conventional result that scarce factors lose from trade may be expected to hold. If trade is mostly motivated by scale economies—which would happen if countries are similar and scale is important, and would be associated with a prevalence of intraindustry trade—we might expect to find that even scarce factors gain.

This insight sounds fairly general. To demonstrate it in any rigorous way is not easy, however. Krugman (1981) develops an example in which there are natural indices of both similarity of countries and the importance of scale economies and shows that one can in fact establish a boundary in terms of these two indices between the case where scarce factors lose and the case where they gain. It is possible to establish as a more general proposition that gains for all factors are more likely the more similar is a country's endowment to that of the world as a whole, and the smaller is the country; this is shown in Krugman (1984).

Intermediate Goods

Ethier (1979, 1982b) has suggested that scale-based international trade is more likely to be important in intermediate goods than in final goods. He argues forcefully that the scope for productive differentiation of products —and the extent to which even the world market is likely to be too small to allow exhaustion of scale gains—is greatest for highly specialized components, capital goods, and so forth, rather than for consumer products.

What difference does this make? The answer is that as long as trade reproduces the integrated economy, as it does in the models of Ethier (1979, 1982b) and Helpman (1985), having trade in intermediate goods rather than final goods does not make much difference at all. The main difference is one of emphasis: It now becomes very clear that the right scale variable to emphasize, when we consider the role of scale in producing gains from trade, is the size of the world industry after trade versus the national industry before trade. We have seen that this is probably the right way to think about the issue even with consumer goods trade, but here the point becomes indisputable. The related nuance is that the doubts that occasionally surface about whether an increase in the diversity of consumer goods really increases welfare seem much less reasonable when it is the diversity of lathes or robots that is at issue.

We may also note a point raised by Helpman and Krugman (1985): if intermediate goods produced with economies of scale are *not* tradeable, the result will be to induce the formation of "industrial complexes"—groups of industries tied together by the need to concentrate all users of a nontradeable intermediate in the same country. In this case the pattern of specialization and trade in the Chamberlinian world will actually come to resemble the pattern in the Marshallian world described previously.

Transport Costs
The exposition that we have presented of the Chamberlinian approach to trade is based heavily on the assumption that trade reproduces the integrated economy, with zero transport costs a key element in this assumption. For some purposes this is clearly an annoying limitation. No general integration of transport costs into the Chamberlinian trade model has been achieved, but some work has been done on special cases, with interesting results.

One way to allow for transport costs with a minimum of complexity is to assume that these costs are either zero or prohibitive, so that we get a strict division of industries into tradeables and nontradeables. If we then assume that there are enough tradeable sectors and that countries are sufficiently similar in their factor endowments, we can still have factor price equalization. In this case, however, factor price equalization need not mean that the integrated economy is reproduced; if differentiated products are included in the set of nontraded goods, the fragmentation of the world economy reduces the scale at which these products are produced as well as the number of varieties available to consumers.

This is a useful observation in itself; it becomes especially interesting when we combine it with some consideration of factor mobility. For if there are nontraded goods produced with increasing returns, this provides an incentive for migration to large economies, a process that will in turn reinforce these economies' size advantage. This point was noted by Helpman and Razin (1984) and elaborated upon in Helpman and Krugman (1985), where it is also noted that the incentive is actually for a change in the location of consumption, not production.

The more realistic case—where transport costs matter, but are not prohibitive— is much harder to analyze, except under very specific assumptions about tastes and technology. A very special model is considered by Krugman (1980) and elaborated upon by Venables (1985). This model generates a result that, upon reflection, looks as though it ought to be more general than the particularity of the assumptions might lead one to believe. The result is this: Other things being equal, countries will tend to be net exporters of goods for which they have relatively large domestic markets.

The logic of this result is quite simple. Suppose there is a product that is sold to two locations and can be produced in either one at equal cost. Suppose further that there are transport costs between the two locations but that economies of scale are strong enough to assure that nonetheless the product will be produced in only one place. Then the location of production will be chosen to minimize transport costs, and this clearly means producing in the location with the larger market and exporting to the smaller market.

Multinationals and Trade in Technology

In addition to allowing a very concise treatment of the role of economies of scale in international trade, the Chamberlinian approach has proved useful as a way to organize thinking about two related issues that do not fit at all well into perfect competition trade models. These are the role of trade in technology and the role of multinational firms.

The reason why trade in technology cannot be treated in conventional models is that investment in knowledge is hard to model except as a kind of fixed cost, which inevitably leads to a breakdown of perfect competition. Once we have a Chamberlinian setup, however, the issue is straightforward. One simply has firms in one country develop products and then sell the knowledge of how to produce these products to firms in another country, who set themselves up as monopolistic competitors. A model along these lines was developed by Feenstra and Judd (1982); their analysis makes clear the point that trade in technology need not be much different in its effects from any trade in which fixed costs play a significant role.

A natural extension of this analysis is to imagine that for some reason licensing or sale of technology is not possible, so that technology can only be transferred within firms. In this case the model of technology transfer can then be reinterpreted as one of multinational firms. A simple model of this type is set forth in Krugman (1980); like the Feenstra-Judd analysis, it suggests that multinational enterprise is more like ordinary trade than one might have supposed.

The identification of direct foreign investment with technology transfer is too narrow, however. A more general approach was suggested by Helpman (1984) and in turn simplified and generalized in Helpman and Krugman (1985). This approach essentially argues that multinational enterprise occurs whenever there exist related activities for which the following is true: There are simultaneously transaction cost incentives to integrate these activities within a single firm and factor cost or other incentives to separate the activities geographically. Suppose, for example, there is a two-stage production process consisting of a capital-intensive upstream activity and a labor-intensive downstream activity and that (for any of the usual causes) there are compelling reasons to combine these activities inside vertically integrated firms. Suppose further that countries are sufficiently different in factor endowments that unless these activities are geographically separated there will be unequal factor prices. Then the result will clearly be the emergence of firms that extend across national boundaries.

Probably the main contribution of the new literature on multinational enterprise has been to clear away some confusions about what multinationals do. What the new models make clear, above all, is that multinational enterprise is not a type of factor mobility. It represents an extension of control, not necessarily a movement of capital. The key lesson is that direct foreign investment is not investment.

Summary

When it was first introduced, the Chamberlinian approach to trade analysis represented a breakthrough. For the first time it became possible to discuss trade issues involving scale economies and imperfect competition intelligibly. At the same time, however, it was difficult to assess how general were the insights gained from the very special models first presented.

Subsequent work has removed some of this uncertainty. Many of the conclusions of the monopolistic competition approach have proved to be independent of the details of the specification. In fact, as we have suggested, in a broad sense many of the insights carry over to other market structures as well. This realization in a way devalues the Chamberlinian approach—it should now be seen as one of several useful analytical devices rather than as *the* alternative to constant returns trade theory. But the simplicity and clarity of monopolistic competition models of trade ensures that they will remain a valuable part of the toolbox for a long time.

5.3   The Cournot Approach

Our first two approaches to trade under conditions of increasing returns may be viewed as being driven by the desire to focus on decreasing costs as a motive for trade while avoiding as much as possible being bogged down in issues of market structure. The Marshallian approach preserves perfect competition despite the presence of scale economies by assuming that these economies are wholly external. The Chamberlinian approach abandons perfect competition but turns instead to the opposite pole of a world of little monopolists, avoiding the awkward middle ground of oligopoly. As a research strategy this artful theoretical dodging is wholly defensible, especially given our continuing lack of anything like a general theory of competition among small numbers of firms. Yet we cannot completely ignore the oligopoly issue, especially if we suspect that the interaction of imperfect competition with trade may give rise to important effects missed by these approaches.

There is no general analysis of oligopoly; but even a special analysis is better than none. Some important insights into international trade have been gained by adopting the admittedly unsatisfactory Cournot assumption that imperfectly competitive firms take each others' outputs as given. Much of the usefulness of this approach has come in the analysis of trade policy, discussed by Dixit (1987); but two themes deserve discussion in this chapter. The first is the role of trade in reducing monopoly power and increasing competition. The second is the possibility that market segmentation and price discrimination can serve as a cause of seemingly pointless trade.

Trade and Market Power

Suppose there is some industry that in each of two countries contains only a few firms. Suppose also that these firms compete in a Cournot fashion, so that (in equilibrium) price will be above marginal cost by a markup that depends on the perceived elasticity of per-firm demand. Finally, suppose that in the absence of trade in this industry the price of the good it produces would be the same in both countries.

Under perfect competition, allowing trade in this industry would have no effect. With Cournot competition, however, this is no longer the case. If trade is opened, each firm will become part of a larger, more competitive market. It will see itself as facing a higher elasticity of demand, leading it to expand output. Thus industry output will expand, and the price will fall. If the countries are, as described, symmetric, then welfare will rise in both, due to the reduction on the monopoly distortion. Interestingly, this effect need not be associated with any actual trade in either direction. It is potential foreign trade (which changes the slope of the demand curve), rather than the actual trade flows, that exerts the procompetitive effect.

The possibility of gains from trade due to increased competition has been understood for a long time. It was emphasized in particular by Caves (1974). However, early analyses usually assumed that the move was from pure monopoly to perfect competition; only with the work of Dixit and Norman (1980) was the more reasonable case—of movement from more to less imperfect competition—formally considered.

Why should there be only a limited number of firms in the industry? The obvious answer is the presence of some form of economies of scale internal to firms. Once we allow this, however, it becomes an obvious possibility that the increase in competition due to trade may leave firms unable to charge a markup on marginal cost sufficient to cover their average cost. The result will be exit. Dixit and Norman develop a simple example in which they show that the effect of opening trade in a Cournot market is to lead to a world industry that has fewer, larger firms than the sum of national industries before trade, but where competition is nonetheless increased. Thus the opening of trade leads not only to a reduction in the monopoly distortion but also to an increase in productive efficiency. Once again, it is the potential for trade (rather than the trade flows themselves) that does the good work.

The procompetitive effect of trade is not exactly a scale economy story. It goes naturally with such a story, however, precisely because decreasing costs are the most natural explanation of imperfect competition.

Market Segmentation and Price Discrimination

At the beginning of this chapter we suggested that trade can always be explained as being due to the combined effects of two motives for specialization, differences between countries and economies of scale. Remarkably, the Cournot approach has actually led to the discovery of a third possible explanation for trade—although arguably not of equal importance in practice. This is the possibility that trade may arise purely because imperfectly competitive firms have an incentive to try to gain incremental sales by "dumping" in each others' home markets.

The seminal paper is by Brander (1981). The model envisages an industry consisting of two firms, each in a different country. These firms are assumed to be able to choose separately their deliveries to each national market and to take the other firm's deliveries to each market as given. Suppose that initially there were no trade in this industry. Then each firm would act as a monopolist, restricting market deliveries to sustain the price. There would, however, then be an incentive for each firm to sell a little bit in the other's home market as long as the price there exceeds the marginal cost. This process will continue until, with symmetric firms, each firm has a 50 percent share of each market.

If the markets are separated by transport costs, the outcome will not be so extreme. Nonetheless, it is shown in Brander and Krugman (1983) that even with transport costs there may be "cross-hauling"—two-way trade in the same product. What sustains this trade is the fact that each firm sees itself as facing a higher elasticity of demand on its exports than it does on domestic sales, because it has a smaller share of the foreign than the domestic market. This means that the firm is willing to sell abroad at a smaller markup over marginal cost than at home, making it willing to absorb the transport cost on foreign sales. Indeed, it is this difference in perceived demand elasticity that drives the determination of the volume of trade: the equilibrium market share of imports is precisely that which makes exporters just willing to absorb transport costs.

This theory of seemingly pointless trade, which is described in Brander and Krugman as "reciprocal dumping," is related in important ways to the traditional industrial organization literature on basing point pricing and cross-hauling (Smithies 1942). What the new models make clear, however, is that despite the waste involved in transporting the same good in two directions, trade can still be beneficial. Against pointless transport costs must be set the increase in competition. Indeed, if there is free entry and exit of firms, it can be shown that the gains from "rationalizing" the industry and increasing the scale of production always outweigh the waste of transport.

Summary

The application of Cournot-type models to trade theory leads to new and important insights about international trade. Papers using the Cournot approach have had a fundamentally different orientation from those using the Marshallian or Chamberlinian approaches. Instead of focusing on economies of scale and treating market structure as (at best) a supporting player, this literature has treated imperfect competition as the protagonist and used economies of scale mostly as an explanation of the existence of oligopoly.

The payoff from this shift in emphasis is substantial. A new source of potential gains from trade is identified—namely, the effect of trade in increasing competition (and, if it induces exit, in rationalizing production). More surprisingly, a new cause of trade is also identified: interpenetration of markets because oligopolists perceive a higher elasticity of demand on exports than on domestic sales.

The major importance of the Cournot approach, however, lies outside the scope of this chapter. This is its versatility and flexibility for the discussion of trade policy. The models we have described under the headings of Marshallian and Chamberlinian approaches depend—as a way to make the analysis tractable—mostly on the assumption that trade reproduces an integrated economy. Tariffs, quotas, and subsidies inevitably break this perfect integration rendering these models unsuitable. The Cournot approach, however, does not have this problem, and has led to a rapidly growing literature on trade and industrial policy under imperfect competition.

5.4   Conclusions

What We Have Learned

Intellectual progress is often hard to perceive. Once new ideas have become absorbed they can seem obvious, and one begins to believe that one always understood them. The ideas that trade can be caused by increasing returns and that increased scale is a source of gains from trade are sufficiently simple that the memory of how little these ideas were appreciated even five years ago is fading fast. Thus it is probably worth restating what we have learned.

It is probably fair to say that a few years ago, if international economists thought at all about the role of increasing returns in trade, they implicitly thought in terms of a 2 × 2 model in which one sector is subject to external economies. In this approach, economies appear as a modification or distortion of comparative advantage, rather than an independent source of trade. The effect of increasing returns is to make it likely, other things being equal, that large countries will export goods subject to scale economies. One can find many writings in which the view is taken that this effect is the only possible role of increasing returns in international trade.

What we have now moved to is a far more satisfactory view, where increasing returns are fully integrated into the trade model rather than grafted on to the Heckscher-Ohlin model as an afterthought. The new approaches allow us to understand clearly that decreasing costs are an independent source of both trade and gains from trade and to have a clear vision of a trading world in which both increasing returns and differences in factor endowments drive the pattern of specialization and trade.

This shift in view was initially brought about largely by the introduction of new models of imperfect competition into trade theory. With some perspective, however, we can now see that the details of these models are less important than might have appeared at first. What is really crucial for the new view of trade is not so much the particular model of market structure but a change in modeling strategy. The key breakthrough has been a willingness to ask different questions and to be satisifed with a somewhat different answer than we were used to.

Traditionally, trade models have given us a precise description of the pattern of trade in goods. In models where there are important increasing returns, however, a characteristic feature is the existence of multiple equilibria. What we have learned to do is essentially to live with multiple equilibria, by focusing on models where a good deal can be said without requiring that we know the precise pattern of specialization and trade. By concentrating on resource allocation rather than goods production; by looking at trade in embodied factor services rather than in the precise goods in which these factor services are embodied; by noting that it may be more important to be able to show that production will be concentrated somewhere than to say where it will be concentrated—thus are we able to bypass the complexities that for many years led trade theory to avoid discussion of increasing returns.

To answer a question by changing it is not to everyone's taste. However, the payoff here has been remarkable: By what (in retrospect) seems a minor shift in emphasis, we have greatly enlarged the range of phenomena that our theory can encompass.

What Needs to Be Done

The theory of trade under increasing returns is not a finished product. Much work still needs to be done, especially in the three following areas.

1. *Dynamic models.* In the real world, many of the advantages of large scale probably take the form of dynamic economies, either in the form of learning

effects or fixed-cost-like R&D. The problem is that dynamic competition in oligopolistic markets may be quite different in character from what static models would suggest; such competition needs further study.

2. *More realistic models of competition.* Not much need be said here. The external economy approach is clearly unrealistic in assuming perfect competition; the Chamberlinian approach relies on fundamentally peculiar cross-restrictions on technology and utility; the Cournot approach is surely far too crude.

3. *The unreproduced integrated economy.* Assuming that trade reproduces the integrated economy does wonders for simplifying the analysis. Now we must edge back toward considering what happens when—especially because of trade barriers and transport costs—trade does not reproduce the integrated economy.

These theoretical extensions are important and needed. What we need even more, however, is to go from qualitative theory to numerical applications. This has always been difficult in international trade. The new work on trade makes it even harder, because once we are no longer assuming perfect competition and constant returns we need far more information to model behavior. In fact, we probably need a whole new methodology for empirical work, possibly mixing case-study evidence and even interview results with econometrics and simulation techniques. Still, now that we have an elegant theory, this is the obvious next step.

II   Cumulative Processes and the Role of History

6   Trade, Accumulation, and Uneven Development

6.1   Introduction

Why is the world divided into rich and poor nations? Most critics of the international economic order would argue that there is some fundamental unequalizing process at work. The argument that there is an inherent tendency for international inequality to increase is often referred to as the doctrine of "uneven development." This doctrine is usually associated with radicals such as Baran (1957), Frank (1967), and Wallerstein (1974), but similar arguments have also been made by less radical authors such as Myrdal (1957) and Lewis (1977).

This chapter sets out a model that attempts to present the essentials of the doctrine of uneven development in schematic form. The model portrays a two-region world in which the industrial sectors of regions grow through the accumulation of capital. Given one crucial assumption—that there are external economies in the industrial sector—a small "head start" for one region will cumulate over time, with exports of manufactures from the leading region crowding out the industrial sector of the lagging region. This process, I would argue, captures the essence of the argument that trade with developed nations prevents industrialization in less developed countries.

In addition to helping synthesize and clarify the arguments of theorists of uneven development, the model set forth in this chapter is of some technical interest. Conventional trade theory has often been criticized for being static and for assuming constant returns to scale. The model developed here meets these objections while continuing to make use of the tools of orthodox theory. One of the surprising things that emerges from the

Originally published in the *Journal of Development Economics* 8 (1981). 149–161. © North-Holland Publishing Company.

analysis is that the theory of uneven development fits in very well with the Heckscher-Ohlin theory of trade.

The chapter is organized in four sections. Section 6.2 lays out the structure of the model. The basic analysis of the model's dynamics is carried out in section 6.3. Section 6.4 considers the role of international investment and shows that the model naturally gives use to a two-stage pattern of development that bears a striking resemblance to a Hobson-Lenin view of imperialism. Finally, section 6.5 extends the analysis to a three-region world.

6.2   The Basic Model

Consider a world consisting of two regions, North and South. These regions will be assumed to be identical in the sense that technological and behavioral relationships are the same. To sharpen the analysis, I will also assume that the regions have equal labor forces and that these labor forces do not grow over time. Thus we have

$$L_N = L_S = \overline{L}. \tag{1}$$

Each region will be able to produce two goods, a manufactured good M and an agricultural product A, and to trade at zero transportation costs. There will thus be a single world price of manufactured goods in terms of agricultural products, P_M. Agricultural products will be produced by labor alone; we will choose units so that one unit of labor produces one unit of agricultural goods.

The growth sector, however, is manufacturing. Manufacturing will require both capital and labor. It will be assumed that, *from the point of view of an individual firm*, the unit capital and labor requirements are fixed.[1] In the aggregate, however, unit capital and labor requirements will not be constant; instead, in each region they will be decreasing functions of the region's aggregate capital stock. Letting c_N, c_S and v_N, v_S be the unit capital and labor requirements in North and South, respectively, we have

$$c_N = c(K_N), \qquad c_S = c(K_S),$$

$$v_N = v(K_N), \qquad v_S = v(K_S), \tag{2}$$

where c', $v' < 0$. I will, however, assume that the absolute value of the elasticity of unit input requirements with respect to output is less than one, so that *total* input requirements rise as manufacturing output rises.

Since the assumption of external economies in the industrial sector is crucial to the dynamic story we are about to tell, it requires some discussion. There are really two questions here. First, can external economies be justified in microeconomic terms? Second, does the concept of external economies really capture the processes theorists of uneven development have in mind?

The justifications for technological externalities have, of course, been familiar since Marshall. Even if economies of scale are internal to firms, internal economies in the production of intermediate inputs can behave like external economies for the firms that buy them. So it is certainly legitimate to make use of the concept. What may be questioned is whether external economies are empirically important or, if they are, whether they are more important in manufacturing than in agriculture. For the sake of argument this paper will assume that there are important external economies specific to the industrial sector.

From a doctrinal point of view it also seems reasonable to use external economies as a key element in a theory of uneven development. Some theorists of uneven development, such as Baran (1957), have explicitly stressed the role of external economies. More generally, the essential argument in any theory of an unequalizing spiral must be that a region with already developed industry has an advantage in industrial production over a region without, and it is hard to see how to model this except in terms of external economies.[2] While many authors have also argued for other factors, such as a distorting effect of the interaction with developed countries on demand in less developed countries, external economies seems to be a useful *minimal* assumption.

Given the relationships (2), then, together with full employment of factors, we can determine the pattern of output. In each country the output of manufactured goods depends on the capital stock:

$$M_N = \frac{K_N}{c(K_N)}, \qquad M_S = \frac{K_S}{c(K_S)}. \tag{3}$$

Output of agricultural goods can then be determined from the agricultural sector's role as a residual claimant on labor:

$$A_N = \bar{L} - v_N M_N, \qquad A_S = \bar{L} - v_S M_S. \tag{4}$$

Note that there is an upper limit, K_{max} to the amount of capital that can usefully be employed in either region, which comes when the region is completely specialized in manufacturing and no more labor can be drawn out of agriculture. We can define K_{max} by noting that $v(K_{max}) \cdot K_{max}/c(K_{max}) = \bar{L}$.

Consider next the distribution of income. There are two cases: the case in which at least some labor is used in agricultural production and the case of complete specialization in manufacturing. If some labor is used in agriculture, this ties down the wage rate, which is 1 in terms of agricultural goods, $1/P_M$ in terms of manufactures. We can then determine the rental per unit of capital as a residual. For simplicity, let us assume (though it is not essential) that capital goods are produced by labor alone; that is we include them as part of "agricultural" output. Then the rental per unit of capital, measured in agricultural (or wage) units, is also the profit rate, and we have

$$\rho_N = \frac{P_M - v_N}{c_N}, \qquad \rho_S = \frac{P_M - v_S}{c_S}, \tag{5}$$

where ρ_N, ρ_S are profit rates North and South. Since c and v are functions of the capital stocks, we can also write (5) as a pair of reduced form equations:

$$\rho_N = \rho(P_M, K_N), \qquad \rho_S = \rho(P_M, K_S), \tag{6}$$

where $\partial \rho / \partial P_M$ and $\partial \rho / \partial K$ are both positive.

When a region is completely specialized in manufacturing, (6) no longer holds. Instead the rate of profit is determined in Kaldorian fashion by the requirement that savings equal zero, if there is no foreign investment, or by the rate of profit on foreign investment if there is such investment. In the latter case the wage rate is residually determined.

To close the model we need to specify the demand side. I will make two strong assumptions for the sake of easy algebra; the conclusions of the model could be derived under weaker but less convenient assumptions. First, saving behavior is classical: all profits and only profits are saved. Second, a fixed proportion μ of wages will be spent on manufactures, $1 - \mu$ on agricultural goods.

The savings assumption means that, if there is no international investment, the rate of growth of the capital stock in each region will just equal the rate of profit.

$$\frac{\dot{K}_N}{K_N} = \rho_N, \qquad \frac{\dot{K}_S}{K_S} = \rho_S. \tag{7}$$

It is easy to see how this can give rise to an unequalizing spiral. Suppose we are at an early stage in the development of the world economy where both regions are nonspecialized but North has accumulated more capital than South. Then, since the regions will face a common relative price of manufactures, by (6) the rate of profit and the rate of growth will be larger in the region that already has more capital. This is the basis for the divergence analyzed in more detail below.

The relative price of manufactured goods will be determined by world demand and supply. Since a fraction μ of wages is spent on manufactures, provided that both countries produce some agricultural goods we have

$$P_M[M_N + M_S] = \mu[L_N + L_S], \tag{8}$$

which can be rewritten as

$$P_M = 2\mu\bar{L}/[K_N/c(K_N) + K_S/c(K_S)]. \tag{9}$$

This gives us a relationship between the two capital stocks and P_M; it is apparent that P_M is decreasing in both capital stocks. Note also that K_N and K_S enter symmetrically, so that where $K_N = K_S$, $\partial P_M/\partial K_N = \partial P_M/\partial K_S$.

Finally, we can combine (6), (7), and (9) to express the rate of change of each region's capital stock as a function of the levels of both capital stocks:

$$\frac{\dot{K}_N}{K_N} = g(K_N, K_S), \qquad \frac{\dot{K}_S}{K_S} = g(K_S, K_N). \tag{10}$$

We know that the effect of an increase in the *other* region's capital stock must be to turn the terms of trade against manufactures and thus reduce profits; so $g_2 < 0$. The effect of an increase in the *domestic* capital stock is, however, ambiguous, since there are two effects: a worsening of the terms of trade and a reduction in unit input requirements. I will assume that the first effect outweighs the second: $g_1 < 0$. In other words, external economies are relatively weak. It is apparent that this is a conservative assumption that weakens the forces for uneven development. Nonetheless, divergence will still occur.

We have now set out a complete dynamic model in which the evolution of the two regions' industrial sectors can be followed from any initial position. The next step is to trace out and interpret the path of the world economy over time.

6.3 Dynamics of Uneven Development

The basic process that drives this model is extremely simple. As long as both countries produce agricultural goods, wage rates will be equalized by trade; while because of the external economies in manufacturing production, whichever country has the larger capital stock will have a higher

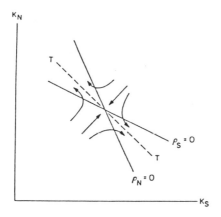

Figure 6.1

profit rate and will therefore grow faster. The result is an ever-increasing divergence between the regions, which ends only when a boundary of some kind has been reached. The outcome can differ slightly, depending on what sort of boundary limits the process.

Figure 6.1 illustrates the essential point, which is that no "interior" equilibrium—where both regions produce both manufactured and agricultural goods—can be stable. (A formal proof is given in the appendix.) The lines $\rho_N = 0$, $\rho_S = 0$ indicate combinations of K_N and K_S, for which profits in North and South respectively are zero. Given the assumptions in section 6.2, these lines are downward-sloping. Also drawn in is a schedule along which the relative price of manufactures is constant, the dotted line TT. As we move northwest along TT, the profit rate must rise in North and fall in South, because of the external economies in manufacturing. As a result, the line $\rho_N = 0$ is steeper than TT, while the line $\rho_S = 0$ is less steep.

If we now recall that each region's capital stock will grow if profits are positive, shrink if they are negative, it is apparent that the behavior of the system near the interior equilibrium must be as indicated by the arrows. There is a knife-edge path leading to the equilibrium; but if either region starts with even a slightly larger stock of capital, there will be an ever-increasing divergence in that direction.

The divergence will continue until a boundary is reached. In this model boundaries are defined by the impossibility of having a negative capital stock and by the fact that when a region's stock of capital reaches K_{max}, profits drop to zero and growth ceases. Figure 6.2 illustrates the boundaries and the interesting possible outcomes.[3] One possibility is indicated by E_N^1,

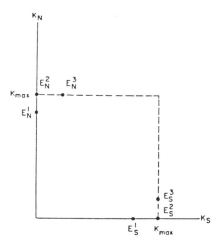

Figure 6.2

E_S^1. In each of these equilibria, the "underdeveloped" region has specialized completely in agriculture while the "developed" region contains both agricultural and industrial sectors. At E_N^2 or E_S^2, by contrast, both regions specialize, the developed in manufactures and the underdeveloped in agriculture. Finally, at E_N^3 or E_S^3 the boundary is given by the exhaustion of investment opportunitites in the developed region at K_{max}, which implies that the region specializes in manufactured goods; meanwhile the underdeveloped region develops some manufacturing capacity but continues to produce and export agricultural products.

Although these three cases differ slightly, they all involve a long-run equilibrium in which the world has become differentiated into industrial and nonindustrial (or at least less industrial) regions. It would run against the spirit of the doctrine of uneven development, however, to conduct the anslysis solely in terms of long-run solutions. Instead we should consider the whole dynamic story. Figure 6.3 illustrates how uneven development occurs, for the case in which both regions end by specializing. We start from an initial position such as A or B, in which one region has slightly more capital. There then follows a period in which both regions grow, but the already more developed region grows faster. As manufacturing capital grows, the relative price of industrial goods falls, until eventually a point is reached when the lagging region's industry cannot compete and begins to shrink. Once this starts, there is no check, because costs rise as the scale of the industry falls; and the lagging region's manufacturing sector disappears.

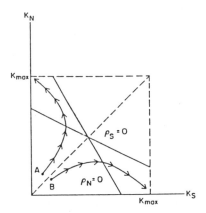

Figure 6.3

This is, of course, precisely what is supposed to have happened to the Indian textile industry in the eighteenth century. In effect the lagging region's nascent industrial sector is destroyed by manufactured exports from the leading region, which is, according to Baran, what "extinguished the igniting spark without which there could be no industrial expansion in the new underdeveloped countries."[4]

There are a number of interesting aspects of this story. Although the character of the long-run equilibrium is determined by tastes and technology, which region takes on which role depends on initial positions, i.e., on "primitive accumulation." Whether one prefers to explain the greater initial accumulation of capital in one region by the slave trade or the Protestant ethic, this is a model in which small beginnings can have large consequences. Another interesting aspect is the role played by trade. The divergence of capital stocks depends on the proposition that as long as both countries are nonspecialized, trade in *goods* leads to equalization of wage rates, that is, of a *factor* price. There is thus a surprising affinity between the theory of uneven development and the Heckscher-Ohlin-Samuelson model of trade.

6.4 International Investment

So far we have assumed that industrial growth must come from capital accumulation out of domestically earned profits. In this section I will open up the model to allow international investment. The easiest way to do this is by making the extreme assumption that capital moves instantly so as to equalize profit rates in the two regions.

Again, we will be interested in the dynamic behavior of the world economy. In particular, we want to know if a Hobson-Lenin view of the process can be justified. Lenin saw the evolution of the capitalist system as a two-stage process: "Under the old type of capitalism, when free competition prevailed, the export of *goods* was the most typical feature. Under modern capitalism, when monopolies prevail, the export of *capital* has become the typical feature.[5] In this model, it turns out that Lenin's "stages" can occur, though this is only a possible outcome.

The working of the model under the assumption of perfect capital mobility is quite straightforward and rests on one basic principle: that it is not possible for both regions to be unspecialized. For if both regions are unspecialized, their wage rates will be equalized by trade in agricultural products. The profit rate will then be higher in whichever region has the larger stock of capital, and capital will flow to that region. In particular, if the world capital stock is less than K_{max}, neither region can specialize in manufactures and the initial position will necessarily be a point on one of the axes of our diagram.

What happens next depends on the particular characteristics of technology and demand, which determine how far industrialization goes. If the long-run equilibrium looks like E_N^1, E_S^1 in figure 6.1, a declining relative price of manufactured goods will drive profits to zero and halt capital accumulation even before the leading region is completely industrialized. Another possibility, corresponding to E_N^2, E_2^S, is that accumulation continues until the developed region is completely industrialized, but that by that time P_M has fallen too far to allow profitable investment in the underdeveloped region.

Finally, if the long-run equilibrium is one in which both regions become at least partially industrialized, we have the Leninist case illustrated in figure 6.4. There are two stages of capital accumulation. In the first stage, from A to B, the rate of profit is sustained and growth able to continue through increasing exports of manufactures to the underdeveloped region. When K_N reaches K_{max}, this process cannot continue. The reserve army of labor in North's agricultural sector is exhausted;[6] the wage rate rises, and the profit rate falls sufficiently to induce capital to flow to the other region. This inaugurates a second stage of accumulation—"imperialism, the highest stage of capitalism"—which depends on capital export from North to South and is shown as the movement from B to C.

In addition to this shift in the mechanism of growth, the move from the first to the second stage of accumulation in this Leninist variant of the

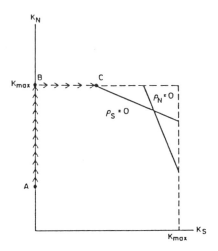

Figure 6.4

model also brings about an important change in the world distribution of income. There are three relevant groups: workers in North, workers in South, and capitalists. As long as we are in the first stage of accumulation, where the industrial region is not yet fully industrialized, the availability of labor from North's agricultural sector keeps wages equal in the two regions. In the "imperialist" stage, however, it is now profits that are equalized, by capital flows. Since industry is more efficient in the industrial region, northern wages are now higher than southern: the northern workforce becomes a "labor aristocracy." This might mean that in addition to exporting capital, the industrial region might, in the second stage of growth, begin importing labor—a point also noted both by Hobson and Lenin.

6.5   A Three-Region World

This final section considers an important extension of the analysis, to a world of three regions. Adding a region allows us to consider the possibility that the trend of international inequality may at some times be ambiguous, with a middle-income region growing faster than either high- or low-income regions.

Let us suppose, then, that there are three regions: Center, Semiperiphery, and Periphery, with capital stocks K_c, K_S, K_P. These regions will, like the two regions of section 6.2, have identical tastes and technology. There will be assumed to be perfect mobility of capital between the regions. Finally, we will assume that Center has an initially larger stock of capital.

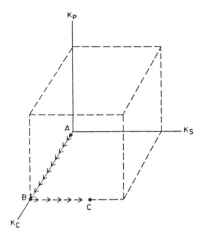

Figure 6.5

The dynamics of the three-region world economy are illustrated in figure 6.5. As before, there is a maximum stock of capital that can usefully be accumulated in any one region, thus defining the boundaries of a cube with a side of K_{max}. At the same time, only one region can be unspecialized at any given time; for if two regions were unspecialized, they would have equal wage rates and capital would flow to the region with the larger capital stock. Thus capital will initially accumulate in only one region, as shown by the movement from A to B. If it is still profitable, industrialization will then spread to *one* of the other regions, as shown by the move from B to C.

This second stage of capital accumulation is interesting in several ways. For one thing, *which* poor region becomes industrialized at this stage is arbitrary, and can be determined by historical accident or by small differences in the conditions of production between the two backward regions. Another interesting point is the direction of international capital movements, which go from the high-income region to the middle-income region, not to the poorest areas. Finally, notice that during this stage of world growth there is simultaneously a narrowing of the differential between the middle-income and the high-income regions and a widening of the differential between the middle-income and low-income regions.

It would clearly be possible, by refining the assumptions of this model, to give it a much more realistic feel. What is remarkable, though, is how much of what has been said about uneven development can be illustrated by an extremely simple model. This suggests that it may be fruitful, and useful to both sides, to apply the tools of orthodox economics to some of the ideas of the economic system's radical critics.

Appendix: Instability of Interior Equilibria

In section 6.3 we stated that no "internal" equilibrium, that is, one with both countries unspecialized, could be stable. This appendix provides a formal demonstration.

Begin by combining (6) with (7); then we have

$$\frac{\dot{K}_N}{K_N} = \rho(K_N, P_M), \qquad \frac{\dot{K}_S}{K_S} = \rho(K_S, P_M), \tag{A1}$$

from which it is immediately apparent that at any equilibrium where $\dot{K}_N = \dot{K}_S = 0$ we must have $K_N = K_S = K^*$. Next consider (4), which we can write in the shorthand form

$$P_M = \pi(K_N, K_S), \tag{A2}$$

with $\pi_1, \pi_2 < 0$. As noted in the text, if $K_N = K_S$, $\pi_1 = \pi_2 = \pi^1$.

Now solve for $\dot{K}_N, \dot{K}_S$ and linearize around K^*:

$$\begin{bmatrix} \dot{K}_N \\ \dot{K}_S \end{bmatrix} = K^* \begin{bmatrix} \rho_1 + \pi^1\rho_2 & \pi^1\rho_2 \\ \pi^1\rho_2 & \rho_1 + \pi^1\rho_2 \end{bmatrix} \begin{bmatrix} K_N - K^* \\ K_S - K^* \end{bmatrix}. \tag{A3}$$

An equilibrium will be unstable if either the trace of the matrix in (A3) is positive or the determinant is negative. But if $\rho_1 + \pi^1\rho_2 > 0$, the trace is positive; while if $\rho_1 + \pi^1\rho_2 < 0$, the determinant is negative. Thus any interior equilibrium is unstable.

Notes

This chapter was stimulated by discussions with Lance Taylor.

1. The fixed-coefficient assumption is made for analytical simplicity, not because it plays any central role. There is nothing in this chapter fundamentally opposed to capital-labor substitution or to the theory of marginal productivity.

2. There is a fairly extensive literature on static trade models with external economies. For a discussion and bibliography, see Chacholiades (1978).

3. There are also some other possibilites. First, there may be several interior equilibria, all of them unstable. There can also be stable equilibria with $K_N = K_S = 0$ and with $K_N = K_S = K_{max}$.

4. The quotation is from Baran, cited by Sutcliffe (1972).

5. Lenin (1939, ch. 4).

6. Actually, this does not quite accord with Lenin, who argued that industrial countries still had a backward agricultural sector. Naturally, the stylized model of this chapter cannot do justice either to the richness or to the internal contradictions of Lenin's work.

7

The Narrow Moving Band, the Dutch Disease, and the Competitive Consequences of Mrs. Thatcher: Notes on Trade in the Presence of Dynamic Scale Economies

7.1 Introduction

When an economist tries to talk with businessmen about international trade, he often senses a frustrating failure to make a connection. Partly this is a matter of differences in vocabulary and style, but it also reflects a more fundamental difference in outlook. Economists, schooled in general equilibrium analysis, have what we might call a "homeostatic" view of international trade. By this I mean that they believe that there is a natural pattern of specialization and trade, determined by underlying characteristics of countries, and that automatic forces tend to restore this natural pattern. Trade policy, exchange rate movements, or other shocks may temporarily distort trade, but when these disturbing factors are removed the natural pattern will reassert itself.

Businessmen, by contrast, are schooled in the competition of individual firms, where equilibrating forces are much less apparent. A wrong decision or a piece of bad luck may result in a permanent loss of market share. Indeed, if large market share itself conveys advantages, the effects of temporary disturbances will grow rather than fade away over time. When businessmen look at international trade, they naturally tend to see competition among nations as competition among firms writ large. As a result, they are far more alarmist in their outlook than economists. They fear that foreign tariffs and subsidies or an overvalued exchange rate will lead to permanent loss of markets, and may indeed propagate into a general loss of competitiveness.

Now it is clear that in this case economists know something that businessmen do not—namely, that there are economywide resource constraints,

Originally published in the *Journal of Development Economics* 27 (1987): 41–55. © 1987, Elsevier Science Publishers B.V. (North-Holland).

and that as a result factor prices are endogenous. Japan cannot have a competitive advantage over the U.S. in everything, because if it did, there would be an excess demand for Japanese labor. Japanese relative wages would rise (perhaps via an exchange rate adjustment), and this would restore U.S. competitiveness in some sectors. It is precisely the recognition of resource constraints that leads economists to emphasize *comparative* rather than *absolute* advantage as the basis for trade.

Yet while businessmen are surely wrong in treating competition among nations as an enlarged version of competition among firms, economists may not have captured the whole of the story either. The homeostatic view of international competition rests ultimately on models that rule out by assumption the kinds of dynamics of competition which are the main concern of corporate strategy. Perhaps if these dynamics were allowed to play a role, something of the businessman's view of competition would turn out to make sense after all. Obviously nations are not firms—they cannot be driven altogether out of business. But perhaps a nation can be driven out of *some* businesses, so that in fact temporary shocks *can* have permanent effects on trade.

The purpose of this paper is to present a simple model of international specialization that incorporates at the national level one of the key elements of strategic analysis at the level of the firm. This is the role of the learning curve. That is, there are dynamic economies of scale in which cumulative past output determines current productivity.[1] In order to bring out the unconventional possibilities clearly, the model is both simplistic and extreme. It can, however, be used to illustrate some of the possibilities missed by more conventional approaches. In particular, I use the model to show how one might justify heterodox analyses of three current policy issues: the effects of Japanese industrial targeting, the consequences of oil discoveries for industrial competitiveness, and the long-run penalties of an overvalued currency.

The chapter is in seven sections. Section 7.2 sets out the model's assumptions. Section 7.3 shows how comparative advantage and the pattern of specialization are determined. Sections 7.4 through 7.6 then provide illustrations of applications of the analysis. Section 7.7 draws conclusions and presents suggestions for further research.

7.2   A Model of Dynamic Comparative Advantage

Consider a world consisting of two countries, Home and Foreign. We will suppose that each of these countries has only one factor of production, labor. Labor can be used to produce any of n traded goods, together with a nontraded good.

At any point in time, we assume that these are constant returns to the production of each traded good,

$$X_i(t) = A_i(t)L_i(t),$$

$$x_i(t) = a_i(t)l_i(t), \qquad i = 1, \ldots, n,$$

(1)

where X_i is output of traded good i in the home coutry, L_i is labor devoted to that good's production, and lower case letters indicate correponding quantities in the foreign country.

While there are constant returns at any point in time, however, we assume that there are dynamic increasing returns, taking the form of an industry learning curve. In each industry in each country, the productivity of resources depends on an index of cumulative experience,

$$A_i(t) = K_i(t)^\varepsilon,$$

$$a_i(t) = k_i(t)^\varepsilon, \qquad 0 < \varepsilon < 1.$$

(2)

I will assume in this paper that the learning curve is entirely an industry phenomenon completely external to firms, so that perfect competition continues to prevail. This is obviously not an ultimately satisfactory formulation, and some discussion of the difference it makes will be given in the concluding section of the paper.

Discussion of external economies in trade often assumes that these economies do not spill across national boundaries. This is, however, not realistic—surely firms can learn from the experience of firms in other countries, though perhaps not as well as they can from other domestic firms. Further, it will be useful as a technical matter to allow for international diffusion of knowledge in our later analysis. Thus I will suppose that both domestic and foreign production enters into the index of experience,

$$K_i(t) = \int_{-\infty}^{t} [X_i(z) + \delta x_i(z)]\,dz,$$

$$k_i(t) = \int_{-\infty}^{t} [\delta X_i(z) + x_i(z)]\,dz, \qquad 0 \leq \delta \leq 1,$$

(3)

where δ can be interpreted as a measure of the internationalization of learning. If $\delta = 0$, we have the often-assumed case of purely national learning effects; if $\delta = 1$, the learning curve should be defined in terms of aggregate world variables. In what follows I will assume that δ in fact lies somewhere between these extremes.

To complete the model, we need to specify how wages are determined, how expenditure is determined, and the what is composition of demand. Later in this paper we will want to explore the consequences of sticky wages and unemployment. For now, however, we will assume full employment. Each country has an exogenously given labor force at any point in time, $L(t)$ and $l(t)$, respectively. These labor forces will be assumed both to grow exponentially at the rate g.[2]

Expenditure will (until section 7.6) be assumed equal to income. A constant share $1 - s$ of income will be assumed spent on nontraded goods. Each traded good will receive a constant and equal share s/n of expenditure.

7.3 Dynamics of Specialization

To analyze international specialization in this model, I proceed as follows. First I analyze the dynamics of relative productivity change, taking the allocation of resources in each country as given. Then I analyze the allocation of resources, taking relative productivities as given. Finally, as a last stage, I show how these interact.

Let us begin, then, with the determination of relative productivities over time. From (2) we know that relative productivity is simply a function of the relative experience indices K and k,

$$\frac{A_i(t)}{a_i(t)} = \left[\frac{K_i(t)}{k_i(t)}\right]^\varepsilon. \tag{4}$$

Thus we must focus on the dynamics of K and k. From (3), we have

$$\frac{dK_i(t)}{dt} = X_i(t) + \delta x_i(t),$$

$$\frac{dk_i(t)}{dt} = x_i(t) + \delta X_i(t). \tag{5}$$

The relative change in the experience indices can therefore be written as

$$\frac{dK_i(t)/dt}{K_i(t)} - \frac{dk_i(t)/dt}{k_i(t)} = \frac{X_i(t) + \delta x_i(t)}{K_i(t)} - \frac{x_i(t) + \delta X_i(t)}{k_i(t)}. \tag{6}$$

Now suppose that the relative labor allocation $L_i(t)/l_i(t)$ is held fixed. Then $K_i(t)/k_i(t)$ will tend to converge on a steady state. Setting the left-hand side of (6) to zero and substituting from (1) and (2), we have

$$\left(\frac{K_i}{k_i}\right)^{\varepsilon-1} = \frac{l_i}{L_i}\left[\frac{1 - \delta k_i/K_i}{1 - \delta K_i/k_i}\right]. \tag{7}$$

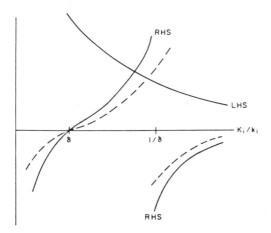

Figure 7.1
Long-run determination of relative productivity

To interpret (7), we can use figure 1. The curve LHS represents the left-hand side of (7), RHS the right-hand side. Clearly, the steady-state value of K_i/k_i always lies between δ and $1/\delta$—which is not surprising given our specification of international spillovers. The steady state value does, however, depend on the allocation of resources. An increase in L_i/l_i is illustrated by the dotted line in the figure; it leads to a higher steady state relative K_i. Since the experience indices in turn determine relative productivity, this means that we can write the steady state relative productivity A_i/a_i as a function of the relative sizes of sectoral labor forces,

$$\frac{A_i}{a_i} = \alpha\left(\frac{L_i}{l_i}\right),\tag{8}$$

where the function $\alpha(\cdot)$ is implicitly defined by (7). From the analysis above it is clear that $\alpha(\cdot)$ is increasing in L_i/l_i, that $\alpha(0) = \delta$, and that $\alpha(\infty) = 1/\delta$.

Now let us turn to the determination of the allocation of labor. At any point in time this model will simply be Ricardian in character. We can rank tradeable industries by their relative productivities $A_i(t)/a_i(t)$. What we then require is that for the marginal industry

$$\frac{A_i(t)}{a_i(t)} = \frac{W(t)}{w(t)},\tag{9}$$

where $W(t)$ is the wage rate at time t. Let $\sigma(t)$ be the share of the world tradeable sector located in the home country, that is, the number of trade-

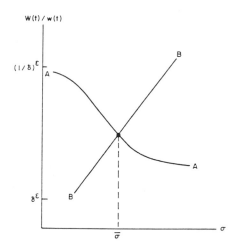

Figure 7.2
Short-run specialization

able sectors in which the home country has a comparative advantage relative to n, the total number of tradeable sectors. Then we can, as in figure 7.2, show the equilibrium condition (9) as the downward sloping schedule AA.

The other equilibrium condition is, of course, balance of payments equilibrium. In a way familiar from Dornbusch, Fischer, and Samuelson (1977) we may write this condition as

$$\frac{W(t)}{w(t)} = \frac{\sigma}{1 - \sigma}\frac{\bar{l}(t)}{\bar{L}(t)}, \tag{10}$$

which yields the upward-sloping schedule BB.

We are now in a position to describe the dynamics of specialization over time. In the absence of any "extrinsic" dynamics— that is, shocks arising from outside sources—these are very simple, almost embarrassingly so. Basically, once a pattern of specialization is established, it remains unchanged, with changes in relative productivity acting to further lock the pattern in. To see this, suppose that at some point the situation looks like that shown in figure 7.2. Some goods are now produced in the home country, some in the foreign country. For those in the first group, we have $L_i(t) = sL(t)/\sigma(t)n$, $l_i(t) = 0$. For those in the second group, $L_i(t) = 0$, $l_i(t) = sl(t)/(1 - \sigma)n$. It is immediately apparent that for the first group, productivity will rise faster in the home country, while for the second group it

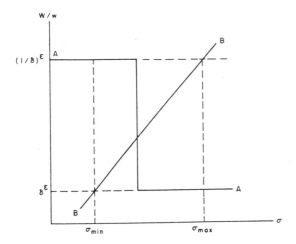

Figure 7.3
Long-run specialization

will rise faster in the foreign country. This means that the part of AA to the left of $\bar{\sigma}$ will rise, that part to the right of $\bar{\sigma}$ will fall. In the long run AA will come to have the "step" shape illustrated in figure 7.3.

Like a river that digs its own bed deeper, a pattern of specialization, once established, will induce relative productivity changes that strengthen the forces preserving that pattern.

Clearly, history matters here even for the long run. In particular, whatever market share $\bar{\sigma}$ the home country starts with will be preserved over time, and so, therefore, will be the relative wage rates associated with that share. Thus there is a whole range of possible steady-state market shares. The boundaries of that range are shown as σ_{min} and σ_{max} in figure 7.3. These are defined by the relative wage rates at which a country will be competitive in a sector even if it has no production experience of its own and must rely entirely on international diffusion of knowledge. Obviously the range of possible outcomes is narrower the larger is δ—that is, the more international are the learning effects.

We have now laid out a simple model where comparative advantage is "created" over time by the dynamics of learning, rather than arising from underlying national characteristics. In the remainder of this paper I will perform a series of thought experiments on this model. What we will see is that a model of this kind can be used to formalize a variety of heterodox arguments about international competition.

7.4   The Narrow Moving Band

The economic success of Japan has been attributed by many to the industrial policies of the Japanese government, and in particular to the use of infant industry protection as a way of gradually broadening the Japanese industrial base. In an effective diatribe, Givens (1982) has described the intervention of the Japanese government as a "narrow moving band" that slices off one industry after another, protecting an industry until it is strong enough to eliminate its U.S. competitors, then moving on to the next target.

The economic reasoning underlying this view of Japanese policy is not completely clear, but our model seems to have the necessary features. It is certainly possible in this model—within limits—for temporary protection to permanently shift comparative advantage.

Suppose that there is some good i in which the foreign country originally has a comparative advantage. Then the labor allocation will be $L_i = 0$, $l_i = s/\sigma n$. Now suppose that the home country closes its market for good i to imports. The effect will be to turn i into a nontraded good, with each country satisfying its own demand,

$$L_i = \frac{sL}{n},$$

$$l_i = \frac{sl}{n}.$$

Clearly, the effect of this market closure will be to accelerate the pace of productivity change in this sector in the home relative to the foreign country. If the protection is continued long enough, this change in relative productivity growth may be enough to give the home country a cost advantage in i. At this point the protection becomes irrelevant, and trade policy has achieved a permanent shift in comparative advantage. We can imagine a government protecting a series of sectors in succcession and thus steadily increasing its market share—a process illustrated in figure 7.4.

There is, however, a limit to this process. As a country acquires more industries, its relative wage rate will rise. This means that the next sector will require higher relative productivity and thus a longer period of protection to become established. In the limit, protectionist policies can at most lead to a relative productivity advantage of $\alpha(L/l)$ and thus cannot push the relative wage above $W/w = \alpha(L/l)$.

Without pursuing the story too much further, this analysis suggests that the use of temporary protection to engineer permanent shifts in compara-

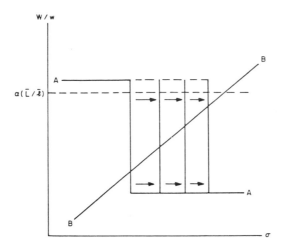

Figure 7.4
The narrow moving band

tive advantage is likely to work best when one is a country with a large labor force but low wages. Small countries will find that the domestic market is not large enough for protection to yield much in the way of accelerated productivity growth; high-wage countries will find that the extra productivity is not enough to provide a cost advantage.

7.5   The Dutch Disease

When a country discovers tradeable natural resources, such as oil, it normally experiences real appreciation of its exchange rate and thus a crowding out of its other tradeable sectors. This phenomenon first drew attention in the case of the Netherlands, where natural gas discoveries clearly hurt the competitiveness of Dutch manufacturing, but the experience is familiar from a number of examples.[3] The interesting question is why it should be regarded as a problem. In conventional trade models, countries should simply specialize in whatever is their comparative advantage. If an oil discovery shifts this comparative advantage, so be it. In parctice, however, there is widespread concern that the contraction of a country's manufacturing sector that follows natural resource discoveries is a bad thing. The worry seems to be that when the natural resources run out, the lost manufacturing sectors will not come back.

Our model does not allow a role for natural resources directly. However, the discussion of the Dutch disease usually treats income earned in the natural resource sector much as if it were a pure transfer payment from abroad. So I will approximate the discussion by considering the implications of a transfer payment from the foreign to the home country.

We need first to rewrite the balance of payments equilibrium condition to take account of the transfer. Following Dornbusch, Fischer, and Samuelson (1977) the condition may be written

$$\sigma(t)s[l - T] = (1 - \sigma(t))s\left\{\left[\frac{W(t)}{w(t)}\right]L + T\right\},$$

where T is the transfer, measured in foreign wage units. This implies the relative wage equation

$$\frac{W(t)}{w(t)} = \frac{\sigma(t)}{1 - \sigma(t)}\frac{l}{L} + \frac{1 - s}{s}\frac{T}{L}. \tag{11}$$

This now defines the BB schedule. As long as $s < 1$—that is, as long as there are nontraded goods—a transfer to the home country will shift the schedule up.

The effects of this transfer depend both on its size and its duration. Let us suppose that we are initially in or near a steady state in which each country has been specialized for a long period. Then the schedule AA will have the shape shown in figure 7.5: a step function. The effect of a small transfer is illustrated by the upward shift of BB to B'B'; this will raise the home country's wage but without altering the pattern of specialization. A

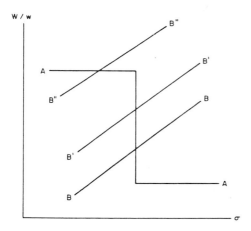

Figure 7.5
Short-run impacts of a transfer

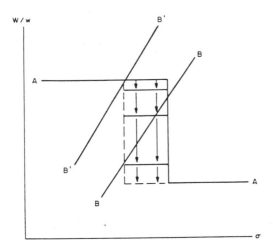

Figure 7.6
Long-run effects of a transfer

larger transfer, however, will raise the schedule to $B'B'$: the rise in the recipient's relative wages will be enough to offset its productivity advantage, so that some sectors move abroad.

The longer run implications now depend on how long the transfer payment lasts. The shift of production from home to foreign will mean declining relative home productivity in those industries over time. Thus AA will develop a middle step, which will deepen over time. The possibilities are illustrated in figure 7.6. There a large transfer is assumed to shift BB up to $B'B'$, resulting in a shift of some industries from the home to foreign country. If the transfer does not last too long, when it ends and BB returns to its previous position, the old pattern of specialization and relative wages will reassert itself. If the transfer lasts longer, however, some of the industries will not come back when it ends. For a transfer of sufficiently long duration, all of the industries that move abroad in the short run will remain abroad even when the transfer ends. In either of the latter cases the home country's market share and relative wage will turn out to have been permanently reduced by its temporary good fortune.

7.6 The Competitive Consequences of Mrs. Thatcher

When countries pursue more contractionary monetary policies than their trading partners, one important channel through which the monetary contraction takes effect appears to be through real appreciation of the exchange rate and a resulting loss of competitiveness in traded goods production. This has been dramatically illustrated by the experience of the U.K. under Margaret Thatcher. When this happens, a major question becomes one of appropriate policy response. Given a consensus on the need for a contractionary monetary policy, say to control inflation, should the tradeable sector be required to bear as much of the burden as seems to be the case? Or should exchange market intervention, capital controls, or such trade policy instruments as tariffs and export subsidies be used to insulate the traded sectors from some of the consequences of a disinflationary transition?

The implication from conventional economic models is that traded sectors should contract along with the rest of the economy. If a certain amount of slack must be created in the conomy, why should it occur only in nontraded sectors? Frankel (1983) has shown that in one simple model a floating exchange rate actually gets it exactly right, producing the optimal mix of output reduction between traded and nontraded sectors.

The counterargument is not usually clearly expressed but hinges on the belief that preserving competitiveness in tradeable sectors is somehow more important than maintaining output in nontraded sectors. While a model with dynamic economies of scale may not capture the whole of this belief, it does provide at least a possible way to make sense of a view that sees the international consequences of tight money as more serious and enduring than the purely domestic consequences.

To examine this issue, we need to modify our model to allow for monetary policy, in particular for monetary policy with real effects. Once again Dornbusch, Fischer, and Samuelson (1977) provide the simplest formulation. Let us assume, first, that nominal expenditure in each country is proportional to that country's money supply (both measured in units of local currency),

$$E(t) = M(t)V,$$
$$e(t) = m(t)v. \tag{12}$$

Let us define $R(t)$ as the exchange rate, defined as the price of foreign currency in terms of home currency. Then the balance of payments equilibrium condition may be written as

$$\sigma(t)R(t)e(t) = [1 - \sigma(t)]E(t). \tag{13}$$

For changes in monetary policy to have a real effect, there must be nominal rigidities somewhere. The simplest assumption is simply to let wage rates be exogenously fixed in local currency,

$$W(t) = \overline{W}, \qquad w(t) = \overline{w}. \tag{14}$$

Combining (13) and (14), we can write an equation for relative wages measured in a common currency,

$$\frac{\overline{W}}{R(t)\overline{w}} = \frac{\sigma(t)}{1 - \sigma(t)} \frac{e(t)}{E(t)}. \tag{15}$$

This will define a BB schedule, just as in previous sections. The AA schedule continues to be defined as before.

Consider, now, the effects of a temporary reduction in the home money supply. A decline in M will reduce E, shifting BB up. As in the last section, if the shock is not large enough there will be no effect on the pattern of specialization. For a sufficiently large reduction in the money supply, however, market clearing will require that some industries move from the home to the foreign country.

At this point the analysis becomes entirely parallel to the analysis in the previous section. If the tight monetary policy is sustained for long enough, when it ends, specialization will remain in its new pattern instead of returning to its previous pattern. As a result the temporary rise in relative wages produced by the monetary contraction will be followed by a permanent reduction in relative wages.

This is a highly simplified model, but it does seem to capture the essentials of an argument that it is dangerous to let tight money be reflected in a very strong currency.

7.7 Conclusions and Implications

The purpose of this chapter has been to suggest that heterdox views about a variety of issues in international economics can be tied together by a single theme: the argument that dynamic economies of scale play a crucial role in international specialization. The three examples given might at first glance seem quite disparate—the use of infant industry protection to expand market share, the problems resulting from natural resource discoveries, and the long-run effects of monetary policy. Yet we were able to show that alarmist concerns in each case can be given their most plausible grounding by a model in which dynamic economies of scale play a crucial role.

This is, however, an exploratory study and by no means intended to give blanket approval to any proposal for protection. There are at least three major reasons to be cautious about the results. Each of these reasons also provides a program for future research.

The first problem with the analysis is the assumption that dynamic scale economies are wholly external to firms. There are certainly both external and internal dynamic scale economies in reality. We have some rough idea how important the internal economies are (varying greatly across sectors); how important the external economies are is highly disputable. A major question is the extent to which the results would go through with imperfectly competitive firms and internal economies. We know from recent work that predatory trade and industrial policies, like those of section 7.4, are possible in a world of imperfectly competitive firms (see Brander and Spencer 1985 and Eaton and Grossman 1986). But it also seems to be the case that in some models the sort of multiple equilibria we have stressed here vanish when economies of scale are wholly internal to firms (see Helpman and Krugman 1985, chs. 3 and 4). The point is that a wage differential between countries with no fundamental differences in their technological capacity may offer a profit opportunity if the differential is not due to wholly external effects.

Second, the model here is clearly too stark in its assumption that dynamic scale economies are the only source of specialization and trade. Allowing for other forces—particularly differences in factor endowments—would surely soften the results. In particular, the complete arbitrariness of the pattern of specialization would be modified, particularly if factor prices shift over time. To return to the geological metaphor of section 7.3, a river may dig its own bed, reinforcing the results of past history, but eventually the larger forces of tectonics will bury that history. Britain's early preeminence in cotton spinning may have been self-reinforcing for the first half of the nineteenth century, but it was eventually overridden by the rising gap between wages in Britain and those in poorer countries.

Finally, while this chapter has addressed policy issues, it has not contained any explicit welfare analysis. We have seen, for example, that in the model presented here a step-by-step policy of infant industry protection can succeed in making a country competitive in an enlarged range of industries. We have not, however, shown that this is necessarily a desirable policy. Formal welfare analysis is bound to be hard in the kind of world envisaged in this chapter, a world of imperfect markets and dynamic effects over time. Nonetheless, we should be careful about making policy prescriptions without such analysis.

This study, then, is an exploration rather than a definitive work. It raises more questions than it answers.

Notes

1. This is not the first such analysis. Bardhan (1970) analyzed trade and industrial policy in the presence of learning effects. His model was, however, oriented more toward development policy in small LDCs than toward the issues addressed in this chapter.

2. A growing population, or technological progress independent of output, is necessary to make the steady-state analysis of this chapter possible.

3. A number of papers have been written on the Dutch disease. See, in particular, Corden and Neary (1982) and Van Wijnbergen (1984).

8   Vehicle Currencies and the Structure of International Exchange

8.1   Introduction

Over most of the past hundred years, some one national currency has had a special role as international money. First the pound sterling and then the U.S. dollar have played at an international level the roles that national monies play in domestic economies. They served as stores of value, with balances held both by central banks and by private individuals; they were used as units of account, in which international obligations were dominated and in terms of which prices of commodities were set; and they were used as media of exchange, becoming "vehicles" through which transactions between other currencies were made.[1]

    This chapter is concerned with this last aspect of international monies: their role as vehicle currencies. Taking the simplest case, that of a three-country, three-currency world, the chapter asks under what conditions payments between two of the countries will be made using the third country's currency. In particular, it is concerned with the relationship between the payments flows between countries, which I will refer to as the *structure of payments*, and the actual transactions on the currency markets, which I will refer to as the *structure of exchange*. The chapter makes three important points that have not been clear in earlier literature on vehicle currencies. First, it clarifies the relationship between transaction costs, the deviation of cross-rates from direct exchange rates, and the extent of triangular arbitrage and shows how these are simultaneously determined. Second, it shows that the currencies of economically dominant countries can normally be expected to take on the vehicle currency role. Third, it explains why a country's currency, once established as an international

Originally published in the *Journal of Money, Credit, and Banking* 12, 3(August 1980): 513–526. © 1980 Ohio University Press.

medium of exchange, can persist in that role even if the country's commercial importance declines.

The argument is put forward in three stages. Section 8.2 sets out a model of payments equilibrium in a three-country world without transaction costs. In this model the structure of payments can be derived, but the structure of exchange is indeterminate. Section 8.3 introduces transaction costs, showing how these costs lead to a determinate exchange structure. In section 8.4 I then show that if transaction costs in turn depend on the volume of transactions, we can develop an interesting and economically plausible account of the relationship between payments structure and exchange structure.

8.2   The Model without Transaction Costs

Consider a world consisting of three countries: A, B, and C. Each country has its own currency, the alpha in A, the beta in B, and the gamma in C. There are three exchange markets on which alphas and betas, betas and gammas, and gammas and alphas can be exchanged. We will call these $\alpha\beta$, $\beta\gamma$, and $\gamma\alpha$ markets, respectively. For the purposes of this section we will assume that exchanging currencies is costless.

Let us define $E_{\alpha\beta}$ as the price of alphas in terms of betas, $E_{\beta\gamma}$ as the price of betas in terms of gammas, and so on. Then because transactions are costless, arbitrage will ensure that the costs of acquiring a currency directly are the same as the costs of acquiring it indirectly, via the third currency. This condition can be written as

$$E_{\alpha\beta}E_{\beta\gamma}E_{\gamma\alpha} = 1. \tag{1}$$

These exchange rates will be determined by the supply and demand for currencies. I will assume that the relevant variables are *flow* demands and supplies. This goes against much recent literature on exchange rates, which views exchange rates as determined by the requirements of *stock* equilibrium. The only justification for the treatment here is simplicity. Asset market equilibrium in the presence of transaction costs is very difficult to model, while if we are willing to adopt a flow model, the analysis remains tractable. The analysis here should therefore be regarded as preliminary, with the integration of this theory with the "asset" view of exchange rates still to be achieved.

The demand for and supply of currencies, then, will be assumed to arise from the desire of residents of the three countries to make payments to other countries. Residents of A wanting to make payments to B, for example, will have to acquire betas. The currency markets will clear if the demand for each currency by foreign residents equals the supply from domestic residents wanting to make payments in foreign currency. Let us define P_{AB} as the desired payment by residents of B to C, and so on. We can write the conditions of equilibrium in the currency markets as

$$P_{BA} + P_{CA} = E_{\alpha\beta}P_{AB} + E_{\alpha\gamma}P_{AC} \tag{2}$$

$$P_{AB} + P_{CB} = E_{\beta\alpha}P_{BA} + E_{\beta\gamma}P_{BC} \tag{3}$$

$$P_{AC} + P_{BC} = E_{\gamma\alpha}P_{CA} + E_{\gamma\beta}P_{CB} \tag{4}$$

for alphas, betas, and gammas, respectively. In each case we have written a condition of aggregate balance of payments equilibrium. Because of budget constraints, if any two countries are in balance of payments equilibrium, the third must also be in balance. Notice, however, that there is no reason why countries must be in *bilateral* balance. If, for example, $P_{AC} > E_{\gamma\alpha}P_{CA}$, that is, C runs a balance of payment surplus with A, we can still have an equilbrium if A runs an offsetting surplus, and C an offsetting deficit, with B.

Now let us consider the structure of payments and the range of possible structures of exchange. It will be helpful if we choose units so that the equilibrium exchange rates are all equal to one. We can then express payments arbitrarily in any of the currencies. Given this normalization, the structure of payments will look like that illustrated in figure 8.1.

In the figure payments by residents of one country to residents of another are indicated by arrows. A is shown as running a surplus of I in its exchange with B; we can relabel B and C if necessary to make this true. The figure then shows that, to maintain balance of payments equilibrium, B must run a surplus of I with C and C a suplus of I with A. Although

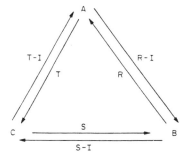

Figure 8.1
The structure of payments for a three-county world

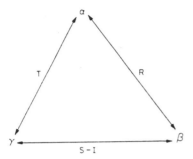

Figure 8.2
Partial indirect exchange

payments need not be bilaterally balanced, then, there is a sort of conservation of imbalance. Once we specify A's surplus with B, we have also determined the imbalances between B and C and between C and A. (This is a special feature of three-country models.)

Our next task is to consider what structures of exchange are possible given this structure of payments. Obviously the structure of exchange is not determinate in the absence of transaction costs. But there are limists on the range of possibilities. In particular, it will not be possible to carry out the payments in figure 8.1 solely through direct exchange. If everyone tried to acquire the desired foreign currency in a single transaction, there would be an excess demand for alphas on the $\alpha\beta$ market, an excess demand for betas on the $\beta\gamma$ market, and an excess demand for gammas on the $\gamma\alpha$ market. So some indirect exchange must take place, because countries will not usually have a "double coincidence of wants."

What kinds of structure of exchange are possible? There are obviously infinite possibilities—for instance, one might exchange gammas for alphas and back again seventeen times, etc.—but once we introduce transaction costs, there will turn out to be only two types of exchange that can actually arise. An example of the first type is given in figure 8.2, where the two-headed arrows represent the volume of transactions on the $\alpha\beta$, $\beta\gamma$, and $\gamma\alpha$ markets. In this example the residents of C make payments of I to B indirectly, first purchasing alphas and then exchanging these for betas. They continue to purchase $S - I$ betas directly, however. At the same time residents of B and A engage only in direct exchange. As is apparent from figures 8.1 and 8.2, this clears all three currency markets, by increasing the supply of gammas on the $\gamma\alpha$ market and the supply of alphas on the $\alpha\beta$ market. Since this structure of exchange involves indirect exchange only

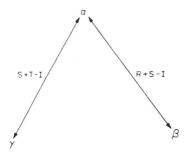

Figure 8.3
Total indirect exchange

for the imbalance in payments, let us call this a case of *partial indirect exchange* using alphas as the vehicle currency, with the understanding that it is the payments imbalance I that is indirectly exchanged. Clearly, we can have partial indirect exchange with any one of the three currencies as vehicle.

Figure 8.3 gives an example of the other possible kind of exchange structure. In this case *all* payments between B and C are made indirectly, through the medium of alphas. The $\beta\gamma$ market disappears, while the $\alpha\beta$ and $\gamma\alpha$ markets have the indicated volume. Since all three countries are in balance of payments equilibrium, it is obvious that both existing currency markets clear. Let us call this a case of *total indirect exchange*, with alphas as the vehicle currency. Again, we can also have total indirect exchange with betas or gammas as the vehicle.

To summarize, I have defined two kinds of structure of exchange, partial indirect exchange and total indirect exchange. Each type of structure involves the use of one currency as a "vehicle" for indirect transactions. So we have to determine which currency is the vehicle and which kind of exchange structure occurs. To do this, we must now introduce transaction costs.

8.3   Transaction Costs and Exchange

In this section I show how transaction costs can determine the structure of exchange. This analysis relies on the assumption that transaction costs are "small," so that we can use a concept of approximate equilibrium, which will be defined in a moment. In essence what this concept allows us to do is determine the structure of exchange while ignoring any feedback from the structure of exchange to the structure of payments.[2]

Let us begin by describing transaction costs. I will assume that in each of the three markets transactors must pay a brokerage fee proportional to the size of the transaction. This proportion will be $t_{\alpha\beta}$, $t_{\beta\gamma}$, and $t_{\gamma\alpha}$ in the $\alpha\beta$, $\beta\gamma$, and $\gamma\alpha$ markets, respectively. It will be assumed (countries will be labeled such that) $t_{\alpha\beta}$ and $t_{\gamma\alpha}$ are both less than $t_{\beta\gamma}$. This will, as we will see, ensure that the alpha is the vehicle currency.

The effect of these transaction costs will be to worsen the effective exchange rate one gets. Thus if $E_{\alpha\beta}$ is the exchange rate on the $\alpha\beta$ market, a transactor purchasing betas will actually get only $E_{\alpha\beta}(1 - t_{\alpha\beta})$ betas per alpha; a transactor purchasing alphas will get only $E_{\alpha\beta}^{-1}(1 - t_{\alpha\beta})$ alphas per beta.

Because of the transaction costs, the arbitrage condition (1) will no longer hold exactly. Instead, there will be a deviation from triangular arbitrage:

$$D = E_{\alpha\beta}E_{\beta\gamma}E_{\gamma\alpha} \neq 1. \tag{5}$$

I will call D, which may be either greater or less than one, the *clockwisdom* of exchange rates. The reason for the name is that an increase in the value of D makes indirect exchange more attractive compared with direct exchange if the indirect exchange proceeds clockwise in figures 8.2 and 8.3, less attractive if the indirect exchange proceeds counterclockwise. Consider, for example, an exchange of alphas for gammas. In direct exchange, the exchange rate is $1/E_{\gamma\alpha}$. In indirect exchange, clock-wise via betas, the rate is $E_{\alpha\beta}E_{\beta\gamma}$. There will thus be a bias in favor of indirect exchange if $E_{\alpha\beta}E_{\beta\gamma} > 1/E_{\gamma\alpha}$, that is, if $E_{\alpha\beta}E_{\beta\gamma}E_{\gamma\alpha} = D > 1$. On the other hand, an exchange of betas for gammas takes place at a rate of $E_{\beta\gamma}$ directly, while the counterclockwise indirect exchange takes place at a rate $1/E_{\alpha\beta}E_{\gamma\alpha}$; thus there is a bias *against* indirect exchange if $E_{\beta\gamma} > 1/E_{\alpha\beta}E_{\gamma\alpha}$, that is, $E_{\alpha\beta}E_{\beta\gamma}E_{\gamma\alpha} = D > 1$. Clearly, then, an individual deciding whether to purchase foreign currency directly or indirectly will take the clockwisdom of exchange rates into account; his decision will not simply be a matter of minimizing transaction costs.[3]

Using the concept of clockwisdom we can now proceed to analyze equilibrium. What I will derive here is an *approximate* equilibrium, which will be close to the actual, provided transaction costs are small. The approximateness comes from considering only the effect of transaction costs on the way payments are made, ignoring the effect of these costs on the payments themselves. Another way of saying this is to say that transaction costs are taken to affect the structure of exchange but that the structure of payments is taken as given.

Specifically, let us define the equilibrium concept as follows. Any particular D will lead to a particular set of choices about how to acquire foreign currency. For example, residents of A might find it cheapest to acquire betas by direct purchase but to acquire gammas by buying betas first, then selling them for gammas. We will consider a value of D to be an equilibrium value if the choices it induces about how to purchase foreign currency would be consistent with market-clearing *in the absence of transaction costs*. These choices will in turn imply for the no-transaction cost case a structure of exchange; we will consider this the equilibrium structure.

Given this concept of equilibrium, we can now state the relationship between transaction costs and the structure of exchange. Recall that $t_{\alpha\beta}$ and $t_{\gamma\alpha}$ are both assumed to be less than $t_{\beta\gamma}$. Then we can state that (1) the alpha will be the vehicle currency; (2) if $(1 - t_{\alpha\beta})(1 - t_{\gamma\alpha}) < (1 - t_{\beta\gamma})$—that is, if indirect exchange is more costly than direct—the equilibrium structure will be one of partial indirect exchange, as defined in section 8.2; (3) if $(1 - t_{\alpha\beta})(1 - t_{\gamma\alpha}) > (1 - t_{\beta\gamma})$— indirect exchange is less costly than direct—the equilibrium structure will be one of total indirect exchange.

The result 1 through 3 make intuitive sense, since what they amount to is saying that the system acts in such a way as to minimize total transaction costs.

Proving the results is a straightforward but rather tedious matter and is carried out in the appendix. Here I sketch out the results.

The basic point here is that, because of the "conservation of imbalance," if exchange is balanced in one currency market, it is balanced in all three markets. Thus we can focus on the $\beta\alpha$ market and look for a value of D that would match the demand for and supply of gammas on that market.[4]

Consider first the case where $(1 - t_{\alpha\beta})(1 - t_{\gamma\alpha}) < (1 - t_{\beta\gamma})$, that is, where indirect exchange is more costly than direct. As the appendix shows, the $\beta\gamma$ market is cleared on a "flat" where transactors exchanging gammas for betas are indifferent between direct and indirect exchange, while all other transactors prefer direct exchange. The result. then, must be one of partial indirect exchange, as defined in section 8.1 and illustrated in figure 8.2. In equilibrium, the clockwisdom D is $(1 - t_{\beta\gamma})/(1 - t_{\alpha\beta})(1 - t_{\gamma\alpha}) > 1$. We can think of this as a situation in which holders of gammas wishing to acquire betas are offered a slightly better exchange rate on indirect transactions, which is just enough to offset the higher transaction cost.

If $(1 - t_{\alpha\beta})(1 - t_{\gamma\alpha}) > (1 - t_{\beta\gamma})$, that is, indirect exchange is *less* costly than direct, the situation is somewhat different. Here D is indeterminate within a certain range. The reason for the indeterminacy becomes clear when we examine the structure of exchange implied by some D in that range, say, $D = 1$. For such a clockwisdom, transactors exchanging betas for gammas and gammas for betas will both prefer indirect exchange, while all other transactors prefer direct exchange. The implied structure must therefore be one of total indirect exchange, as illustrated in Figure 8.3. Since the $\beta\gamma$ market clears with a volume of zero, the exchange rate $E_{\beta\gamma}$ and hence D are, of course, indeterminate. The structure of exchange is, however, fully determined.

In each of these cases the alpha plays a special role as vehicle currency. It enters into more transactions than A's role in world payments would by itself justify. The special role of A's currency arises, of course, from the assumption that transaction costs in the exchange markets differ. We have labeled the currencies so that $t_{\alpha\beta}$ and $t_{\gamma\alpha}$ are both less than $t_{\beta\gamma}$, and this insures the alphas will be used as a vehicle.

What is particularly interesting is that the alpha will play a limited vehicle currency role even when roundabout exchange involves higher transaction costs than direct purchase. The reason is that some indirect exchange is necessary to clear the currency markets, and this necessity is reflected in a deviation of the cross-rate from the direct exchange rate. The cost of this indirect exchange is minimized by the choices of the minimum transaction cost route.

But why should transaction costs be different? We would like some theory to explain this; in particular, we would like to relate the structure of transaction costs to the structure of payments in some way, to make sense of the observed fact that vehicle currencies have historically been the currencies of dominant trading nations. The next section tries to sketch out such a theory.

8.4   Endogenous Transaction Costs

In this section I attempt to explain why differences in transaction costs might arise. The analysis is based on a somewhat ad hoc but simple and surprisingly powerful assumption: that transactions costs a proportion of the transaction are decreasing in the volume of transactions. This turns out to be enough to give us considerable insight both into the way the structure of payments limits the structure of exchange and into the exchange structure's dynamics.

The assumption that average transaction costs decrease with the volume of transactions is apparently a realistic one. Thus Kubarych (1978) writes that the dollar's dominance in the interbank market arises because the larger markets for dollars make it easier to trade large amounts. Notice, however, that I am only concerned here with economies of market size, not with economies to large transactions, which are assumed away.

Let us consider, then, the implications of letting transaction costs depend on volume. If we let $V_{\alpha\beta}$, $V_{\beta\gamma}$, $V_{\gamma\alpha}$ be the values of sales on the three markets, then we have

$$t_{\alpha\beta} = F(V_{\alpha\beta}) \tag{6}$$

$$t_{\beta\gamma} = F(V_{\beta\gamma}) \tag{7}$$

$$t_{\gamma\alpha} = F(V_{\gamma\alpha}), \tag{8}$$

where the function $F(.)$ is assumed the same for all markets and we assume that $F' < 0$.

If the structure of transaction costs depends in this way on the volume of transactions, then it depends on the structure of exchange. But the structure of exchange, as we saw in section 8.3, is determined by the structure of transaction costs. What we must look for, then, is an exchange structure that is an equilibrium in the sense that the pattern of transaction costs produced by transactors' choices of direct versus indirect exchange sustains these choices. There is no reason why there must be only one such equilibrium; there may be as many as six. Exchange might be partially or totally indirect, and any one of the three currencies might serve as the vehicle.

The simultaneous choice of type of exchange structure and of vehicle currency makes for a very complex problem. I will simplify this problem by concentrating on two more limited choices. First, we will take the type of exchange structure as given and consider the choice of vehicle currency. Then we will take the vehicle currency as given and consider the choice of exchange structure. These limited analyses will serve to illustrate the main principles, while the general case can be analyzed only through numerical examples.

Let us begin, then, with the case in which we assume that the exchange structure is one of partial indirect exchange and we are concerned solely with which currency is the vehicle. We start with a structure of payments like that in figure 8.1. When a particular currency is chosen as vehicle, we get a structure of exchange that is an equilibrium if the implied structure of transaction costs confirms that currency's vehicle position. From (6)–(8) this means that choice of a currency as vehicle must make the volume of the two markets in which that currency participates larger than the volume of the third market.

The relationship between choice of vehicle and the volume of transactions, for the structure of payments in figure 8.1, is

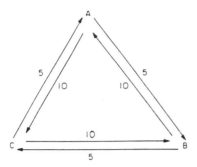

Figure 8.4
A structure of payments without a dominant country

Vehicle currency	$V_{\alpha\beta}$	$V_{\beta\gamma}$	$V_{\gamma\alpha}$
α	R	$S - I$	T
β	R	S	$T - I$
γ	$R - I$	S	T

Each currency market has a "secure" volume arising from counterclockwise payments: the volume is then increased above this level if one of the currencies traded serves as a vehicle. This suggests two things. First, because choosing a currency as vehicle swells the markets on which it is traded, we have a possibility of multiple equilibria. Second, because of the "secure" part of transaction volume, there are some limits on this; the currency of a country, which plays only a minor role in world payments, will not be able to overcome the advantages of other countries' "secure" volumes.

These points are illustrated by the examples in figures 8.4 and 8.5. In figure 8.4 payments are symmetrical and any currency can serve as vehicle. If, for example, the beta were to be the vehicle, we would have $V_{\alpha\beta} = V_{\beta\gamma} = 10$, $V_{\gamma\alpha} =: 5$; this would make $t_{\alpha\beta}$ and $t_{\beta\gamma}$ less than $t_{\gamma\alpha}$ and confirm the beta as the vehicle. On the other hand, in figure 8.5, A's dominance in world payments assures that the alpha will be the vehicle currency. If one were to try to make the beta the vehicle, we would have $V_{\alpha\beta} = 10$, $V_{\beta\gamma} = 2$, $V_{\gamma\alpha} = 9$: the structure of transaction costs would still lead people to carry out indirect exchange through the alpha. Similarly, using the gamma as vehicle would produce $V_{\alpha\beta} = V_{\beta\gamma} = 2$, $V_{\gamma\alpha} = 10$; the alpha would still be preferred for indirect exchange. So the unique equilibrium here is a structure of exchange using the alpha as vehicle, with $V_{\alpha\beta} = V_{\gamma\alpha} = V_{\beta\gamma} = 1$.

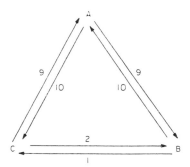

Figure 8.5
A structure of payments with A dominant

In partial indirect exchange, then, only the currencies of countries important in world payments can become vehicles; but there may be more than one such currency. (Notice, by the way, that the relationship between a country's role in payments and the choice of vehicle currency is parallel to the requirement that a domestic medium of exchange be a good widely desired.) We will turn to the implications of these multiple equilibria in a moment.

Before proceeding to this analysis, however, let us consider the other special case mentioned of choice of exchange structure: the choice between partial and total indirect exchange given the choice of vehicle currency. Suppose that we take it as known that the alpha will be the vehicle currency and the structure of payments is again that of figure 8.1. Then the possible structures of exchange are (1) partial indirect exchange: $V_{\alpha\beta} = R$, $V_{\beta\gamma} = S - I$, $V_{\gamma\alpha} = T$; (2) total indirect exchange: $V_{\alpha\beta} = R + S$, $V_{\beta\gamma} = 0$, $V_{\gamma\alpha} = S + T$. We know from section 8.2 that partial indirect exchange can be an equilibrium if $(1 - t_{\alpha\beta})(1 - t_{\gamma\alpha}) < (1 - t_{\beta\gamma})$, or, substituting,

$$[1 - F(R)][1 - F(T)] < [1 - F(S - I)]. \tag{9}$$

This can be the case if F does not decrease too rapidly as volume increases. On the other hand, total indirect exchange requires that $(1 - t_{\alpha\beta})(1_{\alpha\beta} - t) > (1 - t_{\beta\gamma})$, which means that we must have

$$[1 - F(R + S)][1 - F(S + T)] > [1 - F(0)]. \tag{10}$$

This is more likely to be the case if F *does* decrease rapidly with volume. However, the left-hand side of (10) is larger than that of (9), while the right-hand side is smaller; therefore (9) and (10) are not mutually exclusive.

One might expect that total indirect exchange would be more likely if some one country were very dominant in world payments. This is true in the limited sense that predominance of one country may make partial indirect exchange impossible. In (9), increasing R and T while reducing $S - I$ may reverse the inequality. Even this is not certain, however. If $[1 - F(\infty)]^2 < 1 - F(0)$, which is fully consistent with $F' < 0$, the exchange structure will always be only partially indirect no matter how predominant one country is.

To summarize, then, if transaction costs are a decreasing function of the volume of transactions, we can relate the structure of exchange to the structure of payments in economically sensible ways. Only the currency of a country that is important in world payments can serve as an international medium of exchange; the predominance of one country makes it more likely that all transactions between the others will take place indirectly. Although the structure of exchange is limited by the structure of payments, there may still be several possible exchange structures.

Which exchange structure will actually emerge? To give a definitive answer would require a dynamic analysis, which lies beyond this article's scope. But it seems clear that history will matter; once an exchange structure is established, it will persist unless the structure of payments shifts enough to make it untenable or unless the system experiences a shock large enough to shift it from one equilibrium to another. Suppose, for example, that the currency of an economically dominant country becomes established as a vehicle. This role will be self-reinforcing, swelling transactions in the currency. Even if the country's predominant position then vanishes, its currency's special role may then persist. This is presumably the explanation of the persistence of sterling's role as a vehicle long after British commercial preeminence had passed.

When change comes, however, it will be "catastrophic" in the formal sense. Once a currency begins to lose its role as vehicle, there will be a cumulative process in which declining trading volume leads to higher transaction costs and higher transaction costs lead to lower trading volume. Thus gradual change in the underlying structure of payments can, when it reaches a critical point, produce abrupt changes in the structure of exchange.

In this chapter I have attempted to answer in a systematic way the rather subtle question of why some currencies have functioned as international media of exchange. The model set forth in this chapter is, of course, highly simplified. Nonetheless, it gives results that look as if they have something to do with the actual experience of international monetary history. And the model shows that it is possible to deal in at least a rudimentary way with the role of transaction costs in international financial markets.

Appendix

Clockwisdom and the Equilibrium Structure of Exchange

In section 8.2 a concept of approximate equilibrium in the presence of transaction costs was developed, and it was stated that (1) if $(1 - t_{\alpha\beta})$ $(1 - t_{\gamma\alpha}) < (1 - t_{\beta\gamma})$, the approximate equilibrium will be one with $D = (1 - t_{\beta\gamma})/(1 - t_{\alpha\beta})(1 - t_{\gamma\alpha})$, and where the only indirect exchange is of gammas for betas, and (2) if $(1 - t_{\alpha\beta})(1 - t_{\gamma\alpha}) > (1 - t_{\beta\gamma})$, D will be indeterminate in the range $(1 - t_{\beta\gamma})/(1 - t_{\alpha\beta})(1 - t_{\gamma\alpha})$ to $(1 - t_{\alpha\beta})(1 - t_{\gamma\alpha})/(1 - t_{\beta\gamma})$, and all beta–gamma exchanges will take place indirectly. The purpose of this appendix is to demonstrate these propositions.

In making this demonstration, we can use two helpful aspects of the model. First, because of the budget constraints of the countries, it is sufficient to consider only one market, for instance the $\beta\gamma$ market. Second, the excess demand for gammas on the $\beta\gamma$ market is nondecreasing in D, since increases in D can never encourage a shift away from clockwise or toward counterclockwise indirect exchange. This means that if for D slightly less than D_0 we find $X_{\beta\gamma} < 0$, while for D slightly more than D_1 we find that $X_{\beta\gamma} > 0$, *all* equilibrium values of Dt *must lie in the range* D_0 to D_1.

Let us begin by analyzing the choice between direct and indirect exchange. Consider the example of an exchange of alphas for gammas. In direct exchange, after transaction costs one could get $E_{\gamma\alpha}^{-1}(1 - t_{\gamma\alpha})$ gammas per alpha. In indirect exchange one could get $E_{\alpha\beta}E_{\beta\gamma}(1 - t_{\alpha\beta})(1 - t_{\beta\gamma})$ gammas per alpha. Clearly the breakpoint is $E_{\alpha\beta}E_{\beta\gamma}E_{\gamma\alpha} = D = (1 - t_{\gamma\alpha})/(1 - t_{\alpha\beta})(1 - t_{\beta\gamma})$. A similar exercise can be carried out for all such exchanges, yielding critical values of D, as shown in table 8.1. For entries

Table 8.1
Critical values of D for indirect exchange

Initial currency	Final currency, α	β	γ
α		$\dfrac{(1 - t_{\beta\gamma})(1 - t_{\gamma\beta})}{(1 - t_{\alpha\beta})}$	$\dfrac{(1 - t_{\alpha\beta})(1 - t_{\beta\gamma})}{(1 - t_{\gamma\alpha})}$
β	$\dfrac{(1 - t_{\alpha\beta})}{(1 - t_{\beta\gamma})(1 - t_{\gamma\alpha})}$		$\dfrac{(1 - t_{\alpha\beta})(1 - t_{\gamma\alpha})}{(1 - t_{\beta\gamma})}$
γ	$\dfrac{(1 - t_{\gamma\alpha})}{(1 - t_{\alpha\beta})(1 - t_{\beta\gamma})}$	$\dfrac{(1 - t_{\beta\gamma})}{(1 - t_{\alpha\beta})(1 - t_{\gamma\alpha})}$	

below the diagonal in the table the value is that of the *minimum* D that will lead to indirect exchange; for entries above the diagonal it is the *maximum*.

Given a value of D, together with information on the structure of transaction costs, we can determine for each type of exchange whether direct or indirect exchange is preferred. I will use a "+" to indicate a preference for indirect exchange, a "−" to indicate a preference for direct exchange, and a "0" to indicate indifference.

We can now proceed to cases. Recall that we have labeled countries so that $t_{\alpha\beta}$ and $t_{\gamma\alpha}$ are both less than $t_{\beta\gamma}$. Also, the underlying structure of payments is assumed to be that shown in figure 8.2.

Case 1: $(1 - t_{\alpha\beta})(1 - t_{\gamma\alpha}) < (1 - t_{\beta\gamma})$

In this case it is immediately clear that $D = (1 - t_{\beta\gamma})/(1 - t_{\gamma\alpha})$ corresponds to an equilibrium. Referring to table 8.1, we have a matrix of preferred exchanges

$$
\begin{bmatrix}
 & \alpha & \beta & \gamma \\
\alpha & & - & - \\
\beta & - & & - \\
\gamma & - & 0 &
\end{bmatrix}.
$$

Thus exchanges of gammas for betas may take place either directly or indirectly, which is consistent with an equilibrium of partial indirect exchange as illustrated in figure 8.3. This equilibrium is unique. To see this, note that for a slightly higher D the matrix becomes

$$
\begin{bmatrix}
 & \alpha & \beta & \gamma \\
\alpha & & - & - \\
\beta & - & & - \\
\gamma & - & + &
\end{bmatrix},
$$

which leads to $X_{\beta\gamma} = S - I > 0$; while for a slightly lower D we have the matrix

$$
\begin{bmatrix}
 & \alpha & \beta & \gamma \\
\alpha & & - & - \\
\beta & - & & - \\
\gamma & - & - &
\end{bmatrix},
$$

which leads to $X_{\beta\gamma} = S - I < 0$. The unique equilibrium exchange structure, then, is partial indirect exchange with the alpha as vehicle.

Case 2: $(1 - t_{\alpha\beta})(1 - t_{\gamma\alpha}) > (1 - t_{\beta\gamma})$

In this case, any value of D in the range from $D_0 = (1 - t_{\beta\gamma})(1 - t_{\alpha\beta})$ $(1 - t_{\gamma\alpha})$ to $D_1 = (1 - t_{\alpha\beta})(1 - t_{\gamma\alpha})/(1 - t_{\beta\gamma})$ will lead to a matrix of preferred exchanges

$$
\begin{bmatrix}
 & \alpha & \beta & \gamma \\
\alpha & & - & - \\
\beta & - & & + \\
\gamma & - & + &
\end{bmatrix}.
$$

This pattern, which means that all payments between B and C take place indirectly, corresponds to an equilibrium of total indirect exchange, as shown in figure 8.4. This is the unique equilibrium structure, although D is indeterminate. If D were slightly above D_1, the matrix of preferred exchanges would be

$$
\begin{bmatrix}
 & \alpha & \beta & \gamma \\
\alpha & & - & - \\
\beta & - & & - \\
\gamma & - & + &
\end{bmatrix},
$$

which would produce an excess demand for gammas of $S - I$ on the $\beta\gamma$ market. If D were slightly below D_0, the matrix would be

$$
\begin{bmatrix}
 & \alpha & \beta & \gamma \\
\alpha & & - & - \\
\beta & - & & + \\
\gamma & - & - &
\end{bmatrix},
$$

which would produce an excess supply of S gammas on the $\beta\gamma$ market. So the equilibrium structure of exchange must be total indirect exchange with the alpha as vehicle.

Notes

1. The vehicle currency role of the pound sterling before World War I is discussed in Yeager (1976). About the current situation, Kubarych (1978) writes: "Virtually all interbank transactions, by the market participants here and abroad, involve a purchase or sale of dollars for a foreign currency. This is true even if a bank's aim is to buy German marks for sterling." Papers that have discussed the role of vehicle currencies, and stressed the parallel with the use of money in domestic exchange, include Kindleberger (1967), Swoboda (1968), McKinnon (1969), and Chrystal

(1977). Discussions of transaction costs and the structure of exchange in closed economies include Niehans (1969) and Jones (1976), as well as a distinguished tradition going back to Menger (1892) and Jevons (1895).

2. A similar approximation is made by Jones (1976), who assumes in his model of domestic exchange that costs of trading have no effect on Walrasian market-clearing prices.

3. The concept of "clockwisdom"—a single number that measures the deviation from perfect triangular arbitrage—as one might expect, cannot be generalized to models with more than three currencies.

4. Note that we are finding a value of D that would set $X_{\beta\gamma} = 0$ if the implied choices of direct versus indirect exchange took place *without* transaction costs.

III   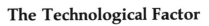The Technological Factor

9   A Model of Innovation, Technology Transfer, and the World Distribution of Income

9.1   Introduction

It is a commonplace that technological innovation in developed countries and the transfer of technology to less developed countries both play an important role in determining the pattern of world trade and changes in that pattern over time. There is an immense empirical and policy literature on innovation and technology transfer in world trade; a literature that draws heavily on simplified, stylized descriptions of these processes at work, notably Vernon's (1966) celebrated concept of the "product cycle." One might have expected that phenomena that are of recognized importance and at the same time display clear empirical regularities would have attracted the attention of theorists. But there have been surprisingly few attempts to introduce technological change into the theory of international trade.[1]

There appear to be several reasons why technological change has received so little emphasis in international trade theory. One is that existing models, while well suited to the analysis of once-for-all changes in technology, are less suited to the analysis of ongoing technical change. Also the kind of technical change that can be analyzed in conventional models involves increased efficiency in production of a given range of goods, while the product cycle literature stresses the development of new products. Related to this is the problem of defining what is meant by a transfer of technology when technical change is assumed to take the form of disembodied increases in the efficiency of factors. Although there have been some useful efforts to solve these problems, notably the recent paper by Findlay (1978), the insights of the empirical workers are still hard to

Originally published in the *Journal of Political Economy* 87, 2 (1979): 253–266. © 1979 by The University of Chicago.

integrate into trade theory. It is not surprising, then, that the role of technology in trade has been relatively neglected.

The purpose of this chapter is to take a first step toward making up for this neglect. It develops a fully worked-out model of international trade in which the pattern of trade is determined by a continuing process of innovation and technology transfer. I postulate a world of two countries: innovating North and noninnovating South. Innovation takes the form of the introduction of new products that can be produced immediately in North but only after a lag in South. The lag in adoption of new technology by South is what gives rise to trade.

The model has a number of interesting implications. There is no fixed pattern of trade; each good is exported by North when first introduced but eventually becomes an export of South instead. The model tends to approach a moving equilibrium in which North exports new products and imports old products. Wages will be higher in North, even if labor in the two countries is equally productive in comparable occupations, because of North's monopoly position in new goods. Finally, because northern wages reflect in part a rent on North's monopoly of new goods, a slowing of innovation or an acceleration of technology transfer narrows the wage differential and may even lead to an absolute decline in living standards of workers in North.

While the results of this chapter are highly suggestive, the limitations of the analysis should be noted. I am concerned with the effects of innovation and technology transfer, not their causes; the rates at which they occur will be taken as exogenous. Also the assumptions are chosen for simplicity and clarity, and no attempt is made at generality. I believe, however, that many of the qualitative results would hold in a more general model.

The remainder of the chapter is in four parts. Section 9.2 develops the basic model. Section 9.3 examines the dynamics of the model and the effects of changes in the rates of innovation and technology transfer. In section 9.4 the model is extended to allow for international investment; the implications of the analysis are then discussed in section 9.5.

9.2   A Model of North–South Trade

There are two things we would like a theory of trade between developed and less developed countries to do. It ought to explain both the pattern of trade and why wages are higher in the developed country. The explanation that much of the literature on technology in world trade seems to be proposing is as follows: The advantage of developed countries does not lie in greater endowments of nonhuman inputs per worker or in superior overall efficiency as much as in a superior ability to exploit *new* technology. As a result, developed countries export newly developed products, and the rent on their monopoly in such products accounts for their higher wages.

In this section I develop a model designed to place this explanation of North–South trade into sharp relief by suppressing all other sources of trade. There is assumed to be only one factor of production—labor—in each country, ruling out differences in factor endowments; at the same time all goods are assumed to be produced with the same cost function, ruling out a Ricardian explanation of trade. Labor productivity in those goods that can be produced in both countries will be assumed to be the same in North and South, so that the special ability of North to produce certain goods will be the only source of inequality in wages.

There are assumed to be two kinds of goods: old goods and new goods. Old goods are goods that were developed some time ago. Their technology is common property, and they can be produced either in North or in South.[2] I choose units so that one unit of labor produces one unit of an old good.

New goods are recently developed products. They can only be produced in the developed country. This is simply assumed here. Vernon (1966) and others have discussed at length the reasons why developed countries may have an advantage in producing new products; the reasons include a more skilled labor force, external economies, and a simple difference in "social atmosphere."

All goods, whether old or new, are assumed to enter demand symmetrically. The utility function, which is shared by all individuals, is assumed to be of the form[3]

$$U = \left\{ \sum_{i=1}^{n} c(i)^{\theta} \right\}^{1/\theta}, \qquad 0 < \theta < 1, \tag{1}$$

where $c(i)$ is the consumption of the ith good and n is the total number of products available. The number of products is the sum of the number of both new and old goods. For the moment we will take these as given, reserving the determination of these numbers to section 9.3.

There is also assumed to be a latent demand for as yet unproduced goods with the additional goods entering into the utility function the same way those previously produced did. That is, if Δn additional goods were made available to consumers, they would now maximize

$$U = \left\{ \sum_{i=1}^{n+\Delta n} c(i)^{\theta} \right\}^{1/\theta} \tag{1a}$$

subject to their budget constraints.

Before proceeding, we ought to note an important point about the assumed utility function. The utility function (1) gives a positive value to the increased variety of available goods. For a given income and prices, an individual will become better off if he is offered a wider selection of goods. In section 9.3 technological change will be assumed to take the form of development of new products. Given the assumed utility function, this is as much an increase in the economy's productive capacity as there would be if there were increased efficiency in production of existing products.

Turning now to the production side, we assume that it takes one unit of labor to produce one unit of any good. All goods will be assumed to be produced under conditions of perfect competition, so that profits will be driven to zero, and we must have

$$P_N = w_N$$
$$P_S = w_S$$

(2)

where w_N, w_S are the wage rates (in arbitrary units) and P_N, P_S are the prices of *any* good produced in North or South, respectively. Which goods are produced where is yet to be determined.

I have already assumed that new goods can only be produced in North; thus North will produce all new goods and South only old goods. The remaining question is whether North produces any old goods or not. This depends on relative wages. If $w_N/w_S = 1$, North will be competitive in old goods; if $w_N/w_S > 1$, it will specialize in new goods.

The relative wage can be determined by looking at the derived demand for northern labor as illustrated in figure 9.1. Suppose that initially $w_N/w_S > 1$, so that the developed country is specialized in new goods, and we lower the relative wage. Then the demand for new goods will rise and with it the demand for northern labor as shown by the line segment DE. At $w_N/w_S =$

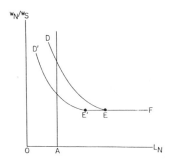

Figure 9.1

1 the demand curve for northern labor will become infinitely elastic, because northern and southern labor are perfect substitutes in the production of old goods. In figure 9.1 the northern labor force is OA, so in equilibrium w_N/w_S is greater than one and North produces only new goods. In the rest of the chapter I will assume that this is true so that we can identify the number of goods produced in each country, n_N and n_S, with the number of new and old goods, respectively.

Now consider what happens if a "technology transfer" takes place, so that some new goods become old goods; in other words, their technology becomes available to South. The effect is to shift the derived demand for northern labor left, to $D'E'F$. This narrows the wage differential; if there were no increase in $n = n_N + n_S$, workers in North may be absolutely worse off.

We can develop these results algebraically. Consider the relative demands for a good produced in North and one produced in South. The utility function (1) implies that the relative demand will depend only on prices:

$$\frac{c_N}{c_S} = \left(\frac{P_N}{P_S}\right)^{-(1/1-\theta)}$$

$$= \left(\frac{w_N}{w_S}\right)^{-(1/1-\theta)} \tag{3}$$

where c_N is consumption of a northern good and c_S consumption of a Southern good. Demand for labor in each country will equal demand for each good times the number of goods, so the relative demand for labor can be written

$$\frac{L_N}{L_S} = \frac{n_N c_N}{n_S c_S}$$

$$= \left(\frac{n_N}{n_S}\right)\left(\frac{w_N}{w_S}\right)^{-(1/1-\theta)}. \tag{4}$$

This can then be turned around to give an expression for relative wages as a function of relative labor forces and the ratio of new to old goods:

$$\frac{w_N}{w_S} = \left(\frac{n_N}{n_S}\right)^{1-\theta}\left(\frac{L_N}{L_S}\right)^{-(1-\theta)}. \tag{5}$$

The important point to notice here is that the relative wage rate in the developed country depends on the relative importance of newly developed products that it can produce and the less developed country cannot. A burst of innovation that increases n_N will raise the relative northern wage. This is in contrast to the result in conventional models in which technological progress in the export sector generally worsens the terms of trade.[4]

We have now seen how momentary equilibrium in the world economy involves exports of new products by North and exports of old products by South with relative wages depending on the numbers of new and old products in existence. Our next step must be to look at the factors determining n_N and n_S—innovation and technology transfer.

9.3   Innovation and Technology Transfer

The stocks of new and old products are determined over time by two processes of technological change—innovation and technology transfer. Innovation is the process by which new products are created; technology transfer is the process by which new products are transformed into old products. Both of these can be assumed to be taking place continually.

In keeping with the general strategy of placing the unconventional aspects of this model in as uncluttered a form as possible, I will assume that *all* technological change takes the form of adding new products or making it possible for southern labor to produce more products. Thus technological change of the kind that is usually supposed to take place—an increase in productivity in the production of a given range of goods—will be assumed away. There will be a technical progress in this model, but it will be entirely in the form of the availability of new products rather than in the form of an increased volume of production of old products.

The process of innovation will mean increases in n, the number of goods produced. We know very little about the factors that affect the rate of innovation. One reasonable guess, though, is that the number of new products invented depends positively on the number already developed: The more you know, the more you can learn. I will assume that innovation is proportional to the number of products already in existence:

$$\dot{n} = i\,n. \tag{6}$$

The reason for making this assumption is the same as the reason for assuming exponential technological change in conventional growth models and has the same justification: It causes the model to approach a long-run steady growth path.

The process of technology transfer turns new goods, which are a Northern monopoly, into old goods, which are in the public domain. Again, we have no good theory of this process. One might suppose that goods would remain new for some fixed period, as if they were patented. On the other hand, the time required for South to adopt a new product might vary considerably from product to product. It may therefore be just as realistic, and certainly more convenient, to represent the process by which new products become old products as one of "radioactive" decay:

$$\dot{n}_S = t\, n_N. \tag{7}$$

Notice that this implies that the average "imitation lag"—the time taken before South learns how to manufacture a new product—is $1/t$.

The rate of change of the number of new products will be the difference between the rate of innovation and the rate of technology transfer:

$$\dot{n}_N = i\, n - t\, n_N. \tag{8}$$

The system of equations (6)–(8) is not stable; it will explode upward in continual technological progress. The composition of the stock of goods will, however, tend toward a stable mix. Let $\sigma = n_N/n$, the share of new goods. Then we have

$$\dot{\sigma} = \frac{\dot{n}_N}{n} - \frac{\sigma \dot{n}}{n} - i - (i + t)\sigma. \tag{9}$$

Thus the system will tend toward an equilibrium at $\sigma = i/(i + t)$.

Finally, we should note that the ratio of new to old goods, which we saw in the last section determined relative wages, is

$$\frac{n_N}{n_S} = \frac{\sigma}{1 - \sigma} = \frac{i}{t} \text{ in equilibrium.} \tag{10}$$

The world economy, then, tends toward a moving equilibrium or steady state. What does this steady state look like? Relative wages are constant, with a fixed differential in favor of the developed country that is an increasing function of the rate of innovation i and a decreasing function of the rate of technology transfer t. The structure of trade remains unchanged in one sense in that North always exports new products and imports old products. But the actual goods involved continually change. Each good is at first produced in and exported by North; then when the technology becomes available to South, the industry moves to the lower wage country. Case studies in such a world would reveal a Vernon-type product cycle.

Now let us move beyond the consideration of the steady state and examine the effects of changes in the rates of innovation and technology

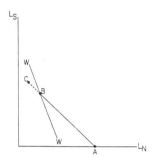

Figure 9.2

transfer. Such changes, by altering the number of goods produced and the location of production, have an efficiency effect that alters world productivity. They also, more interestingly, have effects on the distribution of world income between North and South.

Let us start with the efficiency effects. It is immediately apparent that innovation, by increasing the range of products, represents an increase in real world productivity. It is less obvious but true that technology transfer, allowing production of a wider range of goods in the less developed country, also represents a gain from a global point of view. To see this we can consider the dual of the production problem—the problem of producing the existing output of goods at minimum cost.[5] This is illustrated in figure 9.2, which compares different combinations of northern and southern labor that could be used to produce a given basket of goods. As long as both North and South are producing old goods, northern and southern labor can be freely substituted for one another, as illustrated by the line segment AB. But we have been assuming that the world is at a corner solution; that relative wages, as shown by WW, are such that North and South specialize in new and old goods, respectively, as at B. A transfer of technology, turning some new goods into old goods, makes it possible to substitute southern labor for northern in the production of a given basket of goods as shown by the extension of AB to C. At initial prices this would reduce production cost, which indicates that production possibilities have been expanded.

Both innovation and technology transfer, then, increase world output. But they also alter the world distribution of income.[6] As a result of this, innovation disproportionately benefits the developed country, while technology transfer can actually make the developed country worse off.

These results can easily be seen by referring back to section 9.2. Innovation increases n_N, the number of new goods, while leaving n_S, the number of old goods, unchanged. The resulting increase in the variety of products available benefits both countries. But n_N/n_S increases, which means that the North–South wage differential rises, and the terms of trade move in North's favor. This effect on the terms of trade is a secondary benefit to North and partially offsets the gains to South.[7]

Technology transfer has equally striking distributional impacts. There is no increase in the variety of goods; the increase in n_S equals the reduction in n_N. The terms of trade move against North so that while South gains, northern workers can be worse off.[8]

So far we have considered once-for-all changes in n_N and n_S, instead of changes in rates of innovation and transfer of technology, but the extension is straightforward: we simply compare n_N and n_S with what they would have been if rates of innovation and transfer had not changed. There are, however, some interesting comparative dynamic examples that emerge from this model.

Consider the effects of a slowing in innovation. In a conventional model of growth this might lead to a narrowing of the gap between the developed and less developed country, but the developed country would continue to grow. In this model real income in North might actually decline for a time as its monopoly position in new goods is eroded. We can demonstrate this with an extreme example: If innovation came to a complete halt, while transfer of technology continued, North would eventually lose its wage advantage, leaving northern workers worse off.

An increase in the rate of technological borrowing by the less developed country would work similarly, shifting the terms of trade against North. If this happened fast enough, it could lead to a temporary reduction in northern welfare.

The crucial point in each of these examples is that the incomes of northern residents depend in part on the rents from their monopoly of newly developed products. This monopoly is continually eroded by technological borrowing and must be maintained by constant innovation of new products. Like Alice and the Red Queen, the developed region must keep running to stay in the same place.

9.4 International Investment

The model developed in section 9.2 and 9.3 is concerned only with trade in goods. A simple extension of the model, however, can give us some insights into the relationship between technological change and the international movement of factors of production.

Suppose, then, that there are old and new products entering into demand symmetrically as described by (1) and that North specializes in new goods. The stocks of old and new products will continue to be determined by the processes of innovation and technology transfer described by (6) and (7). We now assume, however, that there are two factors of production in each country: labor, which is assumed to be immobile between countries, and capital, which is assumed to be perfectly mobile internationally. All goods will be produced by capital and labor using the same constant returns to scale production function. I assume that there is a given world stock of capital and assume away net investment in the world as a whole.

To analyze short-run equilibrium in this extended model, we can begin by noticing that new goods as a group and old goods as a group can be regarded as composite commodities, since relative prices will not change within each group. The relative demand for the two composite commodities will depend on the price of the new relative to old goods. The relative supply of the two kinds of goods—which was fixed by the relative labor supplies in section 9.2—will now also be variable because of the possibility of reallocation of the world capital stock. Since capital will move until it earns the same return in both countries, a rise in the relative price of new goods will cause capital to move from South to North.

Figure 9.3 shows how the allocation of the world capital stock is determined. The vertical axis shows the rental price of capital measured in terms of old goods. $D_S D_S$ shows the marginal product of capital in South, which is also the demand for capital. $D_N D_N$ shows the marginal *value* product of capital in North measured in terms of old goods at some *given* relative price of new goods. At that relative price the equilibrium return on capital is r_0, with K_S the stock of capital in South, K_N the stock of capital in North, and $K_S + K_N$ the world stock of capital.

If the relative price of new goods were to rise, the marginal value product of capital in North would increase. In figure 9.3 this is illustrated

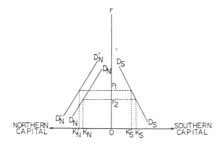

Figure 9.3

by a shift of $D_N D_N$ to $D'_N D'_N$, with the return on capital rising to r_1, northern capital rising to K'_N, and southern capital falling to K'_S. We know that $K'_N + K'_S$ equals $K_N + K_S$, since the world capital stock has not changed. Output of new goods will rise, while output of old goods will fall.

We have, then, relationships between the relative price of new goods and relative demand, on one side, and relative supply, on the other. These relationships determine the relative prices of new goods; this in turn determines factor prices. A rise in the relative price of new goods redistributes income toward northern labor and away from southern labor with an ambiguous effect on the capital share.

The final step in the analysis is to relate changes in relative prices to technological change. Technological change, whether by innovation or transfer, alters the definitions of the composite commodities "new goods" and "old goods," with the result that demand shifts. Innovation, by extending the range of new goods, increases the demand for northern goods at any given relative price. Thus the relative price of northern goods rises and capital moves from South to North. The income of northern workers relative to southern rises for two reasons: The relative prices of the goods they produce rise, and their real wage in terms of their output rises (while that of southern workers falls) because of the reallocation of capital. In the same way technology transfer shifts demand toward goods produced in South so that capital moves south and the relative income of southern workers rises.

What can we learn from these results? There are two major lessons. The first is that technological change will be associated with capital movement: The region experiencing the most rapid technological advance will also experience capital inflow. Notice, though, that the causation runs from technological change to capital movement, not the other way around. Essentially what happens is that technological progress raises the marginal product of capital wherever it occurs and provides an incentive for foreign investment.

The second point we should notice is that rents on North's monopoly of new goods are collected by the immobile factors of production. Migration of mobile factors, which we have called "capital" but could include skilled labor, will equalize incomes of these factors while increasing the inequality of incomes of immobile factors in North and South.[9]

9.5 Implications of the Analysis

This chapter has developed a model of international trade that differs considerably from conventional Ricardian or Heckscher-Ohlin models and draws its inspiration instead from such authors as Vernon (1966) and Hirsch (1974). Distinctive aspects of the model are that it postulates a large number of goods, that it assumes a continuous process of technological change, and that technical progress takes the form of development of new products instead of increased productivity in the manufacture of old products. The assumptions of the model are, like those of conventional models, highly simplified and unrealistic, and the model is not proposed as a replacement of existing theories. Instead, it is a supplement, providing some insight into neglected aspects of the international economy.

The picture of the world that emerges is quite different from what we are accustomed to in trade theory. Although there may be stability in some macroeconomic aggregates, there is continual change at the micro level. New industries are constantly emerging in the developed region, then disappearing in the face of low-wage competition from the less developed region. The picture of trade seems in some ways more like that of businessmen or economic historians than that of trade theorists.

To the extent that the model captures some aspects of the real world, there are some implications for economic policy. One is that the decline of industries in developed countries will be a recurrent event—and one that from the point of view of world productive efficiency, is a desirable event. Another implication is that technical innovation is even more important than it appears to be in conventional models, since developed countries must continually innovate, not just to grow but even to maintain their real incomes.

For less developed countries, there appear to be two major implications of the model. One is that transfer of technology, in addition to its direct benefits, brings the indirect benefit of improved terms of trade. What this means for policy is not clear, since we do not know much about the factors determining the rate at which technological borrowing takes place.

The other implication of the effects of technological borrowing is less encouraging. Success by less developed countries in accelerating their adoption of new techniques can leave workers in developed countries worse off; and it is easy to imagine that by encouraging protectionism such success could be self-defeating.

Notes

1. The effects of technological change in a Ricardian model are discussed by Dornbusch, Fischer, and Samuelson (1977). The effects in a Heckscher-Ohlin model are discussed in Jones (1970).

2. What I call old goods correspond fairly well to what Hirsch (1974) calls Heckscher-Ohlin goods, that is, goods that, unlike what he calls product cycle goods (my new goods), can be produced with the same technology anywhere in the world; and that, unlike his Ricardo goods, do not have special environmental requirements. My model, of course, omits Ricardo goods.

3. This is a restrictive functional form which appears to be necessary if the model is to have a steady-state equilibrium in section 9.3. Something should also be said about the assumption that all goods enter demand symmetrically. This is clearly unrealistic: There is no reason why mopeds and toothbrushes should have identical demand functions. It also assumes away all differences in substitutability among goods, making all goods equally good substitutes for one another. The only justification for the assumption is its simplifying power, which allows us to analyze economies producing many goods. The assumption also has an honorable lineage, since it was adopted by Chamberlin (1962) for the analysis of monopolistic competition. Equation (1) is borrowed from the recent reformulation of Chamberlin's theory by Dixit and Stiglitz (1977).

4. On the relationship between technological change and the terms of trade in a Ricardian model, see Dornbusch, Fischer, and Samuelson (1977).

5. Notice that since tastes are assumed identical and homothetic, we can separate the problem of efficiency in production from that of income distribution. More generally, we would have to assume lump-sum redistribution by some kind of world government for world efficiency to have any meaning.

6. By world distribution of income I mean distribution between nations. This model has nothing to say about distribution within nations.

7. One might suppose that South could actually be made worse off by innovation in North, but given the assumptions of this paper that cannot happen. Letting a "hat" over a variable represent a proportional rate of change, the change in southern welfare can be shown to be

$$\hat{U}_S = \theta^{-1}(1 - \theta)^2 \mu \cdot \hat{n}_N > 0$$

where μ is the share of new goods in expenditure. It is possible, however, that immiserizing effects of innovation could appear in a more general model.

8. Using the same notation as in the previous note, we have

$$\hat{U}_N = \left(1 - \mu + \frac{\mu}{\theta}\right)(1 - \theta)\hat{n}_N + \theta^{-1}(1 - \theta)^2(1 - \mu)\hat{n}_S$$

which is of ambiguous sign. However, if the technology transfer is large enough to lead to equalization of wages, the result will be to make North unambiguously worse off.

9. When capital is mobile, it becomes possible that innovation in North will leave southern *workers* absolutely worse off.

10   A "Technology Gap" Model of International Trade

10.1   Introduction

One of the most important trends in the world economy in recent decades has been the gradual erosion of the technological superiority of the industrial nations in general, and of the United States in particular. To this "closing of the gap" may be attributed the decline of some traditional industries in the advanced countries, the increasing relative importance of high-technology products in the advanced countries' exports, and the secular decline in U.S. relative wages and the U.S. real exchange rate. These effects on trade of technology and technological change are at the heart of the debate on international economic policy. Furthermore there is widespread agreement on certain ways of looking at this issue —such as the common image of a "ladder" of countries whose exports can be ranked on a "scale" of goods—that suggest an implicit model shared by many observers. Yet this model has not been formalized. To a remarkable extent the treatment of technology in formal trade theory has failed to connect with policy concerns.

The purpose of this chapter is to set out a framework for the analysis of technology and trade that is closer than standard models to the way practical men seem to see the issue. The model is basically a many-good Ricardian model similar to those developed by Dornbusch et al. (1977) and Wilson (1980). Some restrictions are, however, placed on the ways in which technology can differ between countries. This is done in such a way as to give a natural meaning to the idea that countries can be ranked by technological level and that goods can be ranked by technology-intensity. The result is a model that is like the Heckscher-Ohlin model in the sense

Orignally published in *Structural Adjustment in Advanced Economies*, edited by K. Jungenfelt and D. Hague. © 1986 Macmillan.

that trade patterns reflect an interaction of the characteristics of countries and goods: technologically advanced countries have a comparative advantage in technology-intensive goods. Within this model we can carry out comparative statics. In particular, we can analyze the effects of a widening or narrowing of the "technology gap," as more or less advanced countries improve their technology. An important asymmetry appears: technical progress in the most advanced country always benefits less advanced countries, but a "catch-up" by a less advanced country may well hurt the technological leader.

The chapter is in four sections. In Section 10.2 I review several approaches that have been taken to the effect of technology on trade and outline the motivation behind the particular approach taken here. In section 10.3 the basic model of comparative advantage is worked out. Section 10.4 then adds a demand side and explores the effects of widening or narrowing the technology gap. Finally, section 10.5 summarizes the argument and discusses some unresolved issues.

10.2 Modeling the Effect of Technology on Trade

Introducing technology into trade models is anything but a new idea. The original Ricardian model is one in which differences in production functions are the cause of trade, even though Ricardo might have attributed them to climate or differences in national character rather than differences in knowledge. The two-factor model can also accommodate differences in technology and technological change, as the elegant papers of Findlay and Grubert (1959) and Jones (1965, 1970) showed. The problem is that the way in which technology is introduced in these papers seems ill-suited to current policy discussion, as we will discuss below. On the other hand, there is an influential body of informal literature on technology and trade, with the work of Posner (1961), Hufbauer (1964), Vernon (1966), and Hirsch (1967) among the best known. This does seem to appeal to practical men but has not been stated in the form of models and is therefore still ambiguous in its implications. Our problem is, if possible, to develop a model that is formal, yet still has the right "feel."

Consider first the two-good, two-country Ricardian model. The problem with this model as a vehicle for discussing technical change is that too many things can happen. In the first place there is no natural ranking of countries by level of technology. A country may have absolute advantage in one sector but not in the other. Even if there is a clear ranking, the effects of technological change depend on the sector in which it occurs (and on whether both countries are specialized or one country produces both goods). That is, technological progress in the Ricardian model is a vector rather than a number. To the question, "what happens if a less advanced country's technology improves?" the Ricardian model replies with another question: "In which sector?"

In the two-factor model, matters are even worse. As Findlay and Grubert (1959) pointed out, the effect of technological progress in the 2 × 2 models depends not only on the sector bias but on the factor bias of the improvement. Capital-saving technical change in the labor-intensive sector can actually cause the progressing sector to contract, as Rybczinski dominates Ricardo. Jones (1965) showed that in the 2 × 2 model technological change must be represented as a *matrix* of changes in unit input requirements in the two sectors.

In either the Ricardian or Heckscher-Ohlin models, going from two goods to many goods adds a further complication: it is no longer possible to identify unambiguously the export- or import-competing sectors. Thus in Dornbusch et al. (1977) technical progress will scramble the comparative advantage ranking on which their analytic method depends. Wilson (1980) has a more general method but still restricts himself to analyzing a uniform technical change that is equivalent to growth in the labor force.

These complications are, of course, not just artifacts of the models but represent real possibilities. It is sometimes argued, for example, that Japan is better than the United States at assembly-line production but not as good in other things, so that there is no unambiguous ranking by productivity. It has actually happened that new labor-saving techniques in farming have led to a reduction in the agricultural labor force; if the techniques are land-using as well, agricultural output could fall too. But one wonders if it is not possible to place some structure on a trade model. We need to do so in a way that is a reasonable approximation to reality that allows us to speak of countries as ranked by the level of their technology and to represent technical progress as a scalar rather than a vector or matrix. The point is not to develop a general theory but to come up with a model that helps to crystalize our intuition.

Consider the following story of a one-factor world. There is a world technological frontier: a sort of best-practice set of techniques of production that is continually improving. The rate at which this improvement takes place is different in different industries. In some industries—call them "technology intensive"—best practice improves rapidly. In other industries it improves more slowly. We will suppose that the ranking of industries by technology intensity in this sense is stable over time; some activities are more amenable to improvement than others.

We do not expect that all countries will be at the technological frontier. A simple assumption would be that each country lags behind best practice by some number of years. A more advanced country might be only three years behind the frontier; a less advanced country might be twenty years behind. We will not get into the deep issue of why some societies do better in this respect than others. Instead, we will take these varying lags as given and point to the consequence: a simple pattern of comparative advantage.

What is this pattern? A more advanced country will be more productive than less advanced countries in all industries. But the productivity advantage will be relatively small in industries where technical progress is slow and a lag in the adoption of best practice does not matter too much. We can, however, say that where the productivity advantage will be large, and where the advanced country's comparative advantage will lie, is in the technology-intensive sectors where best practice is rapidly improving.

10.3 A Model of Comparative Advantage

An Example

A special example may help to provide the intuition for the assumptions of our model of comparative advantage. Suppose, following the informal discussion above, that there is only one factor of production, labor. Let $a_i(z)$ be the unit labor requirement for production of good (z) in country (i). Also let $a^*(z)$ be the best-practice unit labor requirement. We will assume that a^* falls steadily over time:

$$A^*(z) = \exp[-g_z t]. \tag{1}$$

Here, g_z, the rate of progress of best practice technique for good (z), can be regarded as an index of z's technology intensity.

We assume that countries' technologies have a uniform lag (across industries) behind the frontier. Thus suppose country (i) lags λ_i years behind the frontier. Then i's unit labor requirement in producing (z) will be

$$a_i(z) = \exp[-g_z(t - \lambda_i)]. \tag{2}$$

Now compare this country with another country, j, where $\lambda_j > \lambda_i$—that is, (j) lags behind (i) in its adoption of new techniques. Then (i) will be more productive in all goods, but its productivity advantage will not be uniform. Instead, for any good (z) it will be

$$\frac{a_j(z)}{a_i(z)} = \exp[g_z(\lambda_j - \lambda_i)].$$ (3)

That is, i's productivity advantage will be higher, the greater is g_z. The ranking of goods by i's comparative advantage will be same as their ranking by technology intensity.

The General Model

We need not assume as much as we did in the preceding example to have a simple model of technology and comparative advantage. What we do need to assume is the following. First, there is only one factor of production. Thus we rule out the complications introduced by factor-biased technical change, as well as the possibility that factor endowments, as well as technology, determine comparative advantage. Second, we assume that countries may be unambiguously ranked by technological level, so that higher-ranked countries always have an *absolute* advantage in *all* sectors over those with lower ranking. It is natural to follow the informal jargon here and refer to a "ladder" of countries.

Finally, we will assume that it is possible to rank sectors in such a way that a country that is higher on the ladder always has a greater productivity advantage in higher-numbered sectors. That is, we will be able to assign an index (z) to goods such that if country (i) is more advanced than country (j), $a_j(z)/a_i(z)$ is increasing in z. An alternative way of saying this is that as we move up the ladder of countries, productivity always increases more in high-z sectors than in low-z sectors. Again, we can borrow from currently popular jargon to talk of a "scale" of goods.

Now two propositions immediately follow from these assumptions. First, the wage rate must rise as we move up the ladder of countries. Clearly, if one country had a higher wage than another country with more advanced technology, it would have no cost advantage in anything.

Second, the products produced by any country must lie "up-scale" from those produced by less advanced countries and "down-scale" from those produced by more advanced countries. Suppose that some good is cheaper to produce in a less advanced country, that is, this country's productivity disadvantage is outweighed by its lower wage rate. Then any goods of lower technology intensity, for which the productivity difference is smaller

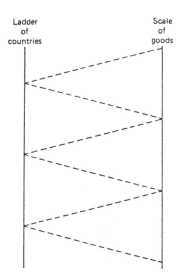

Figure 10.1

still, must also be cheaper to produce there. Conversely, suppose that a good is cheaper to produce in the more advanced country. Then any goods further upscale, where the productivity differential is even greater, must also be cheaper to produce there.

The result is a pattern of specialization like that illustrated in figure 10.1. Each country has a "niche" in the scale of goods; the higher the country is on the technology ladder, the further upscale is the range of goods in which it has a comparative advantage.

To get this result, we have had to impose a great deal of structure on the model, and we must keep in mind how special a model it is. Yet the payoff in terms of insight seems substantial. First, notice that we have a clear description of the pattern of comparative advantage in a many-good, many-country world. This is in contrast to the result in a less structured model where, as McKenzie's (1953) work showed, little of economic interest can be said about the pattern of specialization. Second, we have preserved the appealing feature of Heckscher-Ohlin theory, namely, that comparative advantage reflects an interaction between the characteristics of countries and the characteristics of goods.

Our next step is to examine the effect of technical change on the pattern of specialization and on welfare. To do this, it is necessary to introduce a demand side.

10.4   Effects of Technological Change

Closing the Model: The Demand Side

Although we have determined the pattern of specialization for a many-country world, for the purposes of this paper we will focus on a two-country model. Also, for simplicity, we will assume a very simple form for demand: following Dornbusch et al. (1977), both countries will be assumed to have identical Cobb-Douglas preferences.

We assume, then, that there are two countries, 1 and 2, and a continuum of goods indexed by (z) in order of increasing technology-intensity. Country 1's productivity advantage is

$$A(z) = \frac{a_2(z)}{a_1(z)} \tag{4}$$

and is increasing in (z). There will be some marginal good (z) which is equally costly to produce in country 1 and country 2; the relative wage and (z) are related by

$$w = \frac{w_1}{w_2} = A(\bar{z}). \tag{5}$$

All goods $z < \bar{z}$ are produced in country 2; goods $z > \bar{z}$ in 1.

The implication of Cobb-Douglas preferences is that each good receives a constant share of expenditure. The share of expenditure falling on each country's goods is increasing in the range of products it produces. Thus if (S) is the share of income spent on country 2's products, we have

$$S = S(\bar{z}), \tag{6}$$

increasing in $\bar{z}$.

The second equilibrium condition in the model may be equivalently stated as equality between the supply and demand for 1's labor; equality between the supply and demand for country 2's labor; or balance of payments equilibrium. Letting L_1 and L_2 be the (fully employed) labor forces, we can write the conditions as

$$wL_1S(z) = L_2[1 - S(z)], \tag{7}$$

or

$$w = \frac{L_2}{L_1} \frac{1 - S(z)}{S(\bar{z})}.$$

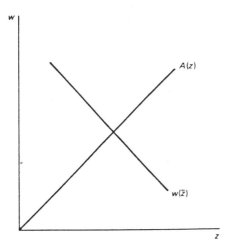

Figure 10.2

Combining the conditions (5) and (7), we can depict equilibrium as in figure 10.2 which is a mirror-image version of a figure from Dornbusch et al. (1977). On the horizontal axis is the index of the marginal good; on the vertical axis the relative wage. Balance of payments equilibrium requires that an increase in the range of goods that 2 produces be offset by a reduction in 1's relative wage; supply-side equilibrium requires the reverse.

Widening the Gap

We are now prepared for our first exercise in comparative statics. What happens if country 1's technology improves, widening the gap between itself and country 2?

It will be useful to restate equilibrium in terms of a different space. In figure 10.3 the horizontal axis represents ln $A(z)$, that is, the percentage productivity advantage of country 1, while the vertical axis now gives the log of the relative wage. The schedules OA and BB correspond to the schedules in figure 10.2; our choice of variables implies that OA is a 45-degree line from the origin.

An improvement in country 1's technology means an increase in its productivity advantage in all sectors; thus OA shifts upward. Given our assumptions about technology, however, this is not a parallel shift: the productivity increase is greater for goods of higher technology intensity, so that OA shifts up more at higher (z). Thus the new schedule must look something like $O'A'$.

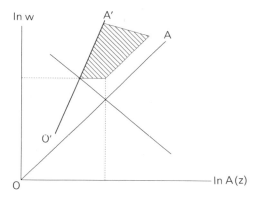

Figure 10.3

The two obvious effects are that the relative wage of the advanced country rises and the range of products produced in the less advanced country falls. Notice, however, that the relative wage increases by less than does the productivity increase on the original marginal good. This is, as we will see, crucial to understanding the effects of this technical advance on real income in the less advanced country.

Who gains and who loses, if anyone? The easiest way to think of this is to look at the purchasing power of each country's labor in terms of goods. For each good (z) there are real wages $w_1/p(z)$, $w_2/p(z)$; if the real wage goes up for all z, a country unambiguously gains.

It is straightforward to show that the advanced country gains. Its real wage in terms of its own products rises because of increased productivity; its real wage in terms of the other country's products rises because the relative wage advantage has risen. There remain the transitional goods; those that were originally produced in country 2 and now move to country 1. These goods would have become cheaper in terms of country 1's labor even if their location of production had not changed; and their production must have shifted because it is cheaper still to produce them in country 1.

Country 2, on the other hand, might at first sight have cause for complaint. In the first place, its relative wage and its share of world income have both fallen. Furthermore the reduction in the range of products that country 2 produces means a loss of its technologically most progressive sectors. In becoming more specialized, country 2 shifts its exports downscale in terms of technological intensity. It is easy to see how one might conclude that progress in the North is occurring at the South's expense.

But this conclusion would be wrong. *The less advanced country is better off.* Consider what happens to the purchasing power of country 2's labor. In terms of its own products, it is unchanged. Since country 1's relative wage rises by less than its productivity increase on the marginal good; and since the productivity increases on transmarginal goods are larger; the prices of country 1's goods in terms of that country's labor fall. As for the "transitional" goods, country 2 still has the option of producing them for itself at unchanged labour cost; if it buys them abroad, it is because they are cheaper.

Geometrically, the increase in country 2's purchasing power may be found by subtracting the rise in ($\ln w$) from country 1's productivity increase; this is shown as the shaded area in figure 10.3.

Technological progress in the leading country, then, even though it widens the gap, benefits the less advanced country as well. The case of technical progress by the less advanced country, however, is not symmetric. A narrowing of the gap need not benefit the advanced country; it may well make it worse off.

Narrowing the Gap

An improvement in country 2's technology means an increase in its productivity in all sectors; OA shifts down. As before, however, the shift is not parallel: the greatest productivity gains are in the more technology-intensive sectors, so that the new schedule $O'A'$ in figure 10.4 is flatter than OA. The wage differential falls, but by less than the productivity increase for the original marginal good. The range of products produced by country 2 increases.

It can be shown that country 2 gains from its own technological progress; the argument is similar to those made above, and we will not repeat

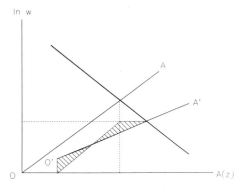

Figure 10.4

it. The interesting question is what happens to real income in the advanced country.

We must consider the advanced country's real wage in terms of three groups of products. First, there are those products that were originally country 1's exports and that continue to be exported by the advanced country. For these, real wages do not change. Second, there are products whose production "moves south." Since these could still have been produced at unchanged labor cost in the advanced country, they must have become cheaper in terms of labor; in figure 10.4 the increase in the real wage on these products is measured by the vertical distance between YZ and OA'.

Finally, there are the products that are produced in the less advanced country throughout. These are made more expensive by the decline in country 1's relative wage, an effect indicated by adding the line XY in figure 10.4, parallel to OA but moved down by an amount showing the decline in $\ln w$. These products are, however, made less expensive by the rise in country 2's productivity, which we have already represented by the shift in OA to $O'A'$.

The net effect is given by the vertical distance between $O'A'$ and XY. Clearly, real wages rise for goods near the original margin but fall for sufficiently inframarginal goods. The pattern of real wage increases and decreases is indicated by the shaded area in figure 10.4 or, equivalently, by figure 10.5: the purchasing power of the advanced country's labor increases for goods near the original margin but falls for traditional imports from the less advanced country. When the Third World learns to make TV sets, the labor price of TV sets falls but the labor price of clothing may well rise.

What is the overall effect on real income in the advanced country? It is possible that Country 1 may gain more from falling prices of medium-technology goods than it loses from worsened terms of trade against low-technology products. But if the closing of the gap is complete, the advanced

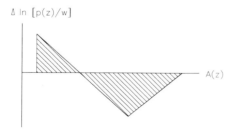

$\Delta \ln [p(z)/w]$

$A(z)$

Figure 10.5

country in effect loses the gains from trade and must be made worse off. It follows that when the technology gap is small, a further narrowing hurts the technological leader.

Interpreting the Results

We have shown that there is a basic asymmetry between the effects of technological progress in more and less advanced countries. Technical advance in the advanced country, which opens a technology gap, benefits the less advanced country as well. "Catch-up" by the less advanced country, which closes the gap, hurts the technological leader.

One way to think about this asymmetry is in terms of the distinction between export- and import-biased growth. In our model, technical progress is always biased toward the technology-intensive industries. These are also the export industries of the leader. So progress in the leading country is in effect biased toward goods that the other country was not producing; while progress in the follower, by contrast, competes with the leader's exports.

The disturbing implication of this analysis is that in a real sense the real income of the technological leader depends on its lead; catching up by other nations can lead to a decline not only in the leader's relative income but in its absolute standard of living as well. If this is read as a spur to continuing innovation, well and good. But it can also be read as a case for technological protectionism, limiting the free flow of information. No doubt there are compelling political and humanitarian arguments against such a policy, but the *economic* case is there.

10.5 Summary and Conclusions

This chapter has developed a simple model of the relationship between technology and trade. The model is basically Ricardian, but "structured" in a way that implies a pattern of interaction between the characteristics of countries and goods. Countries can be ranked by level of technology; goods can be ranked by "technology intensity." Each country finds a niche on the scale of goods which is appropriate to its position on the technology ladder.

The chapter considered the effects of technological progress in two cases: progress in an advanced country that widens the gap between it and another country, and progress in a less advanced country that narrows the gap. In the first case the progress of the leader opens up greater opportunities to trade, and thus raises real income in both countries. "Catch-up" by the follower, however, tends to hurt the leader by eliminating the gains from trade. Thus there is a sense in which the leader's real income depends on preserving its lead, and there is an *economic* case for technological protectionism.

A final point should be made, since this model may be liable to misinterpretation. In this chapter we have seen that technical advance will be accompanied by a rise in the technology intensity of a country's exports. Causation, however, runs from technology to export composition, not the other way around. The increasing technology intensity of a progressive country's exports is a *symptom* of its progress, not a cause. There is nothing in the model that says that subsidising high-technology industries will promote growth. In fact our two exercises in comparative statics showed the technological intensity of exports and real income moving in opposite directions: The less advanced country gained from progress abroad even as it abandoned its most technologically progressive exports; the more-advanced country lost as it abandoned its least progressive industries.

This point—that mimicking the symptoms of progress does not create its reality—is one that needs making. At present nearly every government in the industrial world plans to spur growth by promoting its high-prestige, high-technology industries. The result of this attempt at sympathetic magic will probably be the same as the result when steel and petrochemicals were the talismen of growth: excess capacity, and disappointment.

11   Endogenous Innovation, International Trade, and Growth

The recent interest in models of economic development[1] where technological change is endogenous had primarily been based on the assumption of some kind of technological externality, which makes the social return to investment exceed the private return. This is in the tradition of Arrow (1962), who simply postulated that investment raises the efficiency of future vintages of capital goods, in a way that cannot be captured by firms. The effort of Romer (1986b) to provide a micro-economic foundation for external economies in the growth process returns to an even earlier tradition, that of Young (1928), in which increasing returns in the production of intermediate goods leads to de facto external economies in the production of final goods.

Although external economy models shed an interesting light on some of the possible reasons for self-sustaining economic growth, they share a common feature that is less than satisfactory. In such models technological change is an accidental by-product of economic activities undertaken for other purposes. While this sometimes happens, in the real world much technical change is surely the result of deliberate efforts on the part of firms to improve their products and/or processes—and a key issue of economic policy (perhaps *the* key issue) is how institutions and taxation affect the incentives for such knowledge generation. One would therefore like to have a set of models in which technological change is not only endogenous but also at least in part deliberate, a result of active efforts at innovation.

Now there already exists a tradition in economics that takes just such an approach to economic growth. This is the line of thought associated with Schumpeter (1942), who placed deliberate technological change by firms at the heart of his economic analysis. In the basic Schumpeterian framework, firms are willing to invest in developing knowledge because this knowledge is at least temporarily appropriable and thus allows them to establish monopoly positions that yield private returns. In time, new technologies become public knowledge. But in the meantime innovators have developed still newer technologies, creating a new set of temporary monopolies, and the economy rolls on.

Several recent papers adopt a Schumpeterian framework for thinking about growth. Notable examples include Shleifer (1986) and Murphy, Shleifer, and Vishny (1988). There is also a strong tradition of Schumpeterian models of endogenous technological progress in the international trade literature—perhaps because the analysis of increasing returns in international economics was already well advanced by the time it began to appear in growth theory, and perhaps also because of the traditional emphasis on the role of the "product cycle" in determining patterns of international trade and specialization. In any case there now exists a small literature arising from the international side in which endogenous R&D is the source of technological progress.[2]

Oddly, however, though there now exists a reasonably large Schumpeterian growth literature, few of the papers in this literature focus on the issue of growth per se. The papers by Shleifer and by Murphy, Shleifer, and Vishny focus primarily on the possiblility of multiple equilibria (including dynamic multiple equilibria giving rise to cycles); the international papers focus primarily on the determinants of the pattern of trade, including the product cycle. The purpose of this chapter is to back up from these issues, which I regard as properly the second rather than the first step in development of a Schumpeterian paradigm of growth. Instead, I try to set out in a minimalist form what I regard as the basic insights that arise from a Schumpeterian approach to the growth process.

The first point is a familiar but often misinterpreted one: In a market economy there is a conflict between static efficiency of resource allocation and growth. The Schumpeterian idea is often misinterpreted as the proposition that monopolies are more innovative than competitive firms, but this is not the point. The point is instead that the incentive for innovation depends on the expectation of the innovator that she will be rewarded with a temporary monopoly. In the context of this model we can show that there is a conflict between static efficiency, which would require elimination of monopolies, and the need to provide an incentive for technical change —and we can show that the static costs are worth paying.

The second point is a less familiar one: A Schumpeterian economy is characterized by important dynamic increasing returns. These increasing returns offer a powerful nontraditional case for the gains to a country from participating in an integrated world economy. Quite aside from the usual gains from trade due to comparative advantage and static economies of scale, a Schumpeterian world is one in which international integration increases the incentives for and the benefits from innovation. On one side, access to a world market makes the temporary monopoly of an innovator more valuable, raising the return to innovation. On the other, when temporary monopolies end and knowledge becomes a public good, each country gains from innovations made elsewhere.

In order to bring these points out in as clear and simple a fashion as possible, I offer here a stripped-down model that makes no pretense at realism. In the real world innovation, the exploitation of temporary monopoly positions, and the diffusion of proprietary knowledge to the public at large are all going on simultaneously, and the future stretches out indefinitely. For most of the chapter, I instead assume a world with a finite horizon divided into three neat periods: one during which firms invest in innovation, one in which they reap the rewards of their investment, and one in which their innovations become common property. This formulation brings out the essential principles very clearly, but an obvious next step must be to develop an infinite-horizon model without such arbitrary asymmetries between periods. The chapter concludes with a brief exposition of such a model, focusing only on its steady-state dynamics; the main conclusion of this final exposition is that an integrated economy will not only be more productive than an isolated national economy but will exhibit a permanently higher growth rate.

Section 11.1 lays out the basic assumptions of the model. Section 11.2 derives the equilibrium for a single closed economy. Section 11.3 examines the welfare economics of this equilibrium, focusing on the gains to society from allowing innovators to establish temporary monopolies. Section 11.4 then considers the effects of international integration and the nature of the gains that such integration brings. Section 11.5 then asks whether integration through trade or investment is necessary for these gains, or whether the exchange of ideas is enough. Section 11.6 takes a step toward realism, by describing steady-state growth in an infinite horizon world where innovation, exploitation of monopoly positions, and diffusion of technology are happening at the same time. Section 11.7 concludes the chapter with a discussion of the results and some ideas for future extensions.

11.1 Assumptions of the Model[3]

We consider a world that will last three periods. In this world there are L individuals, who all share identical tastes. These tastes can be represented by a two-level utility function. The upper level may be written

$$U = \theta^{-1}[C_1^\theta + \delta C_2^\theta + \delta^2 C_3^\theta], \qquad \delta, \theta < 1, \tag{1}$$

where C_t is an index of overall consumption in each period. That is, utility is additively separable across periods, and there is a constant elasticity of substitution $1/(1 - \theta)$ between each pair of periods.

Within each period N goods are produced. The aggregate consumption for each period is defined as

$$C_t = \prod_{i=1}^{N} c_{it}^{1/N}, \tag{2}$$

where c_{it} is an individual's consumption of good i in period t. Within-period tastes are therefore Cobb-Douglas, with all N goods receiving equal expenditure shares.

There is only one primary resource: labor. In each period each individual has an endowment of one unit of labor. The unit labor requirement to produce a good depends on whether or not an investment has been made in improving the technology. If no such investment has been made, the unit labor requirement is 1. Once an investment has been made, the new process reduces the labor required to $\gamma < 1$. That is, if a_{it} is the unit labor requirement for good i in period t, we have

$$a_{it} = 1 \qquad \text{if no innovation,}$$

$$= \gamma < 1 \qquad \text{if an innovation has been made.} \tag{3}$$

The economy is assumed to need to go through a rigid sequence of moves. In the first period, labor can be used either to produce goods for current consumption or to invest in innovation, developing improved production technology. We assume that the cost of an innovation is F units of first-period labor. In the second period, innovators have a monopoly of the technology they have developed—although, crucially as it turns out, the original unimproved technology is still available to the general public. Finally, in the third period, the technology developed in the first period becomes common property.

We have now laid out all the assumptions of our model. Surprisingly, even this rudimentary framework can yield some valuable insights about technological change in a market economy, as we will see once we derive the model's equilibrium.

11.2   Intertemporal Equilibrium

To solve the model, we work backward from the third period to the first.

Suppose, then, that in period 1 the economy had invested nF units of labor to pursue technological improvement in $n < N$ goods. Then in the third period these improved technologies will be common property so that the economy will consist of n sectors in which the unit labor requirement is γ, and $N - n$ sectors in which it is 1. All sectors will be perfectly competitive and will price at average cost.

The key variable we need is the period 3 consumption of a representative individual, which may be conveniently expressed as

$$C_3 = \frac{w_3}{P_3}, \tag{4}$$

where w is the wage rate expressed in terns of any numéraire and P_3 the period price index in terms of the same numeraire. In turn we may define

$$P_3 = \prod_{i=1}^{N} P_{i3}^{1/N}, \tag{5}$$

where P_{i3} is the price of good i, and

$P_{i3} = w \qquad$ if there has not been an innovation,

$\quad = \gamma w \qquad$ if there has, $\tag{6}$

implying a consumption index

$$C_3 = \left(\frac{1}{\gamma}\right)^{n/N} = \gamma^{-(n/N)}. \tag{7}$$

Now back up to period 2. In this period the n improved technologies are still proprietary, allowing the innovators to establish monopoly positions. So we need to examine their monopoly pricing.

Assuming that N is a very large number, the elasticity of demand facing each individual monopolist is approximately unity. Now for a pure monopolist a demand elasticity of 1 would imply an infinite markup. However, these are not pure monopolists. They have a monopoly of the improved technique of production, but the original, less productive technique is still available to others. Thus the firms cannot raise their price above the cost of production with $a_{i2} = 1$; and given the unitary elasticity of demand, they will always raise their price up to that point. So the equilibrium is one in which $p = w$ in all sectors—that is, monopolists with higher efficiency charge the same price as competitive industries with lower efficiency, passing none of their lower costs on to consumers.[4]

Per-capita consumption of each good in the second period is the same; it may be expressed as

$$c_{i2} = (1/N)(Y_2/L), \qquad \forall i, \tag{8}$$

where Y_2 is second-period income measured in terms of the (common) price of all goods in that period. This income includes both labor income and the monopoly profits of innovators. Note that each innovator gets to collect as a rent the cost savings from original technology on the product she makes, which are equal to a fraction $(1 - \gamma)$ of sales. Thus Y_2 may be calculated as

$$Y_2 = L + \left(\frac{n}{N}\right)(1 - \gamma)Y_2$$

$$= \frac{L}{1 - (n/N)(1 - \gamma)}. \tag{9}$$

Since the goods produced in period 2 all have the same price, and since all income must be spent in that period, the per-capita consumption in that period may be simply expressed as

$$C_2 = \frac{Y_2}{L} = \left[1 - \left(\frac{n}{N}\right)(1 - \gamma)\right]^{-1}. \tag{10}$$

We now turn to the first period, in which the decision must be made about how much labor to allocate to current production as opposed to innovation. We begin by noting that the price of the aggregate first-period consumption good in terms of labor is 1, since all sectors share the same original technology.

Now consider the incentives for innovation. The developer of an improved production technique gets to have a second-period monopoly that yields rents of

$$R = (1 - \gamma)\frac{Y_2}{N}. \tag{11}$$

The second-period return per unit of first-period consumption foregone is therefore

$$r = \frac{(1 - \gamma)Y_2}{NF} = \frac{(1/NF)[L(1 - \gamma)]}{1 - (n/N)(1 - \gamma)}. \tag{12}$$

The return to innovation, as a function of the volume of innovation, is shown as the curve II in figure 11.1. The curve is upward-sloping, as apparent from inspection of (12). The reason is that the more innovation there is, the larger is second-period income, and thus the larger the market for each good.

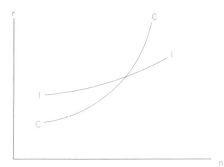

Figure 11.1

To close the model we need another relationship between n and r. This may be derived from the demand side. First, we note that first-period consumption per capita may be written

$$C_1 = \frac{(L - nF)}{L} \tag{13}$$

given the unit labor requirement of 1 in all goods. We also note that the marginal utility of consumption in the first and second periods are

$$\frac{\partial U}{\partial C_1} = C_1^{\theta-1},$$

$$\frac{\partial U}{\partial C_2} = C_2^{\theta-1}. \tag{14}$$

Now r represents the rate at which individuals can trade off period-one consumption for period-two consumption; it must also therefore represent the price of period-one relative to period-two consumption so that

$$r = \frac{\partial U/\partial C_1}{\partial U/\partial C_2} = \delta^{-1}\left(\frac{C_1}{C_2}\right)^{\theta-1}. \tag{15}$$

Substituting from previous equations, we therefore have

$$r = \delta^{-1}\left\{\left(\frac{L}{L - nF}\right)\left[1 - \left(\frac{n}{N}\right)(1 - \gamma)\right]^{-1}\right\}^{1-\theta}. \tag{16}$$

Like (12), this relationship has r increasing in n. At $n = 0$—that is, with no resources devoted to innovation—we have $r = \delta^{-1}$, the rate of return equal to the rate of time preference.

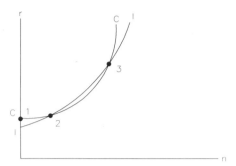

Figure 11.2

The relationship (16) is illustrated in figure 11.1 by the curve CC. As drawn, this curve intersects II in the positive quadrant—which we will assume to be the case—and is steeper than II where they intersect. This assumption amounts to saying that the increase in the rate of return required to induce consumers to release more resources to innovation exceeds the increase in the actual rate of return induced by higher innovation. This seems as though it is a kind of stability condition that we will want to assume is satisfied; in any case a sufficient but not necessary condition for the relative slopes to obey this rule is $\theta < 0$ (i.e., the intertemporal elasticity of substitution less than one).

We should note that there is a possibility of multiple equilibria in this kind of model—this is the lesson of the ingenious papers by Shleifer (1986) and Murphy, Shleifer, and Vishny (1988). The possibility of multiple equilibria may be seen by considering the example of figure 11.2. In that case the CC curve lies above the II curve at $n = 0$. This means that if nobody is expected to innovate, nobody will find it profitable to innovate—so no innovation is a possible equilibrium, illustrated by point 1. However, the more people that innovate, the larger the per-firm sales in period 2, so there may also be equilibria in which innovation does take place, illustrated by points 2 and 3. Of these, 2 will be unstable under most pseudodynamic stories of how equilibrium gets established, so we can think of 1 and 3 as the two possible outcomes. Once we have mutiple equilibria, of course, many stories become possible. For the purposes of this chapter, however, I want to assume that equilibrium is unique, so that I can do comparative dynamic exercises.

We also want to assume that $n < N$, that is, that innovation does not take place in all sectors.

11.3   Welfare Economics of Monopoly

In the world we have now described, innovation in the first period leads to the establishment of temporary monopolies in the second period. This means that there is deviation from static efficiency of resource allocation. What we need to understand is that this deviation is desirable, in the sense that it is better to allow the establishment of temporary monopolies as a way to induce innovation than to seek static efficiency at the cost of technological progress.

First we need to define the static efficiency loss in period 2. This may be most concisely seen by realizing that goods produced in the second period may be divided into two composite commodities: the n "improved" goods whose production technology has been improved by innovations, and the $N - n$ "unimproved" goods where this has not happened. Once the innovative effort has been made, the economy faces an ex-post opportunity cost of improved goods in terms of unimproved goods of γ. This is illustrated by the production possibility frontier in figure 11.3. Given this PPF, the optimal consumption of the two goods is at point 1. However, the temporary monopolies that control the improved technologies will, as we have seen, charge the same price for improved as unimproved goods, so that the relative price consumers face will be 1 instead of γ. This leads to the inferior consumption basket 2.

If the technology in period 2 were exogenous, then, it would be optimal to deny monopoly power to innovators. However, the technology is of course not exogenous. Without the prospective reward of temporary monopoly, firms would not have the incentive to innovate in the first place. In fact we can show that it is unambiguously better to allow the monopoly as the price of innovation than to forbid it.

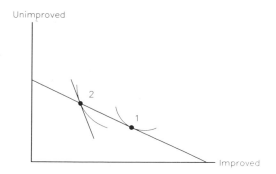

Figure 11.3

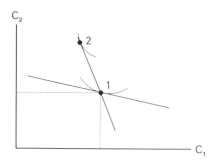

Figure 11.4

To see this, we can break the problem into two parts. First, let us ignore period 3, the period in which new technology becomes common knowledge, and focus on the subutility in periods 1 and 2. We can then return to period 3 and complete the analysis.

Does the equilibrium with temporary monopoly yield a higher subutility in the first two periods than an equilibrium without? To see that it does, rather than explicitly calculating utility, we can use a simple revealed preference argument. Each individual has one unit of labor income to sell in each period. Whether there is innovation or not, the price of consumption in terms of labor in each period is unity. Thus each individual can be thought of as having an endowment of 1 unit each of C_1 and C_2, as illustrated by point 1 in figure 11.4. If there is no ability to convert innovation into temporary monopoly, then individuals will simply consume their endowment in each period. The slope of the indifference curve passing through 1 is $1/\delta$ at that point.

Now suppose that innovation leading to temporary monopoly is allowed. If the intersection in figure 11.1 is in the positive quadrant, that is, if any innovation takes place at all, then the return on innovation is $r > 1/\delta$. The effect is to allow individuals to trade up to a higher level of subutility at point 2.

Nor is this the whole welfare gain. In period 3 any innovations become available to the general public and are thus passed on in lower prices. Since the availability of temporary monopoly shifts n from zero to a positive number, and since n enters positively into period 3 consumption (see equation 7), this represents a further gain.

We see, then, that this model makes the basic Schumpeterian point that monopoly, though distorting the economy at any point in time, may still be socially productive. The ability of innovators to realize a temporary monopoly position as a result of their innovation is a necessary incentive, and the benefits of allowing this incentive outweigh the costs.

It is assumed in this model that the monopoly conferred by innovation lasts one period. In a more realistic model the length of time for which an innovator enjoys a monopoly would be an important parameter, and perhaps a policy variable as well. Clearly the optimal length of monopoly represents a trade-off between the incentive to innovate and the costs of restricting the output of goods whose true marginal cost is less than their price. Nordhaus (1969), working in a partial equilibrium setting, used this trade-off to develop an analysis of optimal patent length. Presumably a more complex general equilibrium model would allow a similar analysis.

11.4   International Integration

We now turn to some less familiar territory, examining the implications of this model for the effects of international integration. Suppose that a country, instead of being an isolated economy, is part of a larger world economy in which residents of other countries are also able to innovate. How does this change the results?

The simplest case is where all countries have the same tastes, original technology, and costs of innovation—and also where the temporary monopoly established by an innovator extends to the international market as well as the domestic market. In this case residents of a country are in effect simploy part of a larger economy than they would be otherwise, and the effects of international integration are the same as the effects of a larger labor force.

To see what these effects are, we examine the two relationships (12) and (16). First, consider (12): How does the II curve in figure 11.1 shift when L is increased? It is immediately obvious that r will be higher for any given n, so the II curve shifts up. The economic intuition for this is that a larger market means more rents per innovation for any given number of innovations; thus the upward shift in II in effect represents the inventives for innovation resulting from increased demand.

Turning to (16), we note that for any given n an increase in L reduces the implied r. That is, the larger the labor force the lower the required rate of return for any given number of innovations. The reason for this is that since there is a fixed cost per innovation, when a given number of innovations are undertaken by a larger economy they require a smaller fraction of

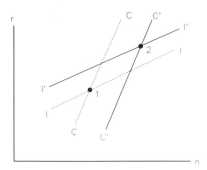

Figure 11.5

first-period resources. This amounts to a kind of supply-side reason why a larger economy will generate more technological progress.

Putting these results together, we have figure 11.5: The upward shift in II and the downward shift in CC imply a shift in the equilibrium from point 1 to point 2. An integrated world economy will generate more innovations, and yield a higher rate of return on these innovations, than any of the national economies that make up this world would do on their own.

Which country does the innovating, and which country produces the goods with improved technology? The answer is that in this model it is indeterminate—and it does not matter. Given the assumptions about identical initial technologies and identical ability to improve technology through innovation, we cannot describe the precise pattern of international innovation and trade. A natural extension would be to introduce some kind of comparative advantage in innovation and/or production of new goods, but this will be left for future research.

An interesting question is whether the integrated world economy will not only generate more innovation than independent national economies but will also devote a higher *share* of its resources to innovation than the national economies. This amounts to asking whether n will increase more or less than proportionately to L. Not too surprisingly, the answer is ambiguous, because both income and subsitition effects are involved. The higher return on innovation both raises wealth, tending to raise first period consumption per capita, and encourages substitution, encouraging saving. A sufficient but not necessary condition for an increase in the share of resources going to innovation is $\theta > 0$ (i.e., a more than unity intertemporal elasticity of substitution).

In any case the benefits of being part of a larger world do not depend on there being an increase in the share of resources devoted to innovation. We

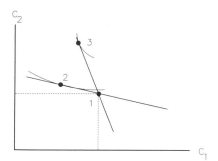

Figure 11.6

can use the same tricks to demonstrate gains from integration that we used
to demonstrate gains from allowing innovators to establish temporary
monopolies. First, we put the third period on one side and consider subutility in the first two periods. The situation is illustrated in figure 11.6. In an
autarchic equilibrium the representative individual would have an endowment at point 1 and would consume at point 2. The effect of making this
economy part of a larger world is to raise the rate of return; this rotates the
budget line clockwise, allowing the individual to achieve a higher subutility
at point 3. Thus utility in the first two periods unambiguously rises. Since
the number of goods with improved technology is increased, consumption
per capita in the third period also unambiguously rises, so that there is a
definite gain from international integration.

We see, then, that it is better to be part of a world economy than to be
isolated, even if all countries are alike and there are no static economies of
scale. The reason is that innovation is in this model is a process that
involves both private increasing returns in a dynamic sense, and an external
economy—the spillover of knowledge when technologies become part of
the public domain—that amounts to a further degree of increasing returns
at the aggregate level.

However, we need to be careful before making this argument a case for
free international trade and investment. The exercise carried out in this part
of the chapter assumed that being part of a world economy is an all-or-
nothing affair in which a country is either completely integrated or shut off
not only from selling its goods but from learning about innovations elsewhere. A natural question is whether such full integration is better or worse
than a world in which countries can learn from each other without necessarily selling freely to one another.

11.5   Are Trade and Investment Necessary?

A key question for assessing the effects of international integration is the extent to which trade and investment flows are associated with flows of knowledge. In practice, no doubt, much knowledge crosses borders only by being embodied in goods and services or by being transferred by multinational firms. However, it is possible to analyze a world in which nonproprietary knowledge diffuses internationally even without trade, simply through countries reading each others' journals and watching each others' television shows. Is such a world necessarily worse off economically than one with trade and/or investment?

To implement this question in our model, suppose that in period 2 innovators cannot establish property rights over their technologies if they sell goods abroad and that they therefore sell only to the domestic market. In period 3, however, improved technology becomes available to foreigners and domestic residents alike.

It is immediately apparent that the equilibrium in the first two periods is the same as in the case of pure autarky. Thus the subutility in these periods is lower than it would be if innovators were able either to export or to produce abroad.

However, it is not certain that consumption in the third period will be lower than with full integration. Two issues arise: How large will be the resources that are devoted to innovation, and how efficiently will these resources be used?

We have already seen that the effect of integration on the *share* of resources devoted to innovation is ambiguous. This implies that a world economy that does not allow innovators to captrue rents in foreign markets might actually devote larger resources to innovation than one that does. As we noted, an intertemporal elasticity of substitution greater than one is sufficient to rule out this case, but it is not impossible.

Suppose that the imperfectly integrated world actually does spend more on innovation than the perfectly integrated one. Does this imply higher third-period consumption? Not necessarily. The reason is the following: As long as the world constitutes an integrated market, there will be no duplication of innovative effort. Remove this integration, and there may well be some overlap, with resources in two or more countries being devoted to the same innovation. This may mean that the number of goods with improved technologies will therefore be less than the number of innovative efforts made.[5]

Putting these arguments together, there would seem to be a presumption but not a certainty that it is better to have an integrated market-place in innovative industries, not simply an efficient international exchange of information. However, this is only a presumption—in the second-best world of Schumpeterian competition, markets don't always do the right thing.

11.6   Long-Term Growth

The analysis in this chapter up until now has been simplified by the assumptions that there is a finite horizon and a rigid sequence of periods in which innovations are made, become temporary monopolies, and then become common knowledge. The next step toward realism is to allow an economy with no end in sight, where our three stages are all taking place simultaneously. In this section I briefly examine such an economy.

Suppose, then, that individuals live forever and maximize a discounted function of future subutilities of the form

$$U = \theta^{-1} \sum_{t=0}^{\infty} C_t^{\theta} \delta^t, \tag{17}$$

where C_t is defined the same way as in (2). The technology of innovation and growth is also assumed to be the same: An innovation in any good requires F units of labor in this period and lowers the unit labor requirement to γ, its former level in all subsequent periods.

For this chapter I restrict analysis to the consideration of steady states. Shleifer (1986), from whose work this model is almost completely derived, has shown that it is possible that non-steady-state paths may occur, and indeed that there may be a multiplicity of cyclical equilibria. I simply ignore these possibilities to focus on the case of steady growth.

The defining feature of a steady state is that there are n sectors in which innovation takes place every period. Thus each period n innovators invest F units of labor, n innovators from the previous period are reaping their reward of temporary monopoly, and n innovations from the period before that become common knowledge. Some of these may be the same goods —that is, a temporary monopoly may have been established in a good where the innovation from two periods back has just become common knowledge, or someone may now be making an innovation in a good where someone else currently has a monopoly. However, given the Cobb-Douglas assumption on demand, plus the fact that prices are constrained by the cost of producing using the most recent common-knowledge technology, this doesn't matter. All that we need to know is the number n, not which goods are playing which roles.

The key point is that in a constant n economy, both consumption and the real wage will grow at a steady rate: The ratio of next period's real wage and consumption to today's is $\gamma^{-n/N}$ (see equation 7). Clearly, the larger is n, the higher the economy's rate of growth.

To analyze the steady state, we follow the same procedure as in the finite-horizon model: We look for two schedules that simultaneously determine the rate of return and the rate of innovation. One such relationship comes from the consumer side. We note, as in equation (15), that

$$r = \frac{\partial U/\partial C_t}{\partial U/\partial C_{t+1}} = \delta^{-1}\left(\frac{C_t}{C_{t+1}}\right)^{\theta-1}, \tag{18}$$

where t is any period. It follows that

$$r = \delta^{-1}\gamma^{-(n/N)(1-\theta)}, \tag{19}$$

which is illustrated as CC in figure 11.7. The intuition behind the upward slope is straightforward: The higher the rate of innovation, the higher is tomorrow's consumption relative to today's, and thus the higher the marginal utility of present realtive to future consumption.

The second schedule comes from the return to investors. To derive this, we first note that in each period the income of $L - nF$ units of labor is spent on consumption goods (the rest being spent on innovation), so that the sales of each good are $(L - nF)/N$ times the wage rate. If the good is sold by a temporary monopolist, she collects a fraction $(1 - \gamma)$ of this so that her return is $(1 - \gamma)(L - nF)/N$ units of labor. However, because of the rising real wage rate, labor next period is more valuable than labor this period; so the real rate of return to innovation is

$$r = F^{-1}N^{-1}(L - nF)\gamma^{-n/N}. \tag{20}$$

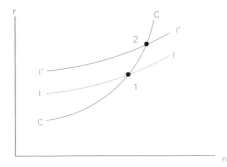

Figure 11.7

This relationship may be either upward- or downward-sloping. In figure 11.7 it is show as II, upward-sloping but less steep than CC. It is apparent from comparison of (19) and (20) that a sufficient but not necessary condition for II to cut CC from above is $\theta < 0$ (i.e., an intertemporal elasticity of substitution less than one).

The intersection of II and CC determines the rate of return and the rate of innovation. It is now straightforward to examine in this context the effect of the size of the economy. From (20), an increase in the labor force will shift II up, as illustrated by the shift to $I'I'$ in figure 11.7. Meanwhile CC will not be affected (a difference from the mechanics of the finite-horizon case). Thus the equilibrium will shift from 1 to 2: the rate of innovation, and thus the rate of growth, will be larger in a larger economy.

As before, we can interpret this as a benefit from international integration. What we learn from this extension is that the gains from being part of an integrated world economy may be more than a one-shot increase in efficiency: In this context they imply a permanently higher rate of growth than each national economy would achieve on its own.

11.7 Conclusions

This chapter has set out just about the simplest possible model of technological progress in a world in which innovators are induced to do their job because they hope to reap the rewards of temporary monopoly. The chapter demonstrates, convincingly I hope, two main points: that the static market distortion of monopoly can play a socially useful role and that endogenous technological development increases the gains from international integration.

There are several directions in which it would be useful to extend this research. The single-economy model would be more attractive if there were room for investment in physical capital as well as knowledge; in the current framework, acquisition of a temporary monopoly is the only form of investment allowed, which is an extreme case. The open-economy model would gain richness if countries were to be allowed to differ, so that comparative advantage would pin down more of the pattern of innovation and trade. However, it is unlikely that either of these extensions would change the basic message very much.

The real problem with this approach, as with the other work in the new growth theory, is going to be one of attaching any empirical substance to these ideas. The new growth theory is currently in a state very similar to that of the new trade theory (with its emphasis on increasing returns and imperfect competition) about six years ago. At that point the new ideas had opened up an exciting new set of concepts, offering a rigorous language for talking about issues that had previously been poorly articulated and ignored by much of the profession. However, once the language and concepts were in place, the next questions became, "How important are these effects? How much difference do they make for policy?" No good answer has yet been provided in the international area, and this has put something of a damper on further work in the area. The same will happen in the near future in the growth area; so the priority is really not how to construct more clever models, but how to build a bridge to reality.

Notes

1. Key papers include Lucas (1985); Romer (1986a, b); Kohn and Marion (1987); Shleifer (1986); Murphy, Shleifer, and Vishny (1988); and Helpman (1988).

2. See, in particular, Feenstra and Judd (1982), Dollar (1986), Jensen and Thursby (forthcoming), Segerstrom, Anant, and Dinopoulos (1987), and Grossman and Helpman (1987).

3. This model is very close in form to the models used in recent work by Shleifer (1986) and Murphy, Shleifer, and Vishny (1988). The main modelling difference is that I assume free-entry zero-profit equilibria, whereas they assume restricted entry that allows some profits to remain. The important difference is, however, in the kind of questions asked; they are primarily concerned with the possibility of mutiple equilibria, whereas I am concerned with comparative dynamics.

In all of these models strong assumptions are made about functional forms that are not really necessary for the results. All that is really needed is additive separability of utility among periods, and symmetry among goods within each period. However, given the unrealistic and illustrative nature of the model in any case, it does not seem worthwhile to take up extra time and space in return for a marginal increase in generality.

4. Nordhaus (1969), in a pioneering analysis of endogenous technical progress, made the useful distinction between "run-of-mill" innovations, in which the innovator does not cut her price, and "major" innovations, in which the optimal monopoly price lies below the cost of producing with older techniques. In this model I have set things up so that innovations are all "run-of-the-mill," which greatly simplifies the analysis. The approach was introduced in the seminal paper of Shleifer (1986), and also in Segerstrom, Anant, and Dinopoulos (1987).

5. Realistically, innovation is not an arbitrary choice from a number of equally attractive areas. Instead, there are some areas where, given the current state of knowledge, an innovative effort looks most promising. This would seem to imply that in practice there will be heavy duplication of effort if there is no market incentive to avoid it.

IV

Imperfect
Competition and
Strategic Trade Policy

12   Import Protection as Export Promotion: International Competition in the Presence of Oligopoly and Economics of Scale

12.1   Introduction

When businessmen try to explain the success of Japanese firms in export markets, they often mention the advantage of a protected home market. Firms with a secure home market, the argument runs, have a number of advantages: They are assured of the economies of large-scale production, of selling enough over time to move down the learning curve, of earning enough to recover the costs of R&D. While charging high prices in the domestic market, they can "incrementally price" and flood foreign markets with low-cost products.

No doubt the argument that import protection is export promotion is often a self-serving position of those who would like protection themselves. Still, there is an undeniable persuasiveness to the argument. Yet it is an argument that economists schooled in standard trade theory tend to find incomprehensible. In a world of perfect competition and constant returns to scale, protecting a product can never cause it to be exported. It may cause some other good that is complementary in production to be exported— but this is hardly what the businessmen seem to have in mind.

The purpose of this chapter is to show that there is a class of models in which the businessman's view of import protection as export promotion makes sense. There are two basic ingredients in these models. First, markets are both oligopolistic and segmented: Firms are aware that their actions affect the price they receive and are able to charge different prices in different markets. As Brander (1981) has shown, and as Brander and Krugman (1983) elaborated, models of this type allow countries to be both

Originally published in *Monopolistic Competition in International Trade*, edited by H. Kierzkoushi. © 1984 by Oxford University Press.

importers and exporters within an industry, because firms will engage in "reciprocal dumping" into each others' home markets.

The second ingredient is some kind of economies of scale. These may take several forms. The simplest would be static economies of scale, namely, a declining marginal cost curve. It is also possible, however, for more subtle forms of scale economies to produce the same results: for example, dynamic scale economies of the "learning curve" type or competition in R&D. As the chapter will stress, the end result is very similar. It is the distinction between increasing and decreasing costs, not the distinction between statics and dynamics, which usually sets the views of practical men and trade theorists apart.

In each case the basic story of protection as promotion remains the same. By giving a domestic firm a privileged position in some one market, a country gives it an advantage in scale over foreign rivals. This scale advantage translates into lower marginal costs and higher market share even in unprotected markets.

The chapter is in six sections. Section 12.2 presents the basic, static model of competition, and section 12.3 shows how protectionism can promote expansion in all markets. Section 12.4 develops an alternative model where there are no static economies of scale but where R&D plays a similar role. In section 12.5 neither of these effects operates, but learning by doing is shown to produce similar effects. Finally, section 12.6 summarizes the results and suggests some conclusions.

12.2   Model 1: Static Economies of Scale

There are two firms: home and foreign. Each firm produces a single product, which it sells in a number of markets in competition with the other firm. The firms' products may but need not be perfect substitutes. The segmented markets in which they compete may be divided by transport costs, border taxes, or type of purchaser; they may include markets in each firm's home country and also markets in third countries.

I will adopt an abbreviated way of representing demand conditions in the different markets; following Spencer and Brander (1982), I will skip the writing of demand functions and go directly to the revenue functions of the firms. In market i $(i = 1, \ldots, n)$ the revenue function of the home firm is

$$R_i = R_i(x_i, x_i^*), \tag{1}$$

where x_i, x_i^* are deliveries to the ith market by the home and foreign firms, respectively. Similarly, the foreign firm's revenue function is

$$R_i^* = R_i^*(x_i, x_i^*). \tag{2}$$

I will assume that each firm's marginal revenue is decreasing in the other firm's output:

$$\frac{\partial^2 R_i}{\partial x_i \, \partial x_i^*} < 0, \tag{3}$$

$$\frac{\partial^2 R_i^*}{\partial x_i^* \, \partial x_i} < 0. \tag{4}$$

Another condition will also be assumed:

$$\Delta = \frac{\partial^2 R_i}{\partial x_i^2} \cdot \frac{\partial^2 R_i^*}{\partial x_i^{*2}} - \frac{\partial^2 R_i}{\partial x_i \, \partial x_i^*} \frac{\partial^2 R_i^*}{\partial x_i \, \partial x_i^*} > 0. \tag{5}$$

The usefulness of this condition will become obvious below; it amounts to saying that "own" effects on marginal revenue are greater than "cross" effects.

On the cost side, each firm will face both production costs and transport costs: thus total costs for each firm will be

$$TC = \sum t_i x_i + C(\sum x_i), \tag{6}$$

$$TC^* = \sum t_i^* x_i^* + C^*(\sum x_i^*), \tag{7}$$

where we assume declining marginal cost of production: C'', $C^{*\prime\prime} < 0$. Notice that transport costs need not be the same for the two firms. For the home firm's domestic market, presumably $t_i < t_i^*$; for the foreign firm's domestic makets, we expect $t_i^* > t_i$; there may also be third-country markets to which either may have lower transport cost.

How do these firms compete? Each firm must choose a vector of deliveries, that is, it must choose x_i or x_i^* for each market. The simplest assumption to make about competition is that each firm takes the other firm's deliveries as given in each market. The result is a multimarket Cournot model, where the firms' decision problems are

$$\max_{\{x_i\}} \prod = \sum R_i(x_i, x_i^*) - \sum t_i x_i - C(\sum x_i), \tag{8}$$

$$\max_{\{x_i^*\}} \prod{}^* = \sum R_i^*(x_i, x_i^*) - \sum t_i^* x_i^* - C^*(\sum x_i^*). \tag{9}$$

The first-order conditions that determine equilibrium are

$$\frac{\partial R_i}{\partial x_i} - t_i - \mu = 0, \qquad i = 1, \dots, n, \tag{10}$$

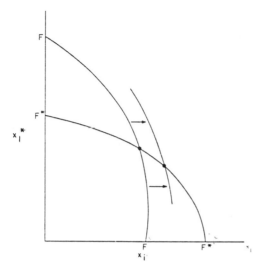

Figure 12.1

$$\frac{\partial R_i^*}{\partial x_i^*} - t_i^* - \mu^* = 0, \qquad i = 1, \ldots, n, \tag{11}$$

where μ, μ^* are marginal production costs. In each market, firms set their marginal revenue equal to marginal cost.

To interpret this equilibrium, it is useful to think in terms of an imaginary iterative process by which we might compute the solution. Specifying this process is purely an expositional device, with no implications for the outcome, but it does help to make clear the underlying logic of the model.

Suppose, then, that we use the following procedure. We begin by making a guess about the firms' marginal cost and play a Cournot game in each market on the basis of that guess. We then sum the chosen levels of deliveries to get total output and compute the implied marginal cost. This estimate of marginal cost is then used for a second round and so on until convergence. The stages of this computation can be represented by the geometric apparatus presented in figures 12.1, 12.2, and 12.3.

Figure 12.1 shows the competition in a representative market for given estimates of marginal cost μ, μ^*. The curves FF and F^*F^* are the reaction functions of the domestic and foreign firm, respectively. Their slopes are

$$\frac{-\partial^2 R_i/\partial x_i^2}{\partial^2 R_i/\partial x_i \, \partial x_i^*} \quad \text{and} \quad \frac{-\partial^2 R_i^*/\partial x_i \, \partial x_i^*}{\partial^2 R_i^*/\partial x_i^{*2}},$$

both negative by (3) and (4) whereas by (5), FF is flatter than F^*F^*.

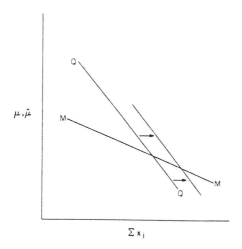

Figure 12.2

Suppose that we reduce μ, the home firm's estimate of marginal cost. The result will be to push FF out, as shown in the diagram; x_i will rise and x_i^* will fall. This will happen in *each* market in which the firms compete, so that total output of the home firm will rise and total output of the foreign firm will fall.

Figure 12.2 illustrates the next step. On one hand, the lower the firm's estimate of marginal cost, the larger its output. On the other hand, the larger the output, the lower its actual marginal cost. These relationships are indicated by the curves QQ and MM. The equilibrium for the firm—conditional on the *other* firm's estimate of marginal cost—is where MM and QQ cross. As drawn, QQ is steeper than MM; this will be true if marginal costs do not fall too steeply, and we will assume that this is the case.

Suppose now that the foreign firm were to raise its estimated marginal cost, μ^*. This would imply a leftward shift of F^*F^* in each market. For a given μ, output of the home firm would rise, that is, the QQ curve shifts right. The end result is that domestic marginal cost is decreasing in foreign marginal cost, and vice versa. This takes us to the final step in determining equilibrium illustrated in figure 12.3.

Domestic marginal cost is decreasing in foreign, foreign marginal cost is decreasing in domestic; an equilibrium is where the schedules $\mu(\mu^*)$ and $\mu^*(\mu)$ cross. The curve $\mu(\mu^*)$ may cut $\mu^*(\mu)$ from above, as in figure 12.3a, or from below, as in figure 12.3b. A simple stability analysis suggests that the latter situation will "almost never" be observed. Suppose that the two firms revise their estimates of marginal cost alternately; then the dynamics

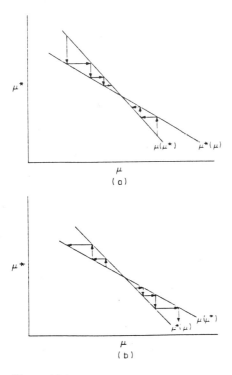

Figure 12.3

will be those indicated by the arrows. If $\mu(\mu^*)$ is steeper than $\mu^*(\mu)$, that is, if "own" effects are again stronger than "cross" effects at this higher level, equilibrium is stable. If $\mu^*(\mu)$ is steeper, the equilibrium is unstable.

It is possible and even important that there may exist no stable equilibrium except where one firm or the other ceases production. For the rest of this chapter, however, we will assume that there is a unique stable equilibrium where both firms produce at positive levels.

We have now described the determination of equilibrium in this model. The essential feature is the circular causation from output to marginal cost to output. Our next step is to show how this circularity makes import protection an export promotion device.

12.3   Effects of Protection

Suppose that the home government excludes the foreign firm from some market previously open to it. This market might be the whole domestic

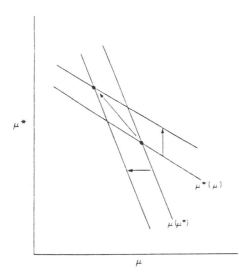

Figure 12.4

market or it might be some piece, say procurement by government-owned firms. For simplicity we consider a complete exclusion of foreign product, although a quota or tariff would have much the same result.

To find the effects of this, we first hold μ constant. The effect under this assumption is solely to raise x_i and lower x_i^* in the newly protected market. This in turn, however, affects marginal cost; in terms of figure 12.2, the home firm's QQ curve shifts right, the corresponding foreign curve shifts left. That is, for a given level of foreign marginal cost, domestic cost falls; for a given level of domestic marginal cost, foreign cost rises. The curve $\mu(\mu^*)$ shifts left, $\mu^*(\mu)$ shifts right; as figure 12.4 shows, the result (assuming stability) is a fall in μ, a rise in μ^*.

It only remains to complete the circle. This is done in figure 12.5, which shows a representative market other than the protected one. The change in marginal cost causes FF to shift out, F^*F^* to shift in; x_j rises, x_j^* falls. *Protecting the domestic firm in one market increases domestic sales and lowers foreign sales in all markets.*

This is the businessman's view, and it should be clear why it is confirmed. There is a positive feedback from output to marginal cost to output. By protecting one market the government gives the domestic firm greater economies of scale while reducing those of its foreign competitor. Thus decreasing costs are at the heart of the story.

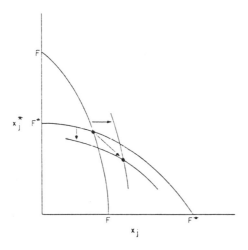

Figure 12.5

Economists tend, however, to be sceptical of the importance of decreasing costs, at least for large industrial countries. Businessmen see more of a role for scale economies than economists do, but the empirical appeal of the protection-as-promotion argument lies in more subtle forms of decreasing cost. These are the dynamic economies of scale involved in the learning curve and in R&D. What I will do in the rest of this chapter is show that these dynamic economies basically have the same implications as static decreasing cost, and that the protection-as-promotion argument remains valid.

12.4   Model II: Competition in R&D

In this section I assume that marginal costs are constant. Firms can, however, reduce their production costs by prior investment in R&D. This turns out to have effects very similar to those of static declining marginal cost.

There are again two firms, competing in a number of markets; demand looks the same as in model I. Costs, however, look somewhat different. Marginal production cost is independent of the level of output but decreasing in the amount of investment each firm does in R&D.

$$\mu = \mu(N) \tag{12}$$

$$\mu^* = \mu^*(N^*), \tag{13}$$

where

$$\frac{\partial \mu}{\partial N}, \frac{\partial \mu^*}{\partial N^*} < 0$$

$$\frac{\partial^2 \mu}{\partial N^2}, \frac{\partial^2 \mu^*}{\partial N^{*2}} < 0.$$

Profits of each firm are revenue, less production and transport costs, and also less R&D expense:

$$\prod = \sum_i R_i(x_i, x_i^*) - \sum_i t_i x_i - \mu(N) \cdot \sum_i x_i - N \tag{14}$$

$$\prod^* = \sum_i R_i^*(x_i^*, x_i) - \sum_i t_i^* x_i^* - \mu^*(N^*) \cdot \sum_i x_i^* - N^*. \tag{15}$$

In determining the outcome of a model like this, there is a question of the appropriate equilibrium concept. The issue is whether firms will adopt "open-loop" strategies, taking the other firm's deliveries as given, or will make sophisticated "closed-loop" calculations that take into account the effect of their own R&D decision on the other firm's subsequent actions. The issue has been repeatedly discussed; Spence (1981) is a recent example. I will opt for simplicity and use the open-loop concept. This also has the advantage of making the parallel between R&D and static scale economies very transparent.

The first-order conditions for the home firm are

$$\frac{\partial R_i}{\partial x_i} - t_i - \mu = 0, \tag{16}$$

$$\frac{\partial \mu}{\partial N} \cdot \sum_i x_i = 1, \tag{17}$$

where we neglect for simplicity the possibility of zero deliveries to some markets.

The important point to notice is that investment in R&D has an effect on profits that is proportional to expected sales. This is a form of increasing returns and is the key to this model.

As in model I, it is useful to think of calculating the equilibrium position iteratively. We first choose levels of R&D expenditure; use the implied marginal cost to compute outputs; recompute the optimal R&D using this; and so on to convergence. The crucial links are illustrated in figures 12.6 and 12.7. In figure 12.6 we show the determination of N given N^*. The higher is N, the lower will be marginal production cost, and thus the higher will be output; the curve QQ captures this relationship. On the other hand,

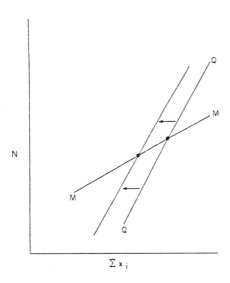

Figure 12.6

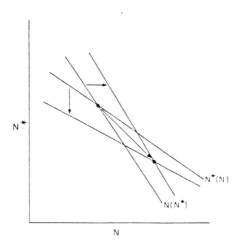

Figure 12.7

the larger the output the greater the marginal profitability of R&D, so N is increasing in output along MM. As in figure 12.2, QQ is assumed steeper than MM.

If the foreign firm were to increase its own R&D, the effect would be to lower its marginal cost and reduce domestic output for any given N. Thus QQ would shift left and N fall. The result is that N is decreasing in N^* and vice versa; in figure 12.7 we show the "stable" or "own effects dominating" case that we assume to prevail.

The effect of reserving some market for the domestic firm is now obvious. At given N and N^* domestic output rises and foreign output falls. The QQ curve shifts out, its foreign counterpart shifts in. Thus $N(N^*)$ shifts right, $N^*(N)$ shifts down; N rises, N^* falls. Reduced marginal production costs for the home firm and higher marginal production costs for the foreign firm mean increased domestic sales in all markets.

The point here is that protection, by increasing the home firm's sales and reducing those of its foreign competitor, increases the incentive for domestic R&D at foreign expense. This in turn translates into a shift in relative production costs, which leads to increased domestic sales even in unprotected markets. Even though there are no static scale economies, the result is exactly the same as in model I.

12.5   Model III: The Learning Curve

In this final model we consider yet another form of economies of scale. In this version there are neither static economies of scale nor explicit investment in R&D; instead, the increasing returns take a dynamic form: higher output now reduces the costs of production later. These learning-by-doing economies turn out to yield results very similar to those in the other models.

The model is a generalized version of one developed by Spence (1981). Again there are two firms, home and foreign. They compete in a number of markets, but now they compete over time as well as space. In each market the revenues of the two firms are

$$R_i = R_i(x_i, x_i^*), \qquad i = 1, \ldots, n, \tag{18}$$

$$R_i^* = R_i^*(x_i^*, x_i), \qquad i = 1, \ldots, n, \tag{19}$$

where x_i, x_i^* now represent rates of delivery per unit time; otherwise they have the same properties we have been assuming all along.

On the cost side, each firm faces constant transport costs t_i, t_i^* to each market. At a point in time, production costs are characterized by constant marginal costs μ, μ^*. These marginal costs are, however, dependent on previous output. Let $Q = \sum x_i$, the home firm's rate of output at a point in time; the home firm's cumulative output to time t is then

$$K(t) = \int_0^t Q \, dz. \tag{20}$$

The learning curve assumption is that marginal costs are a decreasing function of cumulative output to date:

$$\mu = \mu(K). \tag{21}$$

Now consider the firms' maximization problems. Following Spence, we will make the extremely useful assumption that firms maximize cumulative profits over a fixed horizon T *with no discounting*. Thus the home firm takes as its objective to maximize

$$\prod = \int_0^T \left\{ \sum_i [R_i(x_i, x_i) - t_i x_i - \mu(K)_i x] \right\} dt. \tag{22}$$

What does the optimum solution look? By selling another unit in market i, the firm gains two things: the direct marginal revenue and the indirect cost saving on future production costs. On the other hand, it incurs the direct costs of transportation and production. Thus the first-order condition at a point in time is:

$$\frac{\partial R_i}{\partial x_i} - t_i - \mu - \int_t^T \frac{\partial \mu}{\partial K} \cdot Q \, dz = 0. \tag{23}$$

If the left-hand side of (23) is zero at each point in time, it must also be constant over time. So we can differentiate with respect to time to get

$$\frac{d}{dt}\left[\frac{\partial R}{\partial x_i} - \frac{d}{dt}\mu + \frac{\partial \mu}{\partial K} \cdot Q \right] = \frac{d}{dt}\frac{\partial R}{\partial x_i} - \frac{\partial \mu}{\partial K} \cdot Q + \frac{\partial \mu}{\partial K} \cdot Q$$

$$= \frac{d}{dt}\frac{\partial R}{\partial x_i} = 0. \tag{24}$$

The economic implication of this, as Spence points out, is that the firm sets output on the basis of a constant shadow marginal cost. The level of the shadow marginal cost is determined by the terminal condition: at time T, when the firm no longer considers the effect of current output on future cost, the shadow and actual marginal costs converge.

Again we can imagine an iterative procedure for calculating equilibrium. We can make a guess at the firms' terminal marginal costs μ_T, μ_T^*; find the

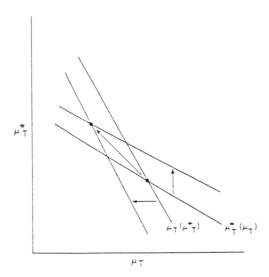

Figure 12.8

cumulative output that results from these guesses, and the corresponding terminal marginal cost; and repeat the process. Without going into detail, it should be obvious that the result will be the same as in our first model. Each firm's terminal marginal cost will be decreasing in the other's; equilibrium is illustrated in figure 12.8, where we assume once again that "own" effects predominate over "cross" effects, so that μ_T (μ_T^*) is steeper than μ_T^* (μ_T).

The effect of protection is now exactly parallel to its effect in the case of static scale economies. Excluding the foreign firm from some market increases the cumulative output of the domestic firm and reduces the cumulative output of the foreign firm for given μ_T, μ_T^*. The result is that μ_T (μ_T^*) shifts left, μ_T^* (μ_T) shift up; μ_T falls, μ_T^* rises. This in turn means that x_i rises and x_i^* falls in all markets, whether they were directly protected or not.

12.6   Summary and Conclusions

The idea that a protected domestic market gives firms a base for successful exporting is one of those heterodox arguments, common in discussions of international trade, that are incomprehensible in terms of standard models yet seem persuasive to practical men. This chapter has developed some simple models that make sense of the argument for protection-as-promotion. To get heterodox conclusions, one needs heterodox assumptions: These models assume oligopoly instead of perfect competition, decreasing costs instead of constant returns. Interestingly, however, the economies of scale need not be simple static production economies but can take fairly subtle dynamic forms.

What is the moral of this chapter? Certainly not that the United States should protect its manufacturers as a general strategy. For one thing, the paper contains no welfare analysis. The reason for this is that it is extremely complex. We are comparing second-best situations in any case, and if markets like the ones portrayed here are prevalent, we will not be able to use the standard tools of consumer and producer surplus.

Also the difference between the conclusions of this chapter and standard conclusions is one based on differences in assumptions; which view is more nearly true is an empirical matter. Showing that heterodox ideas are self-consistent does not show that they are right.

The moral of the chapter, then, is a much more modest one: The things we are talking about here can be modeled. And it is important that we try. It may be that free trade and *laissez-faire* are good policies, and that most interventionist suggestions are self-serving, fallacious, or both. But the argument of trade theorists will remain unpersuasive unless their models begin to contain at least some of the features of the world that practical men accuse them of neglecting.

13

Market Access and International Competition: A Simulation Study of 16K Random Access Memories

with Richard E. Baldwin

The technology by which complex circuits can be etched and printed onto tiny silicon chips is a remarkable one. Until the late 1970s it was also a technology clearly dominated by the United States. Thus it was a rude shock when Japanese competition became a serious challenge to established U.S. firms and when Japan actually came to dominate the manufacture of one important kind of chip, the random access memory (RAM). More perhaps than any other event, Japan's breakthrough in RAMs has raised doubts about whether the traditional American reliance on laissez-faire toward the commercialization of technology is going to remain viable.

There are two main questions raised by shifting advantage in semiconductor production. One is whether it matters who produces semiconductors in general or RAMs in particualr. That is, does the production of RAMs yield important country-specific external economies? This is, of course, the $64K question. It is also an extremely difficult question to answer. Externalities are inherently hard to measure, because by definition they do not leave any trace in market transactions. Ultimately the disscussion of industrial policy will have to come to grips with the assessment of externalities, but for the time being we will shy away from that task.

Here, we instead focus on the other question. This is where the source of the shift in advantage lies. Did Japan simply acquire a comparative advantage through natural causes, or was government targeting the key factor?

Although strong views can be found on both sides, this is also not an easy question to answer. On one side, Japanese policy did not involve large subsidies. The tools of policy were instead encouragement with modest government support of a joint research venture, the very large scale inte-

Originally published in *Empirical Studies of International Trade*, edited by R. Feenstra. © 1988 by Massachusetts Institute of Technology.

gration (VLSI) project, and tacit encouragement of a closure of domestic markets to imports. Given that Japan became a large-scale exporter of chips, a conventional economic analysis would suggest that government policy could not have mattered much.

Semiconductor manufacture, however, is not an industry in which conventional economic analysis can be expected to be a good guide. It is an extraordinarily dynamic industry, where technological change reduced the real price of a unit of computing capacity by 99 percent from 1974 to 1984. This technological change did not fall as manna from heaven; it was largely endogenous, the result of R&D and learning by doing. As a result, competition was marked by dynamic economies of scale that led to a fairly concentrated industry, at least within the RAM market. So semiconductor manufacture is a dynamic oligopoly rather than the static competitive market to which conventional analysis applies.

It is possible to show that in a dynamic oligopoly the policies followed by Japan could in principle have made a large difference. In particular, a protected domestic market can serve as a springboard for exports (Krugman 1984). The question, however, is how important this effect has been. If the Japanese market had been as open as U.S. firms would have liked, would this have radically altered the story, or would it have made only a small difference? There is no way to answer this question without a quantitative model of the competitive process.

Our purpose here is to provide a preliminary assessment of the importance of market access in one important episode in the history of semiconductor competition. This is case of the 16K RAM, the chip for which Japan first became a significant exporter. Our question is whether the alleged closure of the Japanese market could have been decisive in allowing Japan to sell not only at home but also in world markets. The method of analysis is the development of a simulation model, derived from recent theoretical work and "calibrated" to actual data. The technique is in the same spirit as the study on the auto industry by Dixit (1988).

Obviously we are interested in the actual results of this analysis. As we will see, the analysis suggests that privileged access to the domestic market was in fact decisive in giving Japanese firms the ability to compete in the world market. The analysis also suggests, however, that this "success" was actually a net loss to the Japanese economy. Finally, the attempt to construct a simulation model here raises many difficult issues, to such an extent that the results must be treated quite cautiously.

The modeling endeavor has a secondary purpose, however, that might be more important than the first. This is to conduct a trial run of the application of new trade theories to real data. It is our view that RAMs are a uniquely rewarding subject for such a trial run. On one hand, the product is well defined: RAMs are a commodity, in the sense that RAMs from different firms are near-perfect substitutes and can in fact be mixed in the same device. Indeed, successive generations of RAMs are still good substitutes—a 16K RAM is pretty close in its use to four 4K RAMs, and so on. On the other hand, the dynamic factors that new theory emphasizes are present in RAMs to an almost incredible degree. The pace of technological change in RAMs is so rapid that other factors can be neglected, in much the same way that nonmonetary factors can be neglected in studying hyperinflation.

In section 13.1 we provide background on the industry. In section 13.2 we develop the theoretical model underlying the simulation. In section 13.3 we explain how the model was "calibrated" to the data. We describe and discuss simulations of the industry under alternative policies in section 13.4 and we describe the results of some sensitivity analysis in section 13.5. Finally, we conclude with a discussion of the significance of the results and directions for further research.

13.1   The Random Access Memory Market

Technology and the Growth of the Industry

So-called dynamic random access memories are a particular general-purpose kind of semiconductor chip. What a RAM does is to store information in digital form in such a way as to allow that information to be altered and read in any desired order (hence "random access"). The technique of production for 16K RAMs involved the etching of circuits on silicon chips by a combination of photographic techniques and chemical baths, followed by baking. The advantage of this method of manufacture, in addition to the microscopic scale on which components are fabricated, is that in effect thousands of electronic devices are manufactured together, all in a single step. The disadvantage, if there is one, is that the process is sensitive. If a chip is to work, everything—temperature, timing, density of solutions, vibration levels, dust—must be precisely controlled.

The sensitivity of the manufacturing process gives rise to a distinctive form of learning by doing. Suppose that a semiconductor chip has been designed and the manufacturing process worked out. Even so, when production begins, the yield of usable chips will ordinarily be low. That is, chips will be produced, but most of them—often 95 percent—will not work because in some subtle way the conditions for production were not quite right. Thus the manufacturing process is in large part a matter of experimenting with details over time. As the details are worked out, the yield rises sharply. Even at the end, however, many chips still fail to work.

Technological progress in the manufacture of chips has had a more or less regular rhythm in which fundamental improvements alternate with learning by doing within a given framework. In the case of RAMs the fundamental innovations have involved packing ever more components onto a chip through the use of more sophisticated methods of etching the circuits. Given the binary nature of everything in this industry, each such leap forward has inovlved doubling the previous density; because chips are two dimensional, each such doubling of density quadruples the number of components. Thus the successive generations of RAMs have been the 4K (4×2^{10}), the 16K, the 64K, and the 256K. Basically a 16K chip does four times as much as a 4K and, given time, costs not much more to produce, so the succession of generations creates a true product cycle in which each generation becomes more or less thoroughly replaced by the next.

Table 13.1 shows how the successive generations of RAMs have entered the market and how the price has fallen. To interpret the data, bear in mind that one unit of each RAM generation is roughly equivalent to four units of the previous generation. The pattern of product cycles then becomes clear. The effective output of 16K RAMs was already larger than that of 4K RAMs in 1978, and the effective price was clearly lower by 1979. The 16K RAM was in its turn overtaken in output in 1981, in price in 1982. As of the time of this writing, the 64K has not yet been overtaken by 256K RAMs. Missing from the table, as well, is a collapse in RAM prices during 1985, to levels as little as a tenth of those of a year earlier.

From an economist's point of view, the most important question about a technology is not how it works but how it is handled by a market system. This boils down largely to the questions of appropriability and externality. Can the firm that develops a technological improvement keep others from imitating it long enough to reap the rewards of its cleverness? Do others gain from a firm's innovations (other than from its improved product or reduced prices)? When we examine international competition, we also want to know whether external benefits, to the extent that they are generated, are national or international in scope.

From the nature of what is being learned, there seem to be clear differences between the two kinds of technological progress in the semiconduc-

Table 13.1
Prices and total sales of RAMs by generation

Factor	1974	1975	1976	1977	1978	1979	1980	1981	1982	1983	1984
Average price (dollars)											
4K	17.0	6.24	4.35	2.65	1.82	1.92	1.94	1.76	1.62	2.72	3.00
16K			46.4	18.6	8.53	6.03	4.77	2.06	1.24	1.05	0.90
64K					150	110	46.3	11.0	5.42	3.86	3.16
256K									150	47.7	19.9
Total shipments (million units)											
4K	.6	5.3	28	57	77	70	31	13	5	2	2
16K			.1	2	21	70	183	216	263	239	121
64K							13	104	371	853	
256K										2	44
Rate of growth of 16K RAM output					2.35	1.20	0.96	0.17	0.20		

Source: Dataquest.

tor industry. When a new generation of chips is introduced, the knowledge involved seems to be of a kind that is relatively hard to maintain as private property. Basic techniques of manufacture are hard to keep secret and in any case respond to current trends in science and "metatechnology." Thus everyone knew in the late 1970s that a 64K RAM was possible and roughly how it was going to be done. Furthermore even the details of chip design are essentially impossible to disguise: Firms can and do make and enlarge photographs of rivals' chips to see how their circuits are laid out. Also the ability of firms to learn from each other is not noticeably restricted by national boundaries.

The details of manufacture, as learned over time in the process of gaining experience, are, by contrast, highly appropriable. The facts learned pertain to highly specific circumstances and are indeed sometimes plant as well as firm specific. Unlike the design of the chips, the details of production are not evident in the final product. Thus the knowledge gained from learning by doing in this case is a model of a technology that poses few appropriability problems.

It seems, then, that the basic innovations involved in passing from one generation to the next in RAMs are relatively hard to appropriate, whereas those involved in getting the technology to work *within* a generation are relatively easy to appropriate. This observation is the basis of the key untrue assumption that we make in implementing our simulation analysis. We treat product cycles—the displacement of one generation by the next, better one—as completely exogenous. This allows us to focus entirely on the competition within the cycle, in which technological progress takes place by learning. It also allows us to put time bounds on this competition: A single product cycle becomes the natural unit of analysis.

Like any convenient assumption, this one does violence to reality. It is at least possible that the assumptions we make are in fact missing the key point of competition in this industry. For now, however, let us make our simplification and leave the critical discussion to section 13.6.

Market Structure and Trade Policy

Some fourteen firms produced 16K random access memories for the commercial market from 1977 to 1983. Table 13.2 shows the average shares of these firms in world production during the period. Taken as a whole, the industry was not exceptionally concentrated, though far from competitive: The Herfindahl index for all firms, taking the average over the period, was only 0.099. This overstates the effective degree of competition, however,

Table 13.2
Competitors in the 16K RAM
market

Firm	Share of world production, 1977–1983
AMD	5.4
Eurotech	1.5
Fairchild	1.6
Fujitsu	9.5
Hitachi	6.4
Intel	2.4
Mitsubishi	1.2
Mostek	15.3
Motorola	5.4
National	10.6
NEC	15.2
Siemens	3.1
ITT	5.7
TI	12.5
Toshiba	3.6

Source: Dataquest.

for two main reasons. First, some of the firms producing small quantities were probably producing specialized products in short production runs and thus were really not producing the same commodity as the rest. Second, there was, as we will see shortly, a good deal of market segmentation between the United States and Japan, so that each market was substantially more oligopolized than the figures suggest. Nonetheless, when we create a stylized version of the market for simulation purposes, we will want to make sure that the degree of competition is roughly consistent with this data. As it turns out, we will develop a model in which the baseline case contains six symmetric U.S. firms and three symmetric Japanese firms, which does not seem too far off.

Another feature of the semiconductor industry's market structure is not shown in the table. This is the contrast between the nature of the U.S. firms and their Japanese rivals. The major U.S. chip manufacturers shown here are primarily chip producers. (There is also "captive" U.S. production by such firms as IBM and AT&T, but during the period we are considering, little of this production found its way to the open or "merchant" market). The Japanese firms, by contrast, are also substantial consumers of chips in their other operations. The Japanese firms are not, however, vertically integrated

Table 13.3
Average market shares by country of origin[a]

	Source	
Market	United States	Japan
United States	91.2	8.8
Japan	13.7	86.3
Rest of world	56.0	44.0

Source: Author estimates, using tables 2.8, 2.12, and 2.13 from Finan and Amundsen (1985); and Dataquest.
a. We assume that the pattern of consumption for RAMs is the same as for all integrated circuits.

in the usual sense. Each buys most of its chips from other firms and in turn sells most of its chip output to outside customers. There have been repeated accusations, however, that the major suppliers and buyers of Japanese semiconductor production— who are the same firms—collude to form a closed market and exclude foreign sources.

The claim that the Japanese market is effectively closed rests on this difference in market structure. U.S. firms argued that the "buy Japanese" policy of the major firms was tacitly and perhaps even explicitly encouraged by the government so that even in the absence of any formal tariffs or quotas Japan was able to use a strategy of infant-industry protection to establish itself. It is beyond our ability to assess such claims or to determine how important the government of Japan as opposed to its social structure was in closing the market to foreigners. There is, however, circumstantial evidence of a less than open market. The evidence is that of market shares. Consider table 13.3 (the entries should be treated as estimates). We see that U.S. firms dominated both their own home market and third-country markets, primarily in Europe. Yet they had a small share in Japan, probably again in specialized types of RAMs rather than the basic commodity product. Transport costs for RAMs are small; they are, as we have stressed, commoditylike in their interchangeability. So the disparity in market shares suggests that some form of market closure was in fact happening.

Here is where economic analysis comes in. We know that, in an industry characterized by strong learning effects, as we have argued is the case here, protection of the home market can have a kind of multiplier effect. Privileged access to one market can give firms the assurance of moving further down their learning curves and thus can encourage them to price aggressively in other markets as well. Our next task is to develop a simulation model that can be used to ask how important this effect could have been in the case of RAMs.

13.2   A Theoretical Model of Competition in RAMs

The Yield Curve Model of Production

Consider a firm that at the start of a product cycle commits some amount of resources to production. We define one unit of capacity as the resources needed to produce one "batch" per unit of time. Let K be the capacity in which a firm invests.

Now we suppose that production takes the form of "batches": Each period, one unit of capacity can be used to engrave and bake one batch of semiconductor chips. Thus the firm produces batches at a constant rate K throughout the cycle, and the total number of batches produced after t periods has passed is Kt.

In semiconductor production, however, much of a batch of chips will not work. The yield of usable chips per batch rises with experience. We assume specifically that the yield of usable chips per batch $y(t)$ is a function of the total number of batches that a firm has made so far, $K(t)t$, according to the functional form

$$y(t) = [Kt]^\theta. \tag{1}$$

Obviously the functional form (1) cannot be right for the whole range. It implies that the yield of usable chips per batch rises without limit as experience accumulates. In fact yields cannot go above 100 percent so something like a logistic would seem more reasonable. The functional form here is, however, a tremendous help in keeping the problem manageable. So long as the product cycle remains short, it may not be too bad an approximation.

The total number of chips produced by a firm per unit time will then be

$$x(t) = Ky(t) = K^{1+\theta}t^\theta. \tag{2}$$

Now it is immediately and gratifyingly obvious that equation (2) behaves much as if there were ordinary increasing returns to scale. Time enters in a way that is multiplicatively separable from capacity so that the rate of growth of output is in fact independent of the size of the firm. Although we started with a dynamic formulation, the advantages of greater ex- perience show up as the fact that the exponent on K is larger than 1, just as if the economies of scale were static and productivity growth were exogenous.

It is also possible to show the analogy between this formulation and the conventional learning curve. In learning-curve models it is usual to compare current average cost with cumulative experience. Although costs are all sunk in the yield-curve model, current cost as measured would presumably be proportional to the capacity K. Thus current average cost would be measured as proportional to $K/x(t)$. At the same time, cumulative output to date can be found by integrating equation (2). Let $X(t)$ be cumulative output to time t, and let $C(t)$ be the measured average cost of production $cK/x(t)$, where c is the annualized cost of a unit of capacity. Then we have

$$X(t) = \frac{(Kt)^{1+\theta}}{1+\theta},$$

$$C(t) = c(Kt)^{-\theta}$$

$$= c[X(t)(1+\theta)]^{-\theta/(1+\theta)}.$$

If we were to think of this as a conventional learning curve, then $\theta/(1+\theta)$ would be the slope of that learning curve.

The close parallels between our formulation and both static economies of scale and the learning curve are helpful. Usually studies of technological change in semiconductors are framed in terms of learning curves; what we can do is reinterpret the results of those studies in terms of a yield curve, transforming estimates of the learning-curve elasticity to derive estimates of θ. At the same time the parallel with static economies of scale suggests a solution technique for our model, when it is fully specified: Collapse our model into an equivalent static model, and solve that model instead. We need to specify the demand side to show that in fact such a procedure is valid, but this will in the end be the technique we use.

A final point about the assumed technology: The reason for assuming the yield-curve model instead of the learning-curve model is that it implies growing output over the product cycle. Can we say anything more than this? The answer is that the specific formulation adopted here implies also that output grows at a declining rate. By taking logs and differentiating equation (2), we find that the rate of growth of output will decline according to the relationship

$$\frac{dx(t)}{dt}\frac{1}{x(t)} = \frac{\theta}{t}. \tag{3}$$

The prediction of a declining rate of growth in output over the product cycle is borne out, except for a slight reversal at one point, by the data in table 13.1.

Demand and Trade

Turning now to the demand side, we suppose that there are two markets: the United States and Japan. We denote Japanese variables with an asterisk and leave U.S. variables unstarred. In each market there is a constant elasticity demand curve for output, which we write in inverse form as

$$P = AQ^{-\alpha}, \tag{4}$$

$$P^* = A^*(Q^*)^{-\alpha}. \tag{5}$$

We thus assume that the elasticity of demand, $1/\alpha$, is the same in both markets.

Firms are assumed to be located in one market or the other and to be able to ship to the other market only by incurring an additional transport cost. Transport costs will be of the "iceberg" variety, with only a fraction $1/(1 + d)$ of any quantity shipped arriving.

The problem of firms has two parts. First, they must decide on a capacity level. This fixes the path of their output through the product cycle. Second, at each point in time they must decide how much to sell in each market. Let us for the moment take the capacity choice as given and focus only on the determination of the division of output.

This choice can be analyzed as follows (the essence of this analysis is the same as that in the purely static models presented by Brander 1981 and Brander and Krugman 1983). Each firm will want to allocate its current output between markets so that the marginal-revenue, net-of-transport cost of shipping to the two markets is the same. Consider the case of a U.S. firm. The marginal revenue (MR) it receives from shipping an additional unit to the U.S. market is

$$MR_U = P(1 - \alpha S_U V_U), \tag{6}$$

where S_U is the share of the firm in the U.S. market; we will define V_U in a moment. Its marginal revenue from selling in the Japanese market is

$$MR_J = P^*(1 - \alpha S_J V_J)/(1 + d), \tag{7}$$

where S_J is the share of the firm in the Japanese market.

The two terms V_U and V_J—and their counterparts V_{U^*} and V_{J^*} in the decision problem of a Japanese firm—are conjectural variations. They measure the extent to which a firm expects a one-unit increase in its own deliveries to a market to increase *total* deliveries to that market and thus to depress the price. In the simplest case of Cournot competition, we would have all four conjectural variations equal to 1.

The use of a conjectural variations approach in modeling oligopoly is not a favored one. Many authors have pointed out the shaky logical foundations of the approach, and to use it in an empirical application adds an uncomfortable element of "ad-hockery." We introduce these terms now because we have found that we need them; indeed, as soon as we discuss entry, it will become immediately apparent that, to reconcile the industry's structure with its technology, we must abandon the hypothesis of Cournot competition. Whether there are alternatives to the the conjectural variations approach is a question we return to in section 13.6.

Suppose that we suppress our doubts and accept the conjectural variations approach. Then we can notice the following point. Suppose that, for some P, P^*, S_U, and S_J, the first-order condition $MR_U = MR_J$ is satisfied. Then the condition will continue to be satisfied with the same S_U and S_J even for different prices, so long as P/P^* remains the same.

What this means is that if all firms grow at the same rate, so that it is feasible for them to maintain constant market shares, and if prices fall at the same rate in both markets, the optimal behavior will in fact be to maintain constancy of market shares. Fortunately our assumptions on the yield curve ensure that all firms will indeed grow at the same rate. Furthermore, if firms continue to divide their output in the same proportions between the two markets, the fact that all firms grow at the same rate and that the elasticity of demand is assumed constant ensures that prices in the two markets will indeed fall at the same rate. So we have demonstrated that given the initial capacity decisions of the firms, the subsequent equilibrium in the product cycle is a sort of balanced growth in which market shares do not change but output steadily rises and prices steadily fall.

We note finally that, in principle, this equilibrium may be one in which there is two-way trade in the same product. Firms with a small market share (or a low conjectural variation) in the foreign market may choose to "dump" goods in that market, even though the price net of transport and tariff costs is less than at home. Because this may be true of firms in each country, the result can be two-way trade based on reciprocal dumping.

So far we have discussed equilibrium given the number of firms and their capacity choices; our final steps are to consider capacity choice and entry.

Capacity Choice

Following Spence (1981), we assume that the product cycle is short enough that firms do not worry about discounting. Thus the objective of a U.S. firm is to maximize

$$W = \int_0^T \left[Pz(t) + \frac{P^* z^*(t)}{1 + d} \right] dt - cK \tag{8}$$

subject to the constraint

$$z(t) + z^*(t) = K^{1+\theta} t^\theta, \qquad \text{for all } t,$$

where T is the length of the product cycle, $z(t)$ and $z^*(t)$ are deliveries to the U.S. and Japanese markets, respectively, and c is the cost of a unit of capacity.

This maximization problem may be simplified by noting that we have already seen that marginal revenue will be the same for deliveries to the two markets. Thus we can evaluate the returns from a marginal increase in K by assuming that the whole of that increase is allocated to the U.S. market. The first-order condition then becomes

$$(1 + \theta) \int_0^T P(t)(1 - \alpha S_U V_U)(Kt)^\theta \, dt = c. \tag{9}$$

We can rewrite this first-order condition in a revealing form. First, to simplify notation, let us choose units so that the length of the product cycle T is equal to 1. Also we note that given the output path (13.3) and the elasticity of demand, we have

$$P(t) = P(T) \left(\frac{t}{T} \right)^{-\alpha\theta}.$$

By substituting and integrating, we find

$$\left[\frac{1 + \theta}{(1 - \alpha)\theta + 1} \right] P(T)(1 - \alpha S_U V_U) = cK^{-\theta},$$

or

$$P(1 - \alpha S_U V_U) = MC_U, \tag{10}$$

where P is the average price received by the firm over the product cycle; thus the whole left-hand term is the average marginal revenue over the cycle. The term on the right-hand side can be shown to equal the marginal cost of producing one more unit of total cycle output. Thus we see that our problem can be expressed in a form that is effectively the same as one where economies of scale are purely static. Something that looks like marginal revenue is set equal to something that looks like marginal cost.

This means that we can solve for equilibrium by collapsing the problem into an equivalent static problem. Given the balanced-growth character of the equilibrium, there is a one-to-one relationship between total deliveries to each market and the average price, which continues to take a constant elasticity form:

$$P = AQ^{-\alpha}. \tag{11}$$

And we can write an average cost function for cumulative output, which takes the form

$$C = C_U X^{-\theta/(1+\theta)}. \tag{12}$$

A model of the form (10)–(12) may be solved using methods described in Brander and Krugman (1983) and Krugman (1986a). For any given marginal costs we can solve for equilibrium prices and market shares. From prices we can determine total sales, and by using market shares, we can find ouput per firm. This output, however, implies a marginal cost. A full equilibrium is a fixed point where the marginal costs assumed at the beginning are the same as those implied at the end. In practice, such an equilibrium can easily be calculated using an iterative procedure. We make a guess at the marginal costs, solve for output, use this to recompute the marginal costs, and continue until convergence.

Once we have solved this collapsed problem, we can then solve for the implied capacity choices and the whole time path of output and prices.

Entry

Finally, we turn to the problem of entry. Here we assume that there are many potential entrants with the same costs and that all potential entrants have perfect foresight about the postentry equilibrium. An equilibrium with entry must then satisfy two criteria: It must yield nonnegative profits for all those firms that do enter, but any additional firm that might enter would face losses. If we could ignore integer constraints, this would imply a zero-profit equilibrium. In practice, this will not be quite the case. However, as we will see, our estimates of profits turn out to be quite small.

An important point about the relationship between entry and conjectural variations should be noted. This is that the conjectural variations must be high—that is, postentry firms had better not be too competitive—if there are strong increases in yield. To see this, consider a single market with elasticity of demand $1/\alpha$ and yield-curve parameter θ, where all firms are the same. Then the number of firms that can earn zero profits can be shown to be $\alpha(1 + \theta)V/\theta$, where V is the conjectural variation. For the estimates of α and θ that we will be using, this turns out to be $1.98V$. That is, with Cournot behavior only two firms could earn zero profits. Not surprisingly, in order to rationalize the existence of the six large U.S. firms that actually competed and that furthermore faced some foreign competition, we end up needing to postulate behavior a good deal less competitive than Cournot.

We have now described a theoretical model of competition in an industry that we hope captures some of the essentials of the random access memory market. Our next step is to try to make this model operational using realistic numbers.

13.3   Calibrating the Model

Our theoretical model of the random access memory market is recognizably one in which protection of the domestic market will in effect push a firm down its marginal cost curve and lead to a larger share of the export market as well. What we want to do, however, is to quantify this effect. To do this, we need to choose realistic parameter values. We take outside estimates for some of the parameters and then use data on the industry to calibrate the model to fix the remaining parameters.

Parameters from Outside Estimates

The parameters for which we took numbers directly from other sources were the elasticity of demand α, the elasticity of the yield curve θ, and the transport cost d.

Finan and Amundsen (1985) estimate demand elasticity at 1.8 for the U.S. market. In fact we can confirm that this must be at least approximately right by comparing the fall in prices and the rise in quantity from 1978 to 1981, that is, over the period when 16K RAMs were the dominant memory chip. Prices fell by a logarithmic 142 percent over that period, whereas sales rose by 233 percent, 1.6 times as much, despite a recession and high interest rates that depressed investment. In general, it is apparent that the elasticity of demand for semiconductor memories must be more than 1 but not too much more, given that the price per bit has fallen 99 percent in real terms over the past decade. If demand were inelastic, the industry would have shrunk away; if it were very elastic, we would be having chips with everything by now.

The elasticity of the yield curve can, as we noted in our earlier discussion, be derived from the elasticity of the associated learning curve. Discussions of learning curves in general often offer numbers in the 0.2–0.3 range. An Office of Technology Assessment study (1983) estimated the slope of the learning curve for semiconductors at 0.28. Converted to yield-curve form, this implies that $\theta = 0.3889$.

Finally, there is general agreement that costs of transporting semi-internationally are low, as one would expect given the high ratio of value to weight or bulk. We follow Finan and Amundsen's (1985) estimate of $d = 0.05$.

Costs

The data in tables 13.2 and 13.3 show fourteen firms in three markets. If we were to try to represent the complete structure of the industry, we would need to specify fourteen cost functions and forty-two conjectural variations parameters. Instead, we have stylized the market in such a way as to need to specify only two cost parameters and four conjectural variations.

The less important step in this stylization is the consolidation of the U.S. and the rest of world (ROW) markets into a single market. This may be justified on the grounds that transport costs are small, and the crucial issue is the alleged closure of the Japanese market. Also, as our data suggest, the market share of U.S. firms in the U.S. and ROW markets is fairly similar.

The more important step is the representation of the U.S. and Japanese industries as a group of symmetric representative firms. There are many objections to this procedure. The essential problem is that the size distribution of firms presumably has some meaning, and to collapse it in this way means that we are neglecting potentially important aspects of reality. As with our other problematic assumptions, this should be viewed as a simplification that we hope is not crucial.

In table 13.2 we noted that there were nine firms with market shares over 5 percent: six U.S. and three Japanese. We represent the industry by treating it as if these were the only firms and as if all firms from each country were the same. Thus our model industry consists of six equal-cost U.S. firms, which share the entire U.S. market share, and three equal-cost Japanese firms, which do the same for Japan's market shares.

We do not have direct data on costs. Instead, we attempt to infer costs by assuming that in the actual case firms earned precisely zero profits. As

Table 13.4
Market shares and sales per firm

	Producer	
Market	United States	Japan
Market shares		
United States and rest of world	13.5	6.3
Japan	2.3	28.6
Sales (million units)		
United States and rest of world	69.3	32.2
Japan	5.0	62.3

Source: Table 3, Finan and Amundsen (1985); Dataquest.

we know, because of integer constraints this need not have been the case. It should have been close, however, and it allows us to use price and output data to infer costs.

First, we have data on prices. This data shows that from 1978 to 1983 the average price of a 16K RAM was identical in the two markets, at $1.47. There is reason to suspect this data, because the Japanese had been threatened with an antidumping action and the structure of the Japanese industry may have made it easy for effective prices to differ from those posted. Lacking any information on this, however, we will go with the official data.

Next, we use our stylized industry structure to calculate the *per firm* sales in each market. These are shown in the first part of table 13.4. Given this information, we can net out transport costs on foreign sales to calculate the average revenue (*AR*) of a representative firm of each type; that is,

$$AR = \frac{\int_0^T [P(t)z(t) + P^*(t)(z^*(t))/(1 + d)]\,dt}{\int_0^T [z(t) + z^*(t)]\,dt}$$

for a U.S. firm.

But the zero-profit assumption allows us to infer that average cost is equal to average revenue. This in turn implies both the level of marginal cost (*MC*) and the constant term in the average cost function:

$$MC_U = AR/(1 + \theta),$$

$$C_U = AR(X^{\theta/1+\theta}),$$

where X is cumulative output. When we solve these equations we find that

$MC_U = 1.054$, $MC_J = 1.040$,

$C_U = 3.524$, $C_J = 3.733$.

This says that U.S. firms would have had somewhat lower (about 6 percent) costs if they had had the same output as their Japanese rivals but that Japanese firms, thanks to larger scale, ended up with slightly lower marginal costs.

This result confirms what industry experts have claimed in a qualitative sense about the industry. Most estimates based on direct observation have given U.S. firms a larger inherent cost advantage—Finan and Amundsen (1985) suggest 10–15 percent. Given the roundabout nature of our method and the problems of some of our data, we would not quarrel with this.

One might wonder about the coincidence that costs in the two countries appear to be so close. Is there something about our method that forces this? The answer, we believe, is that this is a result of our method of selecting an industry to study. The 16K RAM was the first semiconductor for which Japan became an exporter on a large scale. Not surprisingly, it is a product for which costs were close. Had we done the 4K RAM, for which Japanese firms sold only to a protected domestic market, or the 64K RAM, for which they came to be the dominant producers, we would presumably have found quite different answers.

Conjectural Variations

Our next step is to calculate conjectural variations parameters. We begin with per-firm market shares. These are shown in the second part of table 13.4.

We next note the relationship between average prices, market shares, and marginal cost:

$$(1 - \alpha S_U V_U) \int_0^T P(t)\, dt = MC_U$$

for U.S. firms in the U.S. market, and similarly for Japanese firms in the two markets. Note that we cannot use this method to estimate the conjectural variation for U.S. firms in the Japanese market. The reason is that the whole point of this study is the allegation the U.S. firms were constrained by implicit trade barriers from selling as much as they would have under free trade.

When we solve these equations for the conjectural variations, we find

$$V_U = 3.760, \qquad V_{J^*} = 1.828, \qquad V_{U^*} = 7.345.$$

What about the U.S. conjectural variation in the Japanese market? Here it is impossible to disentangle the effects of U.S. behavior and whatever implicit protection Japan imposed. This is a key point on which there seems to be nothing we can do except make an assumption. Our assumption is this: U.S. firms have the same conjectural variation in the Japanese market that they do at home. Thus we assume that

$$V_J = V_U = 3.760.$$

This conjecture would lead to a substantially higher U.S. market share in Japan than we actually observe. The difference we attribute to protection. This protection can be represented by an implicit tariff. The implicit tariff rate necessary to reproduce the actual market share is 0.2637.

There are two points to note about these results. First, we note that all three estimated conjectural variations are substantially more than 1; that is, the market is less competitive than Cournot. This is an inevitable consequence of the high degree of economies of scale that we have assumed, together with the zero-profit condition. Relatively uncompetitive behavior is needed to rationalize how many firms there are in the market. Second, Japanese firms seem to have been cautious about selling in the U.S. market. Is this number picking up concerns about U.S. trade policy, or is it simply an artifact of our model? In general, the conjectural variations are not too plausible; we consider in section 13.6 what this implies for our general approach.

We have now calibrated the model to the data. That is, when the model is simulated using our assumed parameters, it reproduces the actual prices, outputs, and market shares of the 16K RAM product cycle. We summarize this baseline case in table 13.5. Our next step is to ask how the results change under alternative policies.

13.4   Effects of Alternative Policies

We consider two alternative policies. The first is free trade, represented in our model by a removal of the implicit tariff on U.S. sales to Japan. The second is a trade war, in which both countries block imports. The effects of the two policies are shown next to the baseline case in table 13.5.

It is important to note the underlying assumptions behind these calculations. In each case all parameters are assumed constant, except for the

Table 13.5
Simulation results

Variable	Base case	Free trade	Trade war
Welfare			
United States	1,651.8	1,828.5	1,636.7
Japan	698.4	738.9	225.6
Consumer surplus			
United States	1,651.8	1,822.5	1,636.7
Japan	698.4	738.9	225.6
Price			
United States	1.47	1.30	1.49
Japan	1.47	1.37	2.19
Profit			
United States	0	5	0
Japan	0	—	0
Import shares			
United States in Japan	.14	1.0	0.0
Japan in United States	.19	0.0	0.0
Number of firms			
United States	6	7	7
Japan	3	0	5

implicit tariff on U.S. exports to Japan. In particular, the conjectural variations are assumed to remain unchanged. This is not a particularly satisfactory assumption, but, of course, if we allow these parameters to change, anything can happen.

To solve the model in each case, we followed a two-stage procedure. First, we took the initial number of firms and iterated on marginal cost to get the equilibrium. Then we searched across a grid of numbers of Japanese and U.S. firms to find an entry equilibrium.

Free Trade

Our first policy experiment goes to the heart of the debate over Japanese trade policy. We ask what would have happened if the Japanese market had been open. This is done by removing the implicit tariff on U.S. exports to Japan.

The results, reported in the second column of table 13.5, are quite striking. According to our model, in the absence of protection the Japanese firms that were net exporters in the baseline case do not even enter; only U.S. firms remain in the field. The reason is a sort of circular causation typical in models with scale economies. Japanese firms, deprived of their safe haven in the domestic market, would have smaller cumulative output even with constant marginal cost. The smaller output, however, means a higher marginal cost. This implies still smaller output, which implies still higher marginal cost, and so on. In the end, no Japanese firms find it profitable to enter.

The exit of the Japanese firms and the new access to the Japanese market produce an increase in the profits of the U.S. firms. It turns out that this increase allows an additional U.S. firm to enter. Increased competition, combined with larger output and hence lower marginal cost of the U.S. firms, leads to a fall in price in *both* markets.

The lower price means an increase in consumer surplus in both countries. In the United States this is supplemented with a small rise in profits. The result is a gain in welfare, measured as the sum of consumer and producer surplus, in both nations.

If we reverse the order in which we consider columns 2 and 3 of table 13.5, we can arrive at an evaluation of the effects of Japanese policy. According to our estimates, privileged access to the domestic market *was* crucial, not only in providing Japanese firms with domestic sales but in allowing them to get their marginal cost down to the point where they could successfully export. However, this result of protection was a Pyrrhic victory in welfare terms. It raised Japanese prices, hurting consumers without generating compensating producer gains. The policy was thus not a successful beggar-my-neighbor one, or more accurately it beggared my neighbor only at the cost of beggaring myself as well.

Trade War

Although a Japanese policy of export promotion through home market protection does not seem to be desirable even in and of itself, it is easy to imagine that it could provoke retaliation. The fourth column of table 13.5 asks what would have happened if Japan and the United States had engaged in a "trade war" in 16K RAMs, with each blocking all imports from the other. (For the purposes of the simulation we achieved this by letting each country impose a 100 percent tariff.)

The result of this trade war is unfavorable for both countries. Firms are smaller and thus have higher marginal cost. Prices are therefore higher in both markets, though especially in the smaller Japanese market. Small profits do not compensate for the loss of consumer surplus, so welfare is reduced in both nations.

This trade war example makes a point that has been mentioned in some discussion of high technology industries but needs further emphasis. Although the nonclassical aspects of these industries offer potential justifications for government intervention, they also tend to magnify the costs of protection and trade conflict. We have a case of two countries with similar inherent costs, that is, little comparative advantage. In a constant-returns, perfect-competition situation this would mean that a trade war would have few costs. In this case, however, protection leads to reduced competition and reduced scale, imposing substantial losses.

These results are clearly extremely striking. Furthemore, even though we do *not* find that Japan was successfully pursuing a beggar-thy-neighbor policy at U.S. expense, the implication for market shares is potentially politically explosive. Thus it is important to ask how sensitive the results are to changes in the assumed parameters.

13.5   Sensitivity Analysis

In calibrating the model, we used two sources of information. On one side we used actual data on the industry. Although this data is not ironclad, we did not experiment with how our conclusions might have changed if the data had looked different. Instead, we confined ourselves to analysis of the sensitivity of the results to the value of the parameters we took from outside sources. There are three of these: the elasticity of demand, the transport cost, and the elasticity of learning.

Conducting a sensitivity analysis with respect to these parameters is not simply a matter of rerunning a simulation with a different parameter. If we believe that, say, transport costs are actually twice as large as we assumed in the base case, we must also revise our estimates of the costs of U.S. and Japanese firms and of their conjectural variations. That is, we must recalibrate the entire model before resimulating. Our sensitivity analysis therefore involved a series of recalibrations for different values of the three outside parameters.

The results of these exercises are summarized in table 13.6. Recall that our baseline estimates were that the elasticity of learning $\phi = \theta/(1 + \theta) = 0.28$, the elasticity of demand $\varepsilon = 1.8$, and the transport cost $d = 0.05$. We have treated these as a central case and asked what happens when each of the parameters in turn is varied around the central case. For each recalibration/resimulation exercise we report three numbers: the free trade

Table 13.6
Sensitivity of key results to parameters

Parameter	Free trade, Japanese share in United States	Free trade, U.S. share In Japan	Welfare effect of protection
$\varepsilon = 1.8, d = 0.05$			
$\phi = 0.56$	0	1	−
$\phi = 0.28^a$	0	1	−
$\phi = 0.14$	0	1	0
$\phi = 0.07$	0	1	+
$\phi = 0.28, d = 0.05$			
$\varepsilon = 1.4$	0	1	−
$\varepsilon = 1.8^a$	0	1	−
$\varepsilon = 2.2$	0	1	−
$\varepsilon = 1.8, \phi = 0.28$			
$d = 0.2$	0	1	+
$d = 0.05^a$	0	1	−
$d = 0.025$	0	1	−
Alternative implicit conjectural variation	0	1	−

a. Base case.

share of Japanese firms in the United States, the free trade share of U.S. firms in Japan, and the *sign* of the welfare effect of protection on Japan. In the central case, as we already noted, these entries are 0,1, −: The Japanese industry would not have existed without protection, but nonetheless protection made Japan worse off. The question is whether some plausible variation in the parameters could either reduce the strong implication of the trade policies for market shares or make protection appear to be a successful predatory policy.

The first group of runs holds ε and d at their base levels and varies the elasticity of the learning curve, from twice its central value to only one-fourth as large. It appears that the strong result on market shares is highly robust to this parameter. Somewhat surprising, however, is that Japan might have gained from protection if dynamic scale economies had been fairly *low*. This runs opposite to our intuition, which is that unconventional trade policy answers depend on increasing returns being important. The explanation, as best we can understand it, is that our estimate of relative Japanese costs is inversely related to the degree of scale economies. Our calibration requires that Japanese marginal costs be slightly below those of U.S. firms; in our base case we find nonetheless that underlying Japanese costs are higher, with the greater length of Japanese production runs accounting for the difference. If scale economies are smaller, our calibration makes the underlying costs of Japan's firms closer to those of U.S. firms. When firms in the two countries have similar underlying costs, it then becomes possible for protection actually to lower prices in the protecting country, a point noted by Venables (1985b). That is what seems to be happening.

The second group of runs holds $\phi = 0.28$ and varies the elasticity of demand. As we noted earlier, this is a parameter we are fairly sure of, and the model seems relatively insensitive within a plausible range.

The third group of runs holds ϕ and ε at their central values while varying d. Even implausibly high transport costs do not shake the strong result that Japan's industry would not have existed without protection. With sufficiently high transport costs, however, Japan is better off even with a high-cost domestic industry than importing, and protection actually lowers prices—the Venables effect again.

The last item in table 13.6 addresses one arbitrary assumption we made in our analysis. As we pointed out, it was not possible to disentangle the effects of protection and U.S. behavior in the Japanese market. In the base case we assumed that U.S. firms in the Japanese market would have the same conjectural variation as they did in their home market. Here we try assuming instead that they behave like Japanese firms in the Japanese marekt. The qualitative result is unchanged.

The results of the sensitivity analysis seem to indicate that we need not worry too much about the accuracy of the "outside" parameters. Although we varied these parameters over a wide range, we did not encounter any reversals of the market share result, and only in extreme and implausible cases did the welfare result change. Thus, if there is something wrong with the analysis, it is not in these parameters but in the more fundamental conception of the model.

13.6   Concluding Remarks

The results of our simulation analysis seem fairly clear. What we want to focus on here are the difficulties with the analysis and directions for further work.

The difficulties with the model as it stands are of two kinds. First, it is disturbing that we are forced to rely on conjectural variations to make the model track reality and still more disturbing that the conjectural variations are estimated to be such high numbers. Second, our characterization of the technology, although extremely convenient as a simplification, may simplify too much. As we will argue in a moment, these two difficulties may be related.

Conjectural Variations

Our reliance on conjectural variations, and the large value of these conjectures, is forced by two factors. First is the relatively large number of firms operating in the market. Second is the high learning-curve elasticity we have taken from other sources. These imply that firms can be making only nonnegative profits if they have conjectural variations well in excess of 1.

If this result is wrong, it must be because one of the parameters is mismeasured. One possibility would be that firms are in fact producing imperfect substitutes, so that the elasticity of demand faced by each firm is lower than our perfect-substitutes calculation indicates. This seems implausible, however, given what we know about the applications of RAMs. The alternative possibility is that the degree of scale economies is in some way overstated.

Now we know that, in fact, extremely rapid learning took place and, more important, was expected to take place in RAMs. This would seem to imply large dynamic scale economies. However, it is possible that the pace of learning was more a matter of time elapsed than of cumulative output. If this was the case, large firms would not have had as great an advantage over small firms as we have assumed. A reduction in our estimate of the effective degree of scale economies would in turn reduce the need to rely on conjectural variations to track the data. We should note, however, that the conventional wisdom of the industry is that cumulative output, not time alone, is the source of learning.

Even if the learning curve is as steep as we have assumed, the longer-term dynamics of technological change offer an alternative route by which effective scale economies could have been lower than we say. To see this, however, we need to turn to our second problem, the nature of technological competition.

Technological Competition

In order to simplify the analysis, we have assumed that the competition for each generation of semiconductor memories in effect stands in isolation.

The techniques to construct a new size memory become available, and firms are off in a race to learn. This approach neglects three things. It neglects the R&D that is involved in the endogenous development of each generation and it neglects two technological linkages that might be important. One is the link between successive generations of memories; the other is the link between memories and other semiconductor products.

The endogenous development of new generations, in and of itself, actually adds a further degree of dynamic scale economies. Firms invest in front-end R&D, which acts like a fixed cost. This should actually require still higher conjectural variations to justify the number of firms in the industry.

On the other side, technological linkages could help to explain why so many firms produced 16K RAMs. It has sometimes been asserted that you must produce 16K RAMs to be able to get into 64K RAMs, etc. (although Intel, for example, made a decision to skip a generation so as to leapfrog its competitors). It has also been asserted that firms producing other kinds of semiconductors need a base of volume production on which to hone their manufacturing skills and that commodity products such as memories are the only places they can do this. Either of these linkages could have the effect of making firms willing to accept direct losses in RAM production in order to generate intrafirm spillovers to current or future lines of business.

It should be pointed out, however, that these spillovers can explain the presence of a larger number of firms in RAM production only if they involve a *diminishing* marginal product to memory production. That is, they must take the form of gains that you get by having a foothold in the RAM sector but that do not require a dominant presence. Otherwise, the effect will simply be to make competition in RAMs more intense, with lower prices offsetting the extra incentive to participate.

But if the linkages take this form, they will reduce the degree of economies of scale relevant for competition. Firms will view the marginal cost of production as the actual cost less technological spillovers, but these spillovers will decline as output rises, leaving economic marginal cost less downward sloping than direct cost. Of course, if true marginal costs are less downward sloping than we have estimated, we have less need of conjectural variations to explain the number of firms.

What to Make of the Results

Our concluding remarks have been skeptical about some of the underlying structure of the model. It is at least possible that the data can be reinterpreted in a way that leads us to a substantially lower estimate of dynamic scale economies. If this were the case, the results of our simulation exercises would be much less striking. On the other hand, the view that in such a dynamic industry as semiconductors—where U.S. firms were widely agreed to still have a cost advantage in the late 1970s—protection may have been the key to Japanese success is not implausible.

The final judgment, then, must be that this is a preliminary attempt, not the final word. We believe, however, that it has been useful. It is crucial that study of trade policy in dynamic industries go beyond the unsupported assertions that are so common and attempt quantification. We expect that the techniques for doing this will get much better than what we have managed here, but this is at least a first try.

14   Industrial Organization and International Trade

In retrospect, it seems obvious that the theory of international trade should draw heavily on models of industrial organization. Most of world trade is in the products of industries that we have no hesitation in classifying as oligopolies when we see them in their domestic aspect. Yet until quite recently only a handful of papers had attempted to apply models of imperfect competition to international trade issues. Indeed, in 1974 Richard Caves still felt that a lecture on the relationship between trade and industrial organization needed to begin with an aplolgy for the novelty of the idea.

Only in the last decade have we seen the emergence of a sizable literature that links trade theory and industrial organization. This new literature has two main strands. One is fundamentally concerned with modeling the role of economies of scale as a cause of trade. To introduce economies of scale into the model requires that the impact of increasing returns on market structure be somehow taken into account, but in this literature the main concern is usually to get the issue of market structure out of the way as simply as possible—which turns out to be most easily done by assuming that markets are characterized by Chamberlinian monopolistic competition. Section 14.1 summarizes the main insights from this approach.

Since this chapter is aimed primarily at an audience of I-O researchers rather than trade theorists, most of it will be devoted to the second strand in recent literature, which views imperfect competition as the core of the story rather than an unavoidable nuisance issue raised by the attempt to discuss increasing returns. Here there are four main themes, each represented by a section of the chapter. First is the relation between trade policy and the market power of domestic firms (section 14.2). Second is the role of price discrimination and "dumping" in international markets (section 14.3). Third is the possibility that government action can serve a "strategic" role in giving domestic firms an advantage in oligopolistic competition (section 14.4). Fourth, there is the question of whether industrial organization gives us new arguments in favor of protectionism (section 14.5). A final section (section 14.6) will review some recent attempts at quantifying these theoretical models.

Generality in models of imperfect competition is never easy to come by, and usually turns out to be illusory in any case. In this survey I will not even make the attempt. Whatever is necessary for easy exposition will be assumed: specific functional forms, constant marginal cost, specific parameters where that helps. And at least one part of the tradition of international trade theory will be retained: much of the exposition will be diagrammatic rather than algebraic.

14.1   The Monopolistic Competition Trade Model

Origins of the Model

The monopolistic competition model of trade began with an empirical observation: neither the pattern of trade nor its results seem to accord very well with what traditional trade models would lead us to expect. The most influential of trade models is the Heckscher-Ohlin-Samuelson model, which tells us that trade reflects an interaction between the characteristics of countries and the characteristics of the production technology of different goods. Specifically, countries will export goods whose production is intensive in the factors with which they are abundantly endowed—for example, countries with a high capital-labor ratio will export capital-intensive goods. This model leads us to expect three things: First, trade should typically be between complementary countries—capital-abundant countries should trade with labor-abundant countries. Second, the composition of trade should reflect the sources of comparative advantage. Third, since trade is in effect an indirect way for countries to trade factors of production, it should have strong effects on income distribution—when a country trades capital-intensive exports for labor-intensive imports, its workers should end up worse off.

What empirical workers noticed in the 1960s was that trends in world trade did not seem to accord with these expectations. The largest and rapidly growing part of world trade was trade among the industrial countries, which seemed fairly similar in their factor endowments and were clearly becoming more similar over time. The trade between industrial countries was largely composed of two-way exchanges of fairly similar goods—so-called "intraindustry" trade. Finally, in several important episodes of rapid growth in trade—notably formation of the European Economic Community and the Canadian–U.S. auto pact—the distributional effects turned out to be much less noticeable than had been feared.

From the mid-1960s on, a number of researchers proposed a simple explanation of these observations. Trade among the industrial countries, they argued, was due not to comparative advantage but to economies of scale. Because of the scale economies there was an essentially arbitrary specialization by similar countries in the production of different goods, often of goods produced with the same factor intensities. This explained both why similar countries traded with each other and why they exchanged similar products. At the same time trade based on increasing returns rather than indirect exchange of factors need not have large income distribution effects. Thus introducing economies of scale as a determinant of trade seemed to resolve the puzzles uncovered by exmpirical work.

The problem, of course, was that at the time there was no good way to introduce economies of scale into a general equilibrium trade model. Without being embedded in a formal model, the theory of intraindustry trade could not become part of mainstream international economies. The crucial theoretical development thus came in the late 1970s, when new models of monopolistic competition were seen to allow a remarkably simple and elegant theory of trade in the presence of increasing returns. This marriage of industrial organization and trade was first proposed independently in papers by Dixit and Norman (1980), Krugman (1979), and Lacaster (1980). It was further extended by Helpman (1981), Krugman (1980, 1981), Ethier (1982), and others. Now that a number of years have gone into distilling the essentials of this approach, it is possible to describe in very compact form a basic monopolistic competition model of trade.

The Basic Model

Consider a world economy in which all countries share a common technology. There are two factors of production, capital and labor. These factors are employed in two sectors, Manufactures and Food.

Food we will take to be a homogeneous product, with a constant returns technology and thus a perfectly competitive market structure. Manufactures, however, we assume to consist of many differentiated products, subject to product-specific economies of scale. There is assumed to be a suitable choice of units such that all of the potential products can be made to look symmetric, with identical cost and demand functions. Further the set of potential products is assumed to be sufficiently large, and the individual products sufficiently small, that there exists a free-entry non-cooperative equilibrium with zero profits.

Much effort has gone into the precise formulation of product differentiation. Some authors, including Dixit and Norman (1980), Krugman (1979, 1980, 1981), and Ethier (1982) follow the Spence (1976) and Dixit-Stiglitz (1977) assumption that all products are demanded by each individual, and thus build product differentiation into the utility function. Others, including Lancaster (1980) and Helpman (1981), follow the Hotelling-Lancaster approach in which the demand for variety arises from diversity of tastes. The Hotelling-Lancaster formulation has the advantage of greater realism, and leads to somewhat more plausible formulation of the nature of the gains from trade. However, it is quite difficult to work with. The Spence-Dixit-Stiglitz approach, by contrast, while less convincing, lends itself quite easily to modelling. (A "rock-bottom" model of trade along these lines is given in the appendix.) Fortunately, it turns out that for the purposes of describing trade, it does not matter at all which approach we take. All we need is the result that equilibrium in the Manufactures sector involves the production of a large number of differentiated products and that all profits are competed away.

Now under certain circumstances, which will become clear shortly, international trade allows the world economy to become perfectly integrated, that is, to achieve the same outcome that would occur if all factors of production could work with each other freely. Associated with this integrated equilibrium outcome would be a set of resource allocations to the two sectors, goods prices, factor prices, and so on. Figure 14.1 represents some key features of such an equilibrium. The combined factor endowments

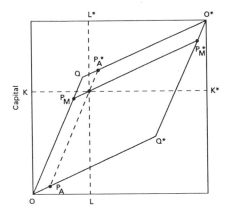

Figure 14.1

of two trading countries are shown as the sides of a box. With full employ-ment this endowment will be exhausted by the resources used in the two sectors. We let OQ be the resources used in Manufactures, and QO^* be the resources used in Food. Thus Manufactures is assumed to be capital-intensive.

Will trade actually lead to this integrated economy outcome? As Dixit and Norman (1980) have shown, the answer depends on whether it is possible to allocate the integrated economy's production among the trad-ing countries in such a way as to fully employ all factors of production while each country produces nonnegative amounts of every good. This has a simple geometric interpretation. Suppose that there are two countries, Home and Foreign. Let us measure Home's resources from the point O, and foreign's from O^*. Then the division of the world's resources among countries can be represented by a point in the box. If the endowment point is E, for example, this means that Home has a capital stock OK and a labor force OL, while Foreign has a capital stock O^*K^* and a labor force O^*L^*. Since E is above the diagonal, Home is capital abundant, and Foreign labor abundant.

What can we now say about the world's production? The answer is that as long as the resources are not divided too unequally—specifically, as long as E lies inside the parallelogram OQO^*Q^*—it is possible to repro-duce the production of the integrated economy without moving resources from one country to the other. We can determine the allocation of produc-tion between the countries by completing parallelograms. Thus Home will devote resources OP_M to Manufactures, OP_A to Food; Foreign will devote $O^*P_M^*$ and $O^*P_A^*$ to Manufactures and Food, respectively.

Now it is immediately apparent that a redistribution of resources from one country to another will have a strongly biased effect on the distribu-tion of world production. Suppose, for example, that Home were to have more capital and Foreign loss. Then it is clear that Home would produce more manufactures and *less* Food—a familiar result for trade theorists. It follows, given identical demand patterns, that capital-abundant Home will be a net exporter of manufactures and a net importer of Food. Thus at the level of *interindustry* trade flows conventional comparative advantage con-tinues to apply.

Where economies of scale and monopolistic competition enter the story is in *intra*industry specialization. When production of Manufactures is split between Home and Foreign, economies of scale will imply that output of each individual differentiated product is concentrated in one country or the other. Which country produces which products is indeterminate (in a fun-damental sense—see the appendix), but the important point is that within

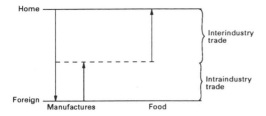

Figure 14.2

the Manufactures sector each country will be producing a different set of goods. Since each country is assumed to have diverse demand, the result will be that even a country that is a *net* exporter of Manufactures will still demand some imports of the manufactures produced abroad.

The resulting pattern of trade is illustrated in Figure 14.2. There will be two-way "intraindustry" trade within the manufacturing sector, as well as conventional interindustry trade. The former will in effect reflect scale economies and product differentiation, while the latter reflects comparative advantage. We can notice two points about this pattern of trade. First, even if the countries had identical resource mixes (i.e., if point E in figure 14.1 were on the diagonal), there will still be trade in manufactures, because of intraindustry specialization. Second, the more similar the countries are in their factor endowments, the more they will engage in intra- as opposed to interindustry trade.

Extensions of the Model

A number of authors have applied the monopolistic competition approach to models that attempt to capture more complex insights than the one we have just described. Many of these extensions are treated in Helpman and Krugman (1985); here I describe a few of the extensions briefly.

Intermediate Goods
Ethier (1982) has emphasized that much intraindustry trade is in reality in intermediate goods. Models that reflect this are Ethier (1982), Helpman (1984), and Helpman and Krugman (1985, ch. 11). As it turns out, this extension makes little difference.

Nontraded Goods
Helpman and Razin (1984) and Helpman and Krugman (1985, ch. 10) introduce nontraded goods into the model. Again, this doesn't make much

difference. The major new implication is that differences in the size of national markets can give rise to new incentives for factor mobility.

Market Size Effects

Krugman (1980), Helpman and Krugman (1985), and Venables (1985b) develop models in which transport costs make the size of the domestic market an important determinant of trade. Specifically, countries tend other things equal to export the products of industries for which they have large domestic markets.

Multinational Firms

Helpman (1985) and Helpman and Krugman (1985) develop models in which it is assumed that economies of scope and/or vertical integration lead to the emergence of multiactivity firms. Within the monopolistic competition framework it is then possible to let comparative advantage determine the location of activitites, allowing models that describe both trade and the extent of multinational enterprise.

Alternative Market Structures

Helpman and Krugman contains some efforts to extend the insights of the monopolistic competition model beyond the highly special Chamberlinian large-group market structure. The insights survive essentially intact when the structure is instead assumed to be one of "contestable markets" in the manner of Baumol, Panzar, and Willing (1982) (see Helpman and Krugman 1985, ch. 4). A much more qualified set of results occurs when the structure is instead assumed to be one of small-group oligopoly (see Helpman and Krugman 1985, chs. 5 and 7).

Evaluation

The monopolistic competition model has had a major impact on research into international trade. By showing that increasing returns and imperfect competition can make a fundamental difference to the way we think about trade, this approach was crucial in making work that applies industrial organization concepts to trade respectable. In effect, the monopolistic competition model was the thin end of the I-O/trade wedge.

From the point of view of I-O theorists, however, the monopolistic competition trade model may be the least interesting part of the new trade theory. In essence, theorists in this area have viewed imperfect competition as a nuisance variable in a story that is fundamentally about increasing returns. Thus the theory has little to teach us about industrial organization itself. By contrast, the other strand of the new trade theory is interested in increasing returns primarily as a cause of imperfect competition, and it is this imperfect competition that is the main story. Thus it is this second stand that will occupy the rest of this survey.

14.2   Protection and Domestic Market Power

Many economists have noted that international trade reduces the market power of domestic firms and have argued that conversely protection increases domestic market power. The interest of trade theorists has been centered on two extensions of this argument. First is the proposition that the effects of protection depend on the form it takes—specifically, that quantitative restrictions such as import quotas create more domestic market power than tariffs. This proposition was first demonstrated by Bhagwati (1965) in a model in which a domestic monopolist faces competitive foreign suppliers; only with recent work by Krishna (1984) has the analysis been extended to the case where both domestic and foreign firms are large agents. More recently still, Rotemberg and Saloner (1986) have argued that when collusive behaviour is backed by the threat of a breakdown of that collusion, import quotas may actually perversely increase competition.

The second proposition is that protection, by initially generating monopoly rents, generates excessive entry and thus leads to inefficiently small scale production. This proposition, originally proposed by Eastman and Stykolt (1960), is backed by substantial evidence and has been modeled by Dixit and Norman (1980).

Bhagwati's Model

Consider an industry in which one firm has a monopoly on domestic production but is subject to competition from price-taking foreign suppliers. Why the domestic market structure should differ from that in the rest of the world is left unexplained; presumably there are unspecified economies of scale that are large relative to the domestic market but not relative to the world market. Although economies of scale may explain the existence of the monopoly, the marginal cost curve is assumed to slope upward. Foreign supply is assumed, for simplicity, to be perfectly elastic (this differs slightly from Bhagwati, who allowed for upward-sloping foreign supply; nothing crucial hinges on the difference. Also Corden (1967) analyzed the

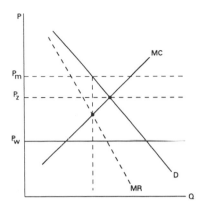

Figure 14.3

case when domestic marginal cost is downward sloping. In this case any tariff sufficient to establish the domestic firm also eliminates imports).

Figure 14.3 can be used to analyze the effects of tariffs in this model. In the figure D is the domestic demand curve facing the monopolist, MC the monopolist's marginal cost curve. P_W is the world price, namely, the price at which imports are supplied to the domestic market. P_Z is the price that would obtain if all domestic demand were supplied by the monopolist but the monopolist were to behave as a price-taker. P_m is the price the monopolist would charge if there were no import competition.

Consider first the case of free trade. The domestic firm cannot raise the price above P_W, so the profit-maximizing strategy is to set marginal cost equal to P_W, producing Q_0. In this case the monopolist has no monopoly power.

Now suppose the government imposes a tariff. The effect is to raise the price at which imports will come into the market. As long as the tariff-inclusive import price lies between P_W and P_Z, however, it remains true that the domestic firm acts like a price-taker, setting output where price equals marginal cost.

In a competitive industry a tariff that raised the import price to P_Z would be prohibitive, and any increase in the tariff beyond that level would have no effect—there would be "water in the tariff." Here the monopoly position of the domestic firm matters. A tariff that raises the price above P_Z allows the firm to raise its own price to the same level, something that will be profitable as long as the tariff price is below P_m. That is, even when no imports actually occur, the *threat* of imports keeps the monopolist from exercising its monopoly power fully, and raising an already prohibitive

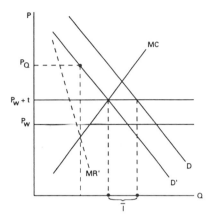

Figure 14.4

tariff therefore leads to domestic price increases. It also follows that such tariff increases actually *reduce* domestic output.

Now consider the effects of an import quota. In perfectly competitive models a quota is equivalent in its effects to a tariff that limits imports to the same level. Once we have domestic market power, however, an important difference emerges. A monopolist protected by a tariff cannot raise its price above the tariff-inclusive import price without losing the domestic market to imports. By contrast, a firm sheltered by quantitative restrictions need not fear increased imports and is free to exercise its market power. The result is that an import quota will lead to a higher domestic price and lower domestic output than an "equivalent" tariff, defined as a tariff that leads to the same level of imports.

Figure 14.4 illustrates the nonequivalence of tariffs and quotas. As before, D is the domestic demand curve, MC marginal cost, P_W the world price. We compare a tariff t that reduces imports to I, and an import quota that restricts imports to the same level.

With a tariff, the domestic firm simply sets marginal cost equal to $P_W + t$. With the equivalent quota, however, the firms now face the demand curve D^1, derived by subtracting I from the domestic demand curve D. Corresponding to D^1 is a marginal revenue curve MR^1. The profit-maximizing price with the quota is therefore P_Q; the quota leads to a higher price and lower output than the tariff.

Bhagwati's model produces a clear and compelling result. Better still, it yeilds a clear policy message: if you must protect, use a tariff rather than a quota. There are, however, two troubling features of the model. On is the asymmetry between domestic and foreign firms; we would like foreigners also to be modeled as imperfectly competitive. The other is the lack of any model of the process of entry that leads to imperfect competition. Both features have been the subject of recent research, the first most notably by Krishna (1984), and the second by Dixit and Norman (1980).

Krishna's Model

To get away from an arbitrary asymmetry between a domestic monopolist and price-taking foreign firms, it seems natural to examine a duopoly. We can let there be a single domestic firm that supplies the market with local production and a single foreign firm that exports to the market. collusion is of course possible, but as a modeling device we would prefer to assume noncooperative behavior. (For some possible implications of collusion, however, see below.)

In modeling noncooperative oligopolies, the choice of strategy variables is crucial. The two main alternatives are of course the Cournot approach, in which firms take each others' outputs as given, and the Bertrand approach, in which prices are taken as given. In analyzing the effects of protection, both approaches turn out to be problematic. The Cournot assumption fails to capture Bhagwati's insight regarding the difference between quotas and tariffs; the Bertrand assumption fails to yield a pure strategy equilibrium.

The problem with the Cournot approach may be simply stated. Bhagwati's model argued that a quota creates more market power than a tariff because the domestic firm knows that an increase in its price will lead to an increase in imports. In the Cournot approach, however, the domestic firm is assumed to take the level of imports as given in any case; so a quota and a tariff that leads to the same level of imports once again have equivalent effects on the domestic firm's behavior.

If Bhagwati's argument for a lack of equivalence between tariffs and quotas is right, however—and most international economists feel that it is—then this approach is missing an important insight. The alternative is a Bertrand approach. What Krishna shows is that this leads to unexpected complexities.

Krishna considers a market in which a domestic and foreign firm produce imperfect substitutes (an assumption that is necessary if Bertrand competition is not to collapse to marginal cost pricing). In the absence of quantitative trade restrictions, that is, either under free trade or with a tariff, Bertrand competition can be treated in a straightforward fashion. Each firm determines a profit-maximizing price given the other firm's price; given reasonable restrictions, we can draw two upward-sloping reaction functions whose intersection determines equilibrium.

But suppose that an import quota is imposed. This creates an immediate conceptual problem, which in turn leads to a problem in the understanding of equilibrium.

The conceptual problem is how to handle the possibility of excess demand. Suppose that at the prices set by the domestic and foreign firms, domestic consumers demand more foreign goods than the import quota allows. What happens? Krishna assumes, plausibly, that an unspecified group of middlemen collects the difference between the price charged by the foreign firm and the market-clearing consumer price. That is, incipient excess demand is reflected in an increased "dealer markup" rather than in rationing.

This now raises the next question, which is how to interpret Bertrand competition in this case. Which price does the domestic firm take as given, the foreign factory price or the dealer price? Here Krishna assumes, again sensibly, that the domestic firm takes the foreign factory price rather than the dealer price as given. This means that the domestic firm recognizes its ability to affect the consumer price of foreign substitutes when the import quota is binding.

But this seemingly innocuous assumption turns out to imply a basic discontinuity in the domestic firm's response function. The domestic firm in effect has two discrete pricing options: an "aggressive" option of charging a low price that limits imports to less than the quota, or a "timid" option of retreating behind the quota and charging a high price. A small rise in the foreign firm's price can shift the domestic firm's optimal response from "timid" to "aggressive".

Figure 14.5 illustrates the point. It shows the demand curve and the associated marginal revenue curve facing the domestic firm for a given foreign firm factory price. The price $\bar{p}$ is the price at which the quota becomes binding. That is, at a domestic firm price above $\bar{p}$ there is an incipient excess demand for imports, which is reflected in dealer markups that the domestic firm knows it can affect. By contrast, at prices below $\bar{p}$ the dealer price of imports is taken as given. That is, at prices below $\bar{p}$ the domestic firm takes the price of the imported substitute as given, whereas at prices above $\bar{p}$ it believes that increases in its own price will increase the price of the substitute as well. The result is a discontinuity in the slope of the perceived demand curve, which is steeper just above $\bar{p}$ than it is just

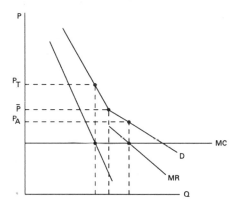

Figure 14.5

below and hence a discontinuity in the *level* of the marginal revenue curve, which jumps up at the quantity corresponding to $\bar{p}$.

What is clear from the figure is that there are two locally profit-maximizing domestic prices: the "timid" maximum p_T, and the "aggressive" maximum p_A. Which maximum is global depends on the price charged by the foreign firm. The profitablility of the timid option is unaffected by what the foreign firm does, but the higher the foreign price, the more profitable is the aggressive option.

The result is a home reaction function looking like *HH* in figure 14.6. At low levels of the foreign price p^*, the domestic retreats behind the quota and therefore chooses a price locally independent of p^*. At a sufficiently high p^*, however, the domestic firm abruptly sallies out from behind the quota with a cut in its price.

The foreign best response function *FF* has no such discontinuity. However, if the quota matters at all, *FF* must, as shown, pass right through the hole in *HH*! Thus no pure strategy equilibrium exists.

A mixed strategy equilibrium does exist. If the foreign firm charges p_E^*, the home firm is indifferent between p_T and p_A; by randomizing its choice of p_A and p_T with the right probabilities, the home firm can induce its competitor to choose p_E^*.

In this mixed strategy equilibrium we notice that the foreign firm, despite its monopoly power, does not always raise its price enough to capture all of the quota rents, a result in contrast to conventional wisdom. We can also note that with some probability the quota will fail to be binding, in the sense that imports are strictly less than the quota—yet both

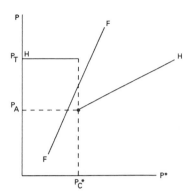

Figure 14.6

domestic and foreign prices are unambiguously higher even in this case than under free trade.

A point stressed by Krishna is that in this duopoly case a quota can easily raise the proftis of *both* firms. Consider, for example, a quota that only restricts imports not to exceed their free trade level. Clearly, if the domestic firm charges p_T, it is because this is more profitable than the free trade price, while the foreign firm will sclll the same output as under free trade, yet at a higher price. On the other hand, if the domestic firm charges p_A, this "aggressive" price is still above the free trade price, so the foreign firm must be earning higher profits. (The domestic firm of course earns the same in both states.) So profitability of both firms increases unambiguously.

Protection versus Collusion

Almost all theoretical work on industrial organization/trade issues assumes that firms act noncooperatively. In industrial organization theory itself, however, there has recently been a drift toward taking the possibility of collusive behavior more seriously. Key to this drift has been the recognition that collusive behavior may be individually rational in an indefinitely repeated game, where each player believes that his failure to play cooperatively today will lead to noncooperative behavior by others tomorrow. The influential experimental work of Axelrod (1983) suggests that reasonable strategies by individuals will indeed lead to cooperative outcomes in a variety of circumstances.

Recently, Davidson (1984) and Rotemberg and Saloner (1986) have proposed analyses of the effects of protection on collusion that seem to stand Bhagwati on his head. They argue that precisely because protection tends to raise profitability in the absence of collusion, it reduces the penalty for cheating on a collusive agreement. By thus reducing the prospects for collusion, the protection actually increases competition.

The case is clearest for an import quota, analyzed by Rotemberg and Saloner. To understand their argument, consider Krishna's model again, but now suppose that the two firms attempt to agree on prices higher than the noncooperative level. Suppose also that the only enforcement mechanism for their agreement is the belief of each firm that if it cheats this period, the other firm will thenceforth play noncooperatively. Then collusion will succeed only if the extra profits gained by cheating now are more than offset by the present discounted value of the profits that will subsequently be lost by the collapse of collusion. A viable price-fixing agreement must therefore set prices low enough to make cheating unappealing.

But as we saw in our discussion of Krishna's model, a quota can actually raise the profitability of both firms in noncooperative equilibrium. This paradoxically makes collusion more difficult to sustain, by reducing the penalty for cheating. If the firms manage to collude nonetheless, they may be forced to agree on lower prices in order to make their collusion sustainable. So in this case an import quota actually leads to more competition and lower prices than free trade!

Davidson considers the case of a tariff that raises the noncooperative profits of the domestic firm but lowers that of the foreign competitor. If the result is to encourage the domestic firm to cheat, the tariff will likewise increase competition.

It remains to be seen whether this argument will shake the orthodox presumption that protection is bad for competition. The modeling of collusive behavior is still in its infancy. To me, at least, the approach taken in this new line of work seems an odd mix of ad-hoc assumptions about retaliation with hyperrational calculations by firms about the consequences of such retaliation. Yet the argument is profoundly unsettling, which means that if must be valuable (though not that it must be right!).

Protection and Excessive entry

In the 1950s, during the honeymoon period of import-substituting industrialization strategies, it was often argued that economies of scale in production provided an argument for protection—a view with a lineage going back to Frank Graham. At first, the point seems obvious: protection raises the sales of domestic firms, and thus allows them to slide down their average cost curves. In an influential paper, however, Eastman and Stykolt (1960) argued that often the reverse is true. In their view, bolstered by an appeal to Canadian experience, protection typically leads to a smaller scale of production and thus reduced efficiency.

The Eastman-Stykolt view was not couched in terms of an explicit model. Basically, however, they considered the typical case to be that where the number of firms permitted by economies of scale is more than one but small enough to allow effective collusion. Such a collusive industry will seek to raise its price to monopoly levels unless constrained by foreign competition. A tariff or quota will thus lead initially to higher prices and profits. The long-run result, however, will be entry of new firms into the industry. If integer constraints do not bind too much, this entry will eliminate profits by driving scale down and average cost up. Thus the effect of protection is to create a proliferation of inefficiently small producers. Such proliferation is indeed one of the favorite horror stories of critics of protection in less-developed countries, with the history of the Latin American auto industry the classic case.

This original version of the inefficient entry problem depended on the assumption of collusion among domestic producers. The problem could, however, arise even with noncooperative behavior, as is clear from a model offered by Dixit and Norman (1980). They show that in a Cournot market with free entry, expanding the size of the market leads to a less than proportional increase in the number of firms and to a fall in average cost. Since international trade in effect links together national markets into a larger world market, it would have the same result. Protection, on the other hand, fragments the world market and hence leads to a proliferation of firms and a rise in costs.

We will return to the inefficient entry problem below. It plays a key role in the debate over "strategic" trade policy and is also central to some attempts to quantify the effects of trade policy.

Evaluation

The basic Bhagwati model of protection and market power is admirably clear and simple, and has been in circulation for long enough to have percolated into practical policy analysis. Market power analysis along Bhagwati's lines has become part of the book of analytical recipes used by the International Trade Commission (Rousslang and Suomeia 1985). Market power considerations have now and then helped dictate the form taken by protection; for example, the trigger price mechanism on steel during the

Carter administration was deliberately designed to minimize the effect of protection on the monopoly power of both domestic and foreign firms. And perceptions of the impact of trade policy on market power seem to be playing a role in antitrust decisions: in the steel industry, for example, it appears that the Justice Department appreciates that foreign competition is less effective a discipline than import penetration would suggest thanks to import quotas and voluntary export restraints.

More sophisticated models have yet to find application. It is at this point hard to see how Krishna's model might be made operational, let alone the inverted logic of the collusion models. The one exception is the excess entry story, which as we will see is the central element in Harris and Cox's (1984) effort to quantify the effect of protection on Canada's economy.

14.3   Price Discrimination and Dumping

The phenomenon of "dumping"—selling exports at less than the domestic price—has long been a major concern of trade legislation. It is also self-evidently an imperfect competition issue. It is therefore not suprising that the new literature on trade and I-O sheds some further light on dumping as a particular case of price discrimination. More surprising, perhaps, is the fact that the new literature on dumping actually identifies a new explanation of international trade, distinct from both comparative advantage and economies of scale.

Much as in the case of protection and market power, the initial insight here comes from an asymmetric model in which a domestic monopolist confronts price-taking foreign firms. This insight becomes both enlarged and transformed when rival oligopolists are introduced. Finally, the welfare effects of trade based on dumping are of some interest.

An Asymmetric Model

An extemely simple model of dumping is presented by Caves and Jones (1985) and illustrated in figure 14.7. As in the case of protection and market power, a single domestic monopolist is assumed to face a given world price P_W. We now, however, reverse the assumptions about the possibilities for trade. Before, we let the firm face import competition while disregarding the possibility of exports. Now we assume that the domestic market is somehow closed to imports, while allowing the domestic firm to export.

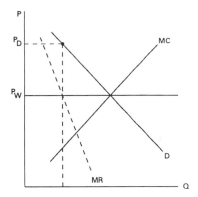

Figure 14.7

In the figure I have drawn a particular case, where with a price-taking domestic firm there would be neither imports nor exports. If the domestic firm acts as a monopolist, however, it will want to set marginal revenue equal to marginal cost in both the domestic and the foreign markets. Marginal revenue on the foreign market is, however, just P_W, so the profit-maximizing solution is the one illustrated. The firm sets a domestic price above P_W, yet it exports, "dumping" on the world market where additional sales do not depress the price received on inframarginal units.

Three points should be noted about this example. The first is that while for simplicity it has been assumed that P_W is given, this is not essential. What is important is that the firm perceives itself as facing a higher elasticity of demand on exports than on domestic sales. That is, dumping is simply international price discrimination.

Second, the figure illustrates a case in which a price-taking domestic firm would not export—in the usual sense of the term, the domestic industry has neither a comparative advantage nor a comparative disadvantage. Yet the firm does in fact export. Clearly we could have an industry that has at least some comparative *disadvantage* and yet dumps in the export market. In other words, dumping can make trade run "uphill" against conventional determinants of its direction.

Third, the difference between the domestic and foreign markets remains unexplained. Why should the domestic firm be a price-setter at home, a price-taker abroad (or more generally, face more elastic demand for exports)? We would like to have a model in which this asymmetry is derived, rather than built in by assumption. In the new I-O trade literature, such models have finally emerged.

Brander's Model

A duopoly model of dumping was developed by Brander (1981), and elaborated on by Brander and Krugman (1983). This model goes to the opposite extreme from the asymmetrical model we just described, by postulating instead a perfectly symmetrical situation. We assume that some good is consumed in two countries, each of which has the same demand, and we assume that there is a single firm in each country and that the two firms have identical costs. There is some positive cost of transporting the good internationally so that in a perfect competition setting there would be no trade.

If the transport costs are not too large, however, and if the firms behave in a Cournot fashion, trade will nevertheless result. To see why, consider figure 14.8, which illustrates what would happen in the absence of trade. We see each firm acting as a monopolist, and thus each country having a price that exceeds marginal costs. The firms do not expand their output, however, because this would depress the price on inframarginal units.

But suppose that the markup over marginal cost exceeds the transport cost between the markets. In this case each firm will have an incentive to absorb the transport cost so as to export to the other's home market. The reason is that an extra unit sold abroad, even though it yields a price net of transportation less than a unit sold domestically, does not depress the price of inframarginal sales (it depresses the price the other firm receives instead). So as long as price less transportation exceeds marginal cost, it is worth exporting.

The result is a mutual interpenetration of markets, described by Brander and Krugman as "reciprocal dumping." With Cournot behavior, equilibrium

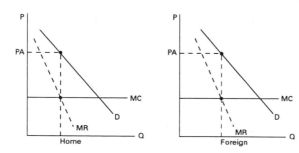

Figure 14.8

will take the following form: each firm will have a larger share of its home market than the foreign market and will thus perceive itself as facing a higher elasticity of demand abroad than at home. The difference in perceived elasticity of demand will be just enough to induce firms to absorb transport costs. The result will therefore be a determinate volume of "cross-hauling": two-way trade in the same product. In the symmetric example considered, this pointless trade will be balanced.

From a trade theorist's point of view, this result is startling: here we have international trade occurring despite a complete absence of comparative advantage and without even any direct role for economies of scale (although an indirect role can be introduced if we suppose that increasing returns is the explanation of oligopoly). From an industrial organization point of view, the result may not seem quite so outlandish, since it bears a family resemblance to the theory of basing-point pricing (Smithies 1942). Nonetheless, the trade-theorist's approach offers the new possibility of an explicit welafare analysis.

Reciprocal Dumping and Welfare

Reciprocal dumping is a totally pointless form of trade—the same good is shipped in both directions, and real resources are wasted in its transportation. Nonetheless, the trade is not necessarily harmful. International competition reduces the monopoly distortion in each market, and the procompetitive effect can outweigh the resource waste.

The welfare effects of reciprocal dumping are illustrated in figure 14.9. Since the countries are assumed to be symmetric, looking at only one

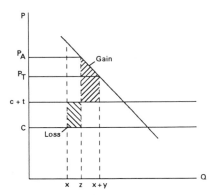

Figure 14.9

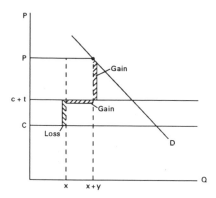

Figure 14.10

market will do. We note two effects. First, some of the exports that are dumped in each country are a net addition to consumption. In the figure this is represented as an increase of total deliveries from an initial level z to the level $x + y$. Since the initial price P_A exceeds marginal cost c plus transportation cost t, this represents a net gain and can be equated with the pro-competitive effect. On the other side, some of the imports displace domestic production for the domestic market. This is represented as a fall of deliveries from the domestic firm to its own market from z to x, with the quantity y both imported and exported. Since this involves a waste of resources on transportation, this constitutes a loss. From the diagram it seems impossible to tell whether the net effect is a gain or a loss.

We know, however, that in one case at least there must be a gain. If transport costs are zero, cross-hauling may be pointless but it is also costless, and the procompetitive effect yields gains. Presumably this remains true for transport costs sufficiently low.

This suggests that we examine how welfare changes as we vary transport costs. Consider the effects of a small reduction in transport costs, illustrated in figure 14.10. There will be three effects. First, there will be a direct reduction in the cost of transporting the initial level of shipments—a clear gain. Second, there will be an increase in consumption, which will be a gain to the extent that the initial price exceeds marginal cost plus transportation cost. Third, there will be a displacement of local production by imports, which will be a loss by the change times the initial transport cost.

Can we sign the total effect? We can do so in two cases: First, suppose that transport costs are near zero. Then the last effect is negligible, and a reduction in transport is clearly beneficial.

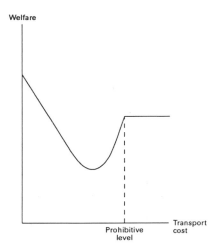

Figure 14.11

More interestingly, suppose that initially transport costs are almost large enough to prohibit trade. Recalling our discussion above, this will be a situation where price is only slightly above marginal cost plus transport and where the volume of trade is very small. This means that when transport costs are near the prohibitive level, the two sources of gain from a small decline in these costs become negligible, and a decline in transport costs thus reduces welfare.

Putting these results together, what we see is the relationship illustrated in figure 14.11. If transport costs are high, but not high enough to prevent trade, trade based solely on dumping leads to losses. If they are low, trade is beneficial.

Evaluation

The new literature on dumping has so far been resolutely nonpolicy and nonempirical. Still, nothing that suggests a previously unsuspected explanation of international trade can be dismissed as without importance. Furthermore the modeling techniques developed in the dumping literature are beginning to find at least some application. As we will see, attempts to calibrate models to actual data have so far relied on assumptions that bear a clear family resemblance to those introduced by Brander and Brander and Krugman.

14.4   Strategic Trade Policy

One of the most controversial ideas of the new I-O/trade literature has been the suggestion that government intervention can raise national welfare by shifting oligopoly rents from foreign to domestic firms. The starting point of this debate was several papers by Brander and Spencer (1983, 1985), who showed that in principle government policies such as export subsidies can serve the same purpose as, for example, investment in excess capacity in the I-O literature on entry deterrence. That is, government policies can serve the "strategic" purpose of altering the subsequent incentives of firms, acting as a deterrent to foreign competitors. The "strategic" analysis seems to offer a possible rationale for trade policies, such as export subsides, that have been almost universally condemned by international economists in the past.

The Brander-Spencer analysis, coming at a time of heated debate over U.S. international competitiveness, appears dangerously topical, and other economists have been quick to challenge the robustness of their results. The critiques are themselves of considerable analytic interest. In this survey I consider four important lines of research suggested by the critique of Brander-Spencer strategic trade policy: First is the dependence of trade policy recommendations on the nature of competition between firms, analyzed by Eaton and Grossman (1986). Second is the general equilibrium issue raised by the fact that industries must compete for resources within a country, analyzed by Dixit and Grossman (1984). Third is the question of entry, studied by Horstmann and Markusen (1986) and Dixit (1989). Finally is the question of who is behaving strategically with respect to whom, analyzed by Dixit and Kyle (1985).

The Brander-Spencer Analysis

As is often the case in the I-O/trade literature, the initial insight in strategic trade policy was obtained by subtraction rather than addition: by simplifying a trade issue to a form where a familiar model of imperfect competition can be easily applied.

Consider an industry in which there are only two firms, each in one country. The clever simplification that Spencer and Brander suggest is to assume that neither country has any domestic demand for the industry's products. Instead, both countries export to a third market. Also distortions other than the presence of monopoly power in this industry are ruled out—namely, the marginal cost of each firm is also the social cost of the

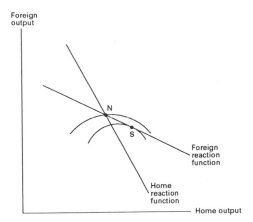

Figure 14.12

resources it uses. The result is that for each country national welfare can be identified with the profits earned by its firm.

Since the firms are themselves attempting to maximize profits, one might imagine that there is no case for government intervention. However, this is not necessarily the case. To see why, we assume for now that the two firms compete in Cournot fashion; we illustrate their competition with figure 14.12.

Each firm's reaction function will, for reasonable restrictions on cost and demand, slope down, and the home firm's reaction function will be steeper than its competitor's. Point N is the Nash equilibrium. Drawn through point N is one of the home firm's isoprofit curves. Given that the reaction function is constructed by maximizing Home's profits at each level of Foreign output, the isoprofit curve is flat at point N.

Now it is apparent that the Home firm could do better than at point N if it could only somehow commit itself to produce more than its Cournot output. Indeed, if the Home firm could precommit itself to any level of output, while knowing that the Foreign firm would revise its own plans optimally, the outcome could be driven to the Stackleberg point S. The problem is that there is no good reason to assign the leadership role to either firm. If no way to establish a commitment exists, the Nash outcome is what will emerge.

What Spencer and Brander pointed out was that a government policy could serve the purpose of making a commitment credible. Suppose that the Home government establishes an export subsidy for this industry. This subsidy will shift the Home reaction function to the right, and thus the outcome will shift southeast along the Foreign reaction function. Because the subsidy has the deterrent effect of reducing Foreign exports, the profits of the home firm will rise by *more* than the amount of the subsidy. Thus Home national income will rise. The optimal export subsidy is of course one that shifts the reaction function out just enough to achieve the Stackleberg point S.

It is possible to elaborate considerably on this basic model. Most notably, we can imagine a multistage competitive process, in which firms themselves attempt to establish commitments through investment in capital or R&D. In these models, considered in Brander and Spencer (1983), optimal policies typically involve subsidies to investment as well as exports. The basic point remains the same, however. Government policy "works" in these models for the same reason that investing in excess capacity works in entry deterrence models, because it alters the subsequent game in a way that benefits the domestic firm.

The Nature of Competition

Eaton and Grossman (1986) have argued forcefully that the argument for strategic trade policy is of limited use because the particular policy recommendation depends critically on details of the model. In particular, they show that the Brander-Spencer case for export subsidies depends on the assumption of Cournot competition. With other assumptions the result may go away or even be reversed.

To see this, suppose instead that we have Bertrand competition, with firms taking each others' prices as given. (As in our discussion of import quotas above, we must assume the the two firms are producing differentiated products if the model is not to collapse to perfect competition.) Then the reaction function diagram must be drawn in price space.

Figure 14.13 shows the essentials. Each firm's best responses describe a reaction function that is upward sloping. With reasonable restrictions, Home's curve is steeper than Foreign's. The Nash equilibrium is at N, and the home isoprofit curve passing through N is flat at that point.

The crucial point is that now Home can increase its profits only by moving northeast along the Foreign reaction function. That is, it must persuade Foreign to charge a *higher* price than at the Nash equilibrium. To do this, it must commit to a higher price than will ex post be optimal. To achieve this, what the government must do is impose, not an export subsidy, but an export *tax*!

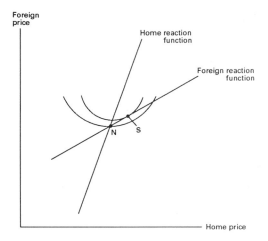

Figure 14.13

So what Eaton and Grossman show is that replacing the Cournot with a
Bertrand assumption reverses the policy recommendation. Given the shaki-
ness of any characterization of oligopoly behavior, this is not reassuring.

Eaton and Grossman go further by embedding both Cournot and Bertrand
in a general conjectural variations formulation. The result is of course that
anything can happen. One case that these authors emphasize is that of
"rational" conjectures, where the conjectures actually match the slope of
the reaction functions (a case that I do not find particularly interesting, given
the problems of the conjectural variation approach in general). In this case,
not too surprisingly, free trade turns out to be the optimal policy.

Competition for Resources

Dixit and Grossman (1984) offer a further critique of the case for stratgeic
trade policy based on the partial equilibrium character of the models. Their
point may be made as follows: an export subsidy works in the Brander-
Spencer model essentially by lowering the marginal cost faced by the
domestic exporter. Foreign firms, seeing this reduced marginal cost, are
deterred from exporting as much as they otherwise would have, and this is
what leads to a shifting of profits. But in general equilibrium an export
industry can expand only by bidding resources away from other domestic
industries. An export subsidy, though it lowers marginal cost in the targeted
industry, will therefore raise marginal cost in other sectors. Thus in industries that are not targeted, the effect will be the reverse of deterrence.

Dixit and Grossman construct a particualr tractable example where a group of industries must compete for a single common factor, "scientists." An export subsidy to one of these sectors necessarily forces a contraction in all the others. As we might expect, such a subsidy raises national income only if the deterrent effect on foreign, competition is higher in the subsidized sector than in the sectors that are crowded out. As the authors show, to evaluate the desirability of a subsidy now requires detailed knowledge not only of the industry in question but of all the industries with which it competes for resources. Their conclusion is that the likelihood that sufficient information will be available is small.

Entry

The strategic trade policy argument hinges on the presence of supernormal profits over which countries can compete. Yet one might expect that the possibility of entry will limit and perhaps eliminate these profits. If so, then even in oligopolistic industries the bone of contention may be too small to matter.

Horstmann and Markusen (1986) have analyzed the Brander-Spencer argument when there is free entry by firms. The number of firms in equilibrium is limited by fixed costs, but they abstract from the integer problem. The result of allowing entry is to restore the orthodox argument against export subsidy, in a strong form: *all* of a subsidy is absorbed either by reduced scale or worsened terms of trade, and thus constitutes a loss from the point of view of the subsidizing country.

Dixit (1989) is concerned with a more dynamic version of the same problem. He notes that in industries characterized by technological uncertainty, there will be winners and losers. The winners—who will actually make up the industry—will appear to earn supernormal profits, but this will not really indicate the presence of excess returns. Ex ante, an investment, say, in R&D, may be either a winner or a loser so that the costs of those who did not make it should also be counted. Dixit develops a technology race model of international competition in a single industry and shows that in such an industry high profits among the winners of the race do not offer the possibility of successful strategic trade policy.

A Larger Game?

The Brander-Spencer analysis assumes that the government, in effect, can commit itself to a trade policy before firms make their decisions. They also leave aside the possible reactions of foreign governments. Yet a realistic analysis would surely recognize that firms also make strategic moves designed to affect government decisions, and that governments must contend with the possibility of foreign reactions. Many of the ramifications of these larger games have been explored by Dixit and Kyle (1985).

To see what difference this extension makes, consider two cases. First, suppose that there is a firm that faces the following situation: it can commit itself to produce by making an irreversible investment. Once this cost is sunk, it will be socially optimal to provide the Brander-Spencer export subsidy, and with this subsidy the firm will find that its entry was justified. From a social point of view, however, it would have been preferable for the firm not to have entered at all.

In this case what is clear is that if the firm can move first, the government will find itself obliged to provide the subsidy. Yet it would have been better off if it could have committed itself not to provide the subsidy, and thus deterred the undesirable entry. The possibility of an export subsidy, though it raises welfare *given* entry, in the end is counterproductive. The government would have been better off if it had never heard of Brander and Spencer, or had a constitutional prohibition against listening to them.

Alternatively, consider the case of two countries, both able to pursue Brander-Spencer policies. It is certainly possible that both countries may be worse off as the result of a subsidy war, yet they will find themselves trapped in a Prisoner's Dilemma.

The point of the extended game analysis, then, is that even though interventionist policies may be shown to be locally desirable, it may still be in the country's interest that the use of such policies be ruled out.

Evaluation

Strategic trade policy is, without doubt, a clever insight. From the beginning, however, it has been clear that the attention received by that insight has been driven by forces beyond the idea's intellectual importance. The simple fact is that there is a huge external market for challenges to the orthodoxy of free trade. Any intellectually respectable case for interventionist trade policies, however honestly proposed—and the honesty of Brander and Spencer is not in question—will quickly find support for the wrong reasons. At the same time the profession of international economics has a well developed immune system designed precisely to cope with these outside pressures. This immune system takes the form of an immediate intensely critical scrutiny of any idea that seems to favor protectionism. So

Brander-Spencer attracted both more attention and more critical review than would normally have been the case.

That said, *does* the marriage of trade and I-O offer an important new case for protectionism? To answer this, we must go beyond the Brander-Spencer analysis of export competition to consider a wider range of models.

14.5   A New Case for Protection?

To the extent that the I-O/trade linkage offers any new comfort to protectionists, it takes the form of four not wholly distinct arguments: First is the possibility that trade policy can be used to extract rent from foreign monopolists. Second is the potential for shifting rent from foreign to domestic firms. Third is the possible use of protectionist policies as a way to get firms further down their average cost curves. Last is the use of protection to promote additional entry, where this is desirable.

Extracting Rent from Foreigners

The possibility of using a tariff to extract gains from a foreign monopolist has been emphasized in two papers by Brander and Spencer (1981, 1984). In its simplest version their analysis considers a foreign monopolist selling to the domestic market without any domestic competition. They point out that under a variety of circumstances a tariff will be partly absorbed by the foreign firm rather than passed onto domestic consumers. For example, suppose that demand is linear and that a specific tariff is imposed: then only half of the tariff will be passed on in prices, with the rest coming out of the firm's markup.

This observation suggests a terms-of-trade justification for tariffs similar to the traditional optimum tariff argument. The difference is that there is no requirement that the tariff-imposing country be large relative to world markets. As long as the foreign seller is charging a price above marginal cost, and as long as it is able to discriminate between the domestic market and other markets, it will be possible for a tariff to lower prices.

In one extension of their analysis, Brander and Spencer go on to consider the case where the foreign firm is attempting to deter entry by a potential domestic competitor. They follow an early Dixit model in which the incumbent firm does this by setting a limit output high enough that if it were to be maintained postentry, this entry would be unprofitable. (In Dixit's model the potential entrant is assumed to believe that the incumbent firm will maintain its preentry output, even though it would not be profit-mazimizing to carry out this threat ex post. Such ad-hoc entry deterrence models are now unfashionable, but this paper was written before Dixit acquired enlightenment and became (subgame) perfect.) The result in this case is that any tariff low enough that the limit-pricing strategy is maintained will be wholly absorbed by the foreign firm.

Rent-Shifting

Clearly a tariff can give domestic firms a strategic advantage in the domestic market, in the same way that export subsidies can give them an advantage in foreign markets. Welfare assessment of strategic tariff policy is, however, complicated by the need to worry about domestic consumers. What Brander and Spencer (1984) point out, however, is that rent shifting will generally reinforce rent extraction. That is, if in the absence of domestic competitors a tariff would be partly absorbed by foreign firms; the presence of domestic competitors will reinforce the case for a tariff.

Reducing Marginal Cost

In Krugman (1984a) it is pointed out that protection of the domestic market can serve as a form of export promotion. The model is a variant of Brander and Krugman (1983), where two firms interpenetrate each others' home markets through reciprocal dumping. Instead of constant marginal cost, however, each firm has downward-sloping marginal cost. Suppose now that one firm receives protection in its home market. The immediate result will be that it sells more and the other firm less. This will reduce the home firm's marginal cost, while raising its competitor's cost; this will in turn have the indirect effect of increasing the Home firm's sales in the unprotected foreign market. In the end "import protection is export promotion": protection of the home market actually leads to a rise in exports. The same results obtain when the economies of scale are dynamic rather than static, arising, for example, from R&D or a learning curve.

Is this policy desirable from the point of view of the protecting country? We can surmise that it might be because it is in effect a strategic export policy of the kind with which we are now familiar. A numerical example in Krugman (1984b) shows at least that such a policy could be worth carrying out—if there is no retaliation.

Prompting Entry

Venables (1985a) considers another variant of the Brander-Krugman model in which marginal cost is constant, but there are fixed costs. This time, however, he allows free entry and waives integer constraints on the number of firms. He now asks what the effects of a small tariff imposed by one country would be.

It is immediately apparent that such a tariff would raise the profitability of domestic firms and lower the profitability of foreign, leading to entry on one side and exit on the other. This makes the home market more competitive, and the foreign market less competitive. What Venables is able to show, surprisingly, is that for a small tariff this indirect effect on competition has a stronger effect on prices than the direct effect of the tariff itself. The price of the protected good will *fall* in the country that imposes the tariff, while rising in the rest of the world!

To understand this result, first note the first-order condition for a firm's deliveries to each market:

$$p + x\left(\frac{dp}{dx}\right) = c,$$

where x is the firm's deliveries to the market and c is marginal cost. In a Cournot model dp/dx as perceived by the firm will be the slope of the market demand curve and thus will itself be a function of the market price p. Thus x will be a function of p, as will the revenues earned by the firm in that market.

Since everything is a function of p, we can write the zero-profit condition that must hold with free entry as a function of p and of p^*, the price in the foreign market. In figure 14.14 the schedule HH represents the combinations of p and p^* consistent with zero profits for a representative firm

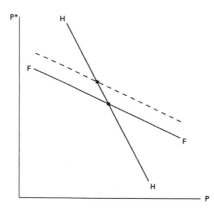

Figure 14.14

producing in Home, FF the zero-profit locus for a firm producing in Foreign. In the presence of transport costs it will ordinarily be true that HH is steeper than FF, that is, Home firms are relatively more affected by the Home price than Foreign firms. A free entry equilibrium will occur when both zero-profit conditions are satisfied.

Now suppose that a tariff is imposed by Home. The zero-profit locus for Home firms will not be affected, but Foreign firms will face increased costs on shipment to Home. They will have to receive a higher price in at least one market to make up for this, so FF shifts out. We now see Venables' result: the price in Home must actually fall, while that in Foreign rises.

The welfare calculation is now straightforward. Profits are not an issue, because of free entry. Consumers are better off in the protecting country. And there is additional government revenue as well.

Evaluation

The new literature on I-O and trade certainly calls into question the traditional presumption that free trade is optimal. Whether it is a practical guide to productive protectionism is another matter. The models described here are all quite special cases; small variations in assumptions can no doubt reverse the conclusions, as was the case in the Brander-Spencer model of export competition.

It may be questioned whether our understanding of how imperfectly competitive industries actually behave will ever be good enough for us to make policy prescriptions with confidence. What is certain is that purely theoretical analyses will not be enough. Until very recently, there was essentially no quantification of the new ideas in trade theory. In the last two years, however, there have been a handful of preliminary attempts to put numbers into the models. I conclude with a discussion of these efforts.

14.6   Quantification

Efforts to quantify the new theoretical models have been of three kinds. First have been econometric studies of some of the aggregate predictions of the intraindustry trade model described in section 14.1. Second, and most recent, have been efforts to "calibrate" theoretical models to fit the facts of particular industries. Finally, and most ambitiously, Harris and Cox have attempted to introduce industrial organization considerations into a general equilibrium model of the Canadian economy.

Testing the Intraindustry Trade Model

The empirical analysis of intraindustry trade, in such studies as that by Grubel and Lloyd (1975), long predates the monopolistic competition theory described in this survey. Without a theoretical base, however, discussion of intraindustry trade often seemed confused. Only once formal models became available was it possible for empirical workers to concentrate on propositions derived from these models.

Two studies focus on the most direct proposition, that the proportion of intraindustry as opposed to interindustry trade should be positively correlated with the degree of similarity between countries' capital–labor ratios. Loertscher and Wolter (1980) use differences in per capita income as a proxy for differences in resource endowments and confirm the correlation using a cross section for a single year. Helpman (1985) uses a more extended data set to confirm the proposition over a number of years; he also shows that as the industrial countries became more similar over time the relative importance of intraindustry trade grew, just as the model would suggest.

Havrylyshyn and Civan (1984) study a proposition that is less clearly implied by the model, but in the same spirit: namely, that intraindustry trade is likely to be more prevalent in the trade between advanced countries than in trade among LDCs, on the presumption that advanced countries produce more differentiated products. They find that this is, indeed, the case.

These regression studies suffer from a common problem of lack of congruence between the data and the concepts in the theoretical model. In the theory an "industry" is a group of products produced with similar factor intensities, so that trade within an industry cannot be explained by conventional comparative advantage. Whether this concept of an industry has anything to do with a three-digit Standard International Trade Classification category—the unit to which the analysis is in each case applied—is anybody's guess. What is clear is that the data do not provide a very good correspondence to the theorectical concept.

Calibrated Models

The newest development in the I-O/trade field is the attempt to quantify models by calibrating them to data from actual industries. This style of analysis seems likely to grow, and needs a name; for now we may call these studies Industrial Policy Exercises Calibrated to Actual Cases (IPECACs).

The pioneering work here is Dixit's (1988) model of the auto industry. The U.S. auto market is represented as a noncooperative oligopoly, with foreign autos differentiated from domestic. Demand functions are derived from published studies; constant terms and cost parameters are derived from actual industry data. In order to make the model fit, Dixit is also obliged to adopt a conjectural variations approach, with the conjectures derived in the process of calibrating the model.

Once the model is calibrated, it is possible to perform policy experiments on it. In particular, Dixit calculated the optimal trade policy when a tariff is the only available instrument, and the optimal trade-*cum*-industrial policy when a production subsidy is also available. He finds that a modest tariff is in fact justified, for the reasons we described above. The gains from this optimal tariff are, however, fairly small. When a production subsidy is allowed, the additional role for a tariff is greatly reduced, with the gains from adding tariffs as an instrument extremely small.

A model similar in spirit but quite different in detail is Baldwin and Krugman (1988), which studies the competition in 16K Random Access Memories. The model is a variant of Krugman (1984a), with strong learning-by-doing providing the increasing returns. As in the Dixit analysis the model's parameters are partly drawn from other published studies and partly estimated by calibrating the model to actual data. Also as in Dixit's study it proves necessary to adopt a conjectural variations approach in order to match the observed industry structure.

In the Baldwin-Krugman analysis the policy experiment is a historical counterfactual. How would the competition in 16K RAMs have been different if the Japanese market, which appears to have been de facto closed to imports, had been open? The model yields a striking result: instead of being substantial net exporters, the Japanese firms would not even have been able to compete in their own home market. Thus import protection was export promotion with a vengeance.

The welfare implications of this counterfactual can also be computed. According to the model Japanese market closure, although it succesfully promoted exports, did not benefit Japan. Because Japanese firms appear to have had inherently higher costs than their U.S. rivals, market closure was a costly policy that hurt both the United States and Japan.

At the time of writing, the only other IPECAC is a study by Venables and Smith (1986). They apply methods that combine those of the Dixit and Baldwin-Krugman papers, as well as an interesting formulation of multi-model competition, to study the U.K. refrigerator and footwear industries. The results are also reminiscent to some degree of both other studies:

modest tariffs are welfare improving, and protection has strong export-promoting effects.

The calibrated trade models are all this point rather awkward constructs. They rely on ad-hoc assumptions to close gaps in the data, and they rely to an uncomfortable degree on conjectural variations—an approach that each of the papers denounces even as it is adopted. To some extent the results of this literature so far might best be regarded as numerical examples informed by the data rather than as studies that are seriously meant to capture the behavior of particular industries. Nonetheless, the confrontation with data does lend a new sense of realism and empirical discipline to the I-O/trade literature.

General Equilibrium

The most ambitious attempt to apply industrial organization to trade policy analysis is the attempt by Harris and Cox to develop a general equilibrium model of Canada with increasing returns and imperfect competition built in. This effort, reported in Harris (1984) and Harris and Cox (1984), stands somewhat apart from much of the other literature reviewed here. Although some elements of the monopolistic competition model are present, the key to the results is the adoption of the Eastman-Stykolt pricing assumption, that firms are able to collude well enough to raise the domestic price to the foreign price plus tariff.

Given this assumption, it is naturally true that Canadian import-competing industries are found to have excessive entry and inefficiently small scale. The authors also offer a fairly complex analysis of pricing and entry in export markets, which leads them to believe that inefficient scale in Canadian export industries results from U.S. protection. Combining these effects, the authors find that the costs to Canada from its partial isolation from the U.S. market are several times higher than those estimated using conventional computable general equilibrium models. Thus the Harris-Cox analysis makes a strong case for free trade between the United States and Canada.

The Harris-Cox study has not yet been followed by a body of work that would enable us to evaluate the robustness of its conclusion. It is unclear, in particular, how much the assumption of collusion-*cum*-free-entry is driving the results; Would a noncooperative market structure still imply comparably large costs from protection? It is a fairly safe bet, however, that over the next few years workers in this area will attempt to fill in the space between Harris-Cox and the calibrated models, building more or loss general equilibrium models that also have some detailing of the process of competition in individual industries.

Evaluation

The attempts at quantification described here are obviously primitive and preliminary. However, the same could be said of attempts to apply industrial organization theory to purely domestic issues. The problem is that the sophistication of our models in general seems to have outrun our ability to match them up with data or evidence. The first efforts in this direction in international I-O are therefore welcome. One might hope that this effort will be aided by an interchange with conventional I-O research that poses similar issues, such as the analysis of the effects of mergers.

14.7 Concluding Comments

The rapid growth in the application of industrial organization concepts to international trade seems to be remaking trade theory in I-O's image. Traditional trade theory was, by the late 1970s, a powerful monolithic structure in which all issues were analyzed using variants of a single model. The new literature has successfully broken the grip of that single approach. Increasingly international economics, like industrial organization, is becoming a field where many models are taught and research is an eclectic mix of approaches.

This transformation of the subject has been extremely valuable in several ways. First of all, the fundamental insight is right—markets are often not perfectly competitive, and returns to scale are often not constant. Beyond this, the new approaches have brought excitement and creativity to an area that had begun to lose some of its intellectual drive.

At this point, however, the central problem of international trade is how to go beyond the proliferation of models to some kind of new synthesis. Probably trade theory will never be as unified as it was a decade ago, but it would be desirable to see empirical work begin to narrow the range of things that we regard as plausible outcomes.

Appendix: Some Basic Models

Applications of industrial organization to international trade so far rely on fairly simple models, so that it is still possible to describe most research in this field verbally and graphically. For completeness, however, this appendix offers formal presentations of simple versions of the two "workhorse"

models of the new field: the monopolistic competition model of international trade resulting from economies of scale and the homogeneous-
product duopoly model.

Monopolistic Competition

The simplest version of the monopolistic competition model of trade is one
in which there is only one factor of production and countries have identical
technologies, so that economies of scale are the only reason for trade. We
further assume that product differentiation takes the Spence-Dixit-Stiglitz
form in which each individual has a taste for variety, rather than letting the
demand for variety arise from difference between consumers. The model
can be further simplified by assuming particular forms for both production
and utility functions. The result is a "rock-bottom" model that reveals the
essentials of the approach in the simplest possible form.

Let us assume, then, that there is a very large number of potential
products N (it would be more rigorous to assume a continuum of products,
but this would complicate the exposition with no gain in insight). These
products enter symmetrically into the utility of all consumers, with the
utility function taking the specific convenient form

$$U = \sum_{i=1}^{N} c_i^{\theta}, \qquad 0 < \theta < 1, \tag{1}$$

where c_i is an individual's consumption of good i, and θ measures the
degree of substitution between varieties; note that (1) can be monotonically
transformed into a CES function with elasticity of substitution $1/(1 - \theta)$.

There is only one factor of production, labor. Not all goods will, in
general, be produced. For any good that is produced, the labor employed is

$$l_i = \alpha + \beta x_i, \qquad \alpha, \beta > 0, \tag{2}$$

where x_i is output of good i. The presence of the fixed cost α introduces
economies of scale into the model. As we will see, it is this fixed cost that
limits the number of varieties that any one country actually produces, and
therefore leads to both trade and gains from trade.

Let L be an economy's total labor force. Then full employment requires
that

$$L = \sum_{i=1}^{n} (\alpha + \beta x_i), \tag{3}$$

where n is the number of goods actually produced.

A Closed Economy

First, we consider equilibrium in a single economy that does not trade with the rest of the world. Each consumer will maximize welfare subject to his budget constraint; the first-order conditions from that maximization problem will take the form

$$\theta c_i^{\theta-1} = \lambda p_i, \tag{4}$$

where λ is the marginal utility of income. This may be rewritten in the form

$$c_i = \left[\left(\frac{\lambda}{\theta}\right)p_i\right]^{-1/(1-\theta)}. \tag{4'}$$

If the number of available products is sufficiently large, the marginal utiltiy of income of each will be negligibly affected by changes in its price, so that the demand for each good will have a constant elasticity $1/(1 - \theta)$.

Next we turn to the problem of firms. We begin by noting that as long as there are more potential varieties than are actually produced, there will be no reason for more than one firm to produce any given variety; since the varieties are symmetrical, a firm will always prefer to switch to a different variety rather than compete with another firm head to head. Thus each good will be produced by a monopolist. Since the monopolist faces demand with an elasticity $1/(1 - \theta)$, her optimal price is

$$p = \left(\frac{\beta}{\theta}\right)w, \tag{5}$$

where w is the wage rate. Notice that there is no subscript. Given the symmetry assumed among the goods, they will all have the same price, p. We can choose labor as the numéraire and write the price equation as

$$\frac{p}{w} = \frac{\beta}{\theta}. \tag{5'}$$

Next we introduce the possibility of entry and exit. If firms are free to enter and exit, and we ignore integer constraints, then profits will be driven to zero. But the profits of a representative firm are

$$\pi = (p - \beta w)x - \alpha w, \tag{6}$$

or

$$\frac{\pi}{w} = \frac{p}{w} - \beta x - \alpha = 0.$$

This implies that the output of a representative firm is

$$x = \frac{\alpha \theta}{\beta(1 - \theta)}. \tag{7}$$

Using the full-employment condition, we can then conclude that the number of firms, which is also the number of goods actually produced, is

$$n = \frac{L}{\alpha + \beta x} = \frac{L(1 - \theta)}{\alpha}. \tag{8}$$

Note that it is the fixed cost α that limits the number of goods produced. If there were no fixed cost, or the fixed cost were very small, the product space would become saturated, and our assumption that each good is produced by a single firm would break down.

Also note that although we can determine the *number* of goods n that is produced, we cannot determine *which* n goods are produced. This indeterminacy cannot be eliminated without spoiling the simplicity of the model. It arises precisely because of the assumed symmetry of the goods, which in turn is what allows us to find a zero-profit equilibrium.

Finall, we can determine the utility of a representative household. Let us assume that each household owns one unit of labor. Then it is has an income w, which it will divide equally among all available products. Utility is therefore

$$U = n \left(\frac{w}{np} \right)^{\theta} = \left(\frac{w}{p} \right) n^{1-\theta} = \left(\frac{\theta}{\beta} \right) n^{1-\theta}. \tag{9}$$

Welfare is therefore increasing in the number of goods available.

A Trading World

Now consider a world of two countries: Home, with a labor force L, and Foreign, with a labor force L^*. In the absence of trade, each of these countries would be described by the analysis just developed. Suppose, however, that the countries are able to trade with each other at zero cost. Then wages will be equalized, and the countries will in effect constitute a single larger economy with a labor force $L + L^*$. Home will produce $n = L(1 - \theta)/\alpha$ goods, and Foreign $n^* = L^*(1 - \theta)/\alpha$ goods. Since firms will still never compete over a market, these will be different goods—that is each good that is produced will be produced in only one country. Thus the countries will be specialized in producing different ranges of goods, and will trade with each other.

There are three important points to note about this trade: First, since it is indeterminate who produces what, the pattern of trade is indeterminate. We know that the countries specialize, but not in what. This indeterminacy is at first disturbing, but it is characteristic of models with increasing returns.

Second, although the pattern of trade is indeterminate, the volume of trade is fully determined. Each household will spend the same share of income on each good, and each household will spend a share $n/(n + n^*)$ on Home-produced goods, and $n^*/(n + n^*)$ on Foreign goods. The total income of Home is wL, and the total income of Foreign wL^*. Thus the value of Home's imports from Foreign is $wLL^*/(L + L^*)$, which is also the value of Foreign's imports from Home. Trade is balanced, as it must be in a model with not saving.

Finally, trade is mutually beneficial. In the absence of trade, Home households would have had only n products available; as a result of trade, the number available increases to $(n + n^*)$. Letting U_A be welfare in the absence of trade and U_T be welfare with trade, we have

$$\frac{U_T}{U_A} = \left(\frac{n + n^*}{n}\right)^{1-\theta} > 1. \tag{10}$$

Foreign households similarly gain. Note that the gain from trade is larger, the smaller is θ (i.e., the greater the gains from variety).

Homogeneous Product Duopoly

The other most widely used model in applications of industrial orgainzation to international economics is the simple model of homogeneous product duopoly. This model can be used to demonstrate the procompetitive effect of trade, the motivations behind dumping, the potential for strategic trade policy, and the possibility that protection promotes exports. I present here a simple linear version and then indicate how it can be extended.

Suppose that there are two countries, Home and Foreign, that both demand some product. For simplicity, they will be assumed to have identical, linear demand curves, which we write in inverse form as

$$p = A - Bz, \tag{11}$$

$$p^* = A - Bz^*, \tag{12}$$

where z, z^* are total deliveries to the Home and Foreign markets, respectively.

Each of the countries is also the base of a single firm producing the good. Each firm can deliver to either country; we let x be the Home firm's deliveries to its own market, and x^* its deliveries to the Foreign market. Then its costs will depend on its shipments,

$$C = F + cx + (c + t)x^*, \tag{13}$$

where marginal cost is for the moment assumed constant, and t may be interpreted as transport cost. Also let y be the Foreign firm's deliveries to the Home market, and y^* its deliveries to its own market; if the firms have identical costs, we then have

$$C^* = F + cy^* + (c + t)y. \tag{14}$$

In the absence of trade, each firm would be a monopolist, and we would have $z = x$ and $z^* = y^*$. In that case it is straightforward to see that the price in each market would be

$$p = c + \frac{A - c}{2}. \tag{15}$$

If the markup $(A - c)/2$ exceeds the transport cost t, however, each firm will have an incentive to ship into the other firm's market, since it will be able to sell goods there at above its marginal cost of delivery. Thus we need to analyze an equilibrium in which each firm may ship to both markets, and therefore

$$z = x + y, \tag{16}$$

$$z^* = x^* + y^*. \tag{17}$$

Each firm must choose its levels of shipments to each market based on its beliefs about the other firm's actions. The simplest assumption is that each firm takes the other firm's deliveries to *each* market as given—the Home firm maximizes profits, taking y and y^* as given, and vice versa. Then the model breaks into two separate Cournot games in the two markets. Since these games are symmetric, it is sufficient to examine only what happens in the Home market. The Home firm's reaction function is

$$x = \frac{A - c}{2B} = \frac{y}{2}, \tag{18}$$

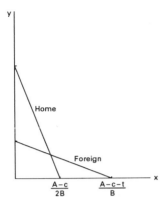

Figure 14.15

whereas the Foreign firm's reaction function is

$$y = \frac{A - c - t}{2B} = \frac{x}{2}. \tag{19}$$

These reaction functions are shown in figure 14.15. Note that there is a positive intersection if and only if $(A − c)/2 > t$ that is, if the monopoly markup in the absence of trade of trade would have exceeded the transport cost.

If there is a positive intersection, there will be trade. That is, the Foreign firm will have positive sales in the Home market. Given the symmetry of the markets, furthermore this will be two-way trade in the same product: the Home firm will ship the same product to the Foreign market.

Interpretation and Effects of Trade

We have described this trade as "reciprocal dumping." In what sense is this dumping? The point is that the price that each firm receives on its export sales is the same that it receives on domestic sales, and therefore it does not compensate for transport cost. Equivalently, we can observe that if the firm simply sold all its output at a fixed price at the factory gate, private shippers would not find it profitable to export. It is only because the firm is willing to absorb the transport cost, receiving a lower net price on export sales than on domestic sales, that trade takes place.

Why are firms willing to do this? *Price* net of transport cost is lower on export sales than on domestic sales. In equilibrium, however, each firm will have a smaller share of its export market than of its domestic market and will therefore perceive itself as facing a higher elasticity of demand abroad than at home. This is what makes the marginal revenue on export sales equal that on domestic sales, despite the lower net price.

What are the effects of this seemingly pointless trade? First, it unambiguously lowers the price in both markets and hence raises consumer surplus. This procompetitive effect is strongest in the case of zero transport costs, in which the markup over marginal cost falls from $(A - c)/2$ to $(A - c)/4$ as a result of trade.

Second, trade leads to a waste of resources in seemingly pointless cross-hauling of an identical product—except in the case where transport costs are zero.

Finally, trade leads to a fall in profits both because the price falls and because firms incur transport expenses.

The net welfare effect is ambiguous, except in the case of zero transport cost. The procompetitive effect reduces the monopoly distortion, but against this must be set the waste of resources in transportation. For this linear model, it is possible to show that trade leads to gains if t is close to zero, but to losses if t is close to $(A - c)/2$, the monopoly markup in the absence of trade.

Extensions

One extension is to add government policy to the model, in the form of a tax on imports, a subsidy on exports, and so forth. The simplest Brander-Spencer model takes this basic framework but assumes that, instead of selling to each other, both countries sell to a third market. This means that each country's welfare can be identified with the profits earned from these exports. It is then straightforward to show that an export subsidy will raise profits at the expense of the other country.

A second extension is to vary the linear cost function. Specifically, assume that each firm's costs take the form

$$C = C(x + x^*) + tx^*, \tag{20}$$

with $C'' < 0$, declining marginal costs. This now introduces an interdependence between the two markets: the more the Home firms sells in one market, the lower are its marginal costs of shipment to the other market. In this case protection of the domestic market has the effect of increasing exports. A tariff or import quota increases the protected firm's sales in its domestic market while lowering the sales of its rival. This in turn lowers the marginal cost of the protected firm, raises the marginal cost of the other firm, and thus leads to a rise in sales abroad as well as at home.

References

Axelrod, R. 1983. *The Evolution of Cooperation*. New York: Basic Books.

Balassa, B. 1966. "Tariff Reductions and Trade in Manufactures." *American Economic Review*, 56: 466–473.

Balassa, B. 1967. *Trade Liberalization among Industrial Countries: Objectives and Alternatives*. New York: McGraw-Hill.

Baldwin, R. and P. R. Krugman. 1988. "Market Access and International Competition: A Simulation Study of 16K Random Access Memories." In R. Feenstra (ed), *Empirical Research in International Trade*. Cambridge: MIT Press.

Baran, P. 1957. *The Political Economy of Growth*. New York: Monthly Review Press.

Bardhan, P. 1970. *Economic Growth, Development, and Foreign Trade*. New York: Wiley.

Barker, T. 1977. "International Trade and Economic Growth: An Alternative to the Neoclassical Approach", *Cambridge Journal of Economics* 1, 2: 153–172.

Baumol, W. J., J. C. Panzar, and R. D. Willig. 1982. *Contestable Markets and the Theory of Industry Structure*. New York: Harcourt Brace Jovanovich.

Bhagwati, J. 1965. "On the Equivalence of Tariffs and Quotas." In R. E. Baldwin (ed.), *Trade, Growth, and the Balance of Payments*. Amsterdam: North-Holland.

Brander, J. A. 1981. "Intra-industry Trade in Identical Commodities." *Journal of International Economics* 11: 1–14.

Brander, J. A., and P. R. Krugman. 1983. "A 'Reciprocal Dumping' Model of International Trade." *Journal of International Economics* 15: 313–321.

Brander, J. A., and B. J. Spencer. 1981. "Tariffs and the Extraction of Foreign Monopoly Rents under Potential Entry." *Canadian Journal of Economics* 14: 371–389.

Brander, J. A., and B. J. Spencer. 1983. "International R&D Rivalry and Industrial Strategy." *Review of Economic Studies* 50: 707–722.

Brander, J. A., and B. J. Spencer 1984. "Tariff Protection and Imperfect Competition." In H. Kierzkowski (ed.), *Monopolistic Competition and International Trade*. Oxford: Oxford University Press.

Brander, J. A., and B. J. Spencer. 1985. "Export Subsidies and International Market Share Rivalry." *Journal of International Economics* 18: 83–100.

Burenstam-Linder, S. 1961. *An Essay on Trade and Transformation*, New York: Praeger.

Caves, R. E. 1974. *International Trade, International Investment, and Imperfect Markets*. Princeton Special Papers in International Economics No. 10. Princeton University.

Caves, R. E., and R. W. Jones. 1985. *World Trade and Payments*. Boston: Little Brown.

Chacholiades, M. 1970. "Increasing Returns and the Theory of Comparative Advantage." *Southern Economic Journal* 37, 2: 157–162.

Chacholiades, M. 1978. *International Trade: Theory and Policy*. New York: McGraw-Hill.

Chamberlin, E. 1962. *The Theory of Monopolistic Competition*. Cambridge: Harvard University Press.

Chrystal, K. A. 1977. "Demand for International Media of Exchange." *American Economic Review*, December 67: 840–1850.

Corden, W. M. 1967, "Monopoly, Tariffs and subsidies." *Economica* 34: 59–68.

Corden, W. M. 1970. "A Note on Economies of Scale, the Size of the Domestic Market and the Pattern of Trade." In I. A. McDougall and R. H. Snape (eds.), *Studies in International Economics*. Amsterdam: North-Holland.

Corden, W. M. 1974 *Trade Policy and Economic Welfare*. Oxford: Clarendon.

Corden, W. M. 1982. "Booming Sector and De-industrialization in a Small Open Economy." *Economic Journal* 92: 825–848.

Davidson, C. 1984. "Cartel Stability and Trade Policy." *Journal of International Economics* 17: 219–237.

Dixit, A. K. 1984. "International trade Policy for Oligopolistic Industries." *Economic Journal*, supplement, 1–16.

Dixit, A. K. 1987. "Strategic Aspects of Trade Policy." In T. F. Bewley (ed.) *Advances in Economic Theory, Fifth World Congress*. Cambridge: Cambridge University Press, 329–362.

Dixit, A. K. 1988, "Optimal trade and Industrial Policy for the U.S. Automobile Industry." In R. Feenstra (ed.), *Empirical Methods for International Trade*. Cambridge: MIT Press.

Dixit, A. K. 1989. "The Cutting Edge of International Technological Competition." *American Economic Review*, forthcoming.

Dixit, A. K., and G. M. Grossman. 1984. "Targeted Export Promotion with Several Oligopolistic Industries." Discussion Paper in Economics No. 71. Woodrow Wilson School, Princeton University.

Dixit, A. K., and A. S. Kyle. 1985. "The Use of Protection or Subsidies for Entry Promotion and Deterrence." *American Economic Review* 75: 139–152.

Dixit, A. K., and V. Norman. 1980. *Theory of International Trade*. Cambridge: Cambridge University Press.

Dixit, A. K., and J. E. Stiglitz. 1977. "Monopolistic Competition and Optimum Product Diversity." *American Economic Review* (June), 67: 297–308.

Dollar, D. 1986. "Technological Innovation, Capital Mobility, and the Product Cycle in North–South Trade." *American Economic Review* 76: 177–190.

Dornbusch, R., S. Fischer and P. Samuelson. 1977. "Comparative Advantage, Trade and Payments in a Ricardian Model with a Continuum of Goods." *American Economic Review* December 67: 823–839.

Eastman, H., and S. Stykolt. 1960. "A Model for the Study of Protected Oligopolies." *Economic Journal* 70: 336–347.

Eaton, J., and G. M. Grossman. 1986. "Optimal trade and Industrial Policy under Oligopoly." *Quarterly Journal of Economics* (May), 2: 383–406.

Ethier, W. 1979. "Internationally Decreasing Costs and World Trade." *Journal of International Economics* (February), 9: 1–24.

Ethier, W. 1982. "Dumping." *Journal of Political Economy* 90: 487–506.

Ethier, W. 1982a. "Decreasing Costs in International Trade and Frank Graham's Argument for Protection." *Econometrica* 50: 1243–1268.

Ethier, W. 1982b. "National and International Returns to Scale in the Modern Theory of International Trade." *American Economic Review* 72: 389–405.

Feenstra, R., and K. Judd. 1982. "Tariffs, Technology Transfer, and Welfare." *Journal of Political Economy* 90: 1142–1165.

Findlay, R. 1978. "Relative Backwardness, Direct Foreign Investment, and the Transfer of Technology: A Simple Dynamic Model." *Quarterly Journal of Economics* (February), 92: 1–16.

Findlay, R., and H. Grubert. 1959. "Factor Intensities, Technological Progress, and the Terms of trade." *Oxford Economic Papers* 11: 111–112.

Frank, A. G. 1967. *Capitalism and Underdevelopment in Latin America*. New York: Monthly Review Press.

Frankel, J. 1983. "The Desirability of a Dollar Appreciation Given a Contractionary US Monetary Policy." National Bureau of Economic Research Working Paper No. 1110.

Friedman, J. W. 1977. *Oligopoly and the Theory of Games.* Amsterdam: North-Holland.

Givens, N. L. 1982. "The US Can No Longer Afford Free Trade." *Business Week* (November) 22: 15.

Graham, F. 1923. "Some Aspects of Protection Further Considered." *Quarterly Journal of Economics* 37: 199–227.

Gray, P. 1973. "Two-Way International Trade in Manufactures: A Theoretical Underpinning." *Weltwirtschaftliches Archiv* 109: 19–39.

Grossman, G., and E. Helpman. 1988. "Product Development and International Trade." Mimeo.

Grubel, H. G. 1967. "Intra-industry Specialization and the Pattern of Trade." *Canadian Journal of Economics* August, 33: 374–388.

Grubel, H. G. 1970. "The Theory of Intra-industry Trade." In I. A. McDougall and R. H. Snape (ed.), *Studies in International Economics.* Amsterdam: North-Holland.

Grubel, H. G., and P. J. Lloyd. 1975. *Intra-industry Trade: The Theory and Measurement of International Trade in Differentiated Products.* New York: Wiley.

Harris, R. 1984. "Applied General Equilibrium Analysis of Small Open Economies with Scale Economies and Imperfect Competition." *American Economic Review* 74: 1016–1033.

Harris, R., and D. Cox. 1984. *Trade, Industrial Policy, and Canadian Manufacturing.* Toronto: University of Toronto Press.

Havrylyshyn, D., and E. Divan. 1984. "Intra-industry Trade and the State of Development." In P. K. M. Tharakan (ed.), *The Economics of Intra-industry Trade.* Amsterdam: North-Holland.

Helpman, E. 1981. "International Trade in the Presence of Product Differentiation, Economies of Scale, and Monopolistic Competition: A Chamberlinian-Heckscher-Ohlin Approcah." *Journal of International Economics* 11: 305–340.

Helpman, E. 1982. "Increasing Returns, Imperfect Markets, and Trade Theory." Discussion Paper. Tel Aviv University.

Helpman, E. 1984. "A Simple Theory of Trade with Multinational Corporations." *Journal of Political Economy* 92: 451–472.

Helpman, E. 1988. "Imperfect Competition and International Trade: Evidence From Fourteen Industrial Countries." In H. Hazard and A. M. Spence (ed.), *International Competitiveness.* Cambridge: Harvard University Press.

Helpman, E. 1985. "International Trade in Differentiated Middle Products." In D. Hague and K. G. Jungenfeldt (ed.), *Structural Adjustment in Developed Open Economies*. New York: Macmillan.

Helpman, E. 1988. "Growth, Technological Progress and Trade." Mimeo.

Helpman, E., and P. R. Krugman. 1985. *Market Structure and Foreign Trade: Increasing Returns, Imperfect Competition, and the International Economy*. Cambridge: MIT Press.

Helpman, E., and A. Razin. 1984. "Increasing Returns, Monopolistic Competition, and Factor Movements: A Welfare Analysis." In H. Kierzkowski (ed.), *Monopolistic Competition and International Trade*, Oxford: Oxford University Press.

Hirsch, S. 1974. "Hypotheses Regarding Trade between Developing and Industrial Countries." In H. Giersch (ed.), *The International Division of Labor*. Tubinger: Mohr.

Hobson, J. A. 1902. *Imperialism: A Study*. London: Nibset.

Horstmann, I., and J. R. Markusen. 1986. "Up Your Average Cost Curve: Inefficient Entry and the New Protectionism." *Journal of International Economics* (May), 20: 225–248.

Hufbauer, G. 1964. *Synthetic Materials and the Theory of International Trade*. Cambridge: Harvard University Press.

Hufbauer G., and J. G. Chilas. 1974. "Specialization by Industrial Countries: Extent and Consequences." In H. Giersch (ed.), *The International Division of Labour: Problems and Perspectives*. Kiel: Institut für Weltwirtschaft.

Jensen, R., and M. Thursby. 1989. "Strategic Approach to the Product Life Cycle." *Journal of International Economics*, forthcoming.

Jevons, S. 1895. *Money and the Mechanism of Exchange*. London: Appleton.

Jones, R. A. 1965. "The Structure of Simple General Equilibrium Models." *Journal of Political Economy* (December), 73: 6.

Jones, R. A. 1970. "The Role of Technology in the Theory of International Trade." In R. Vernon (ed.), *The Technology Factor in International Trade*. New York: National Bureau of Economic Research.

Jones, R. A. 1976. "The Origin and Development of Media of Exchange." *Journal of Political Economy* (August), 84: 757–776.

Kemp, M. 1964. *The Pure Theory of International Trade*. Englewood Cliffs, NJ: Prentice-Hall.

Kemp, M., and T. Negishi. 1970. "Variable Returns to Scale, Commodity Taxes, Factor Market Distortions, and Their Implications for Trade Gains." *Swedish Journal of Economics* 72: 1–11.

Kierzkowski, H. (ed.). 1984. *Monopolistic Competition and International Trade*. Oxford: Oxford University Press.

Kindleberger, C. 1967. "The Politics of International Money and World Language." *Princeton Essays in International Finance*, 61.

Kindleberger, C. 1973. *International Economics*. Homewood, IL: Irwin.

Kohn, M., and N. Marion. 1987. "The Implications of Knowledge-Based Growth for the Optimality of Open Capital Markets." Mimeo.

Kravis, I. 1971. "The Current Case for Import Limitations," in Commission on International Trade and Investment Policy. *United States Economic Policy in an Interdependent World*. Washington: Government Printing Office.

Krishna, K. 1989. "Trade Restrictions as Facilitating Practices." *Journal of International Economics*, forthcoming.

Krugman, P. R. 1979. "Increasing Returns, Monopolistic Competition, and International Trade." *Journal of International Economics* (November), 9: 469–479.

Krugman, P. R. 1980. "Scale Economies, Product Differentiation, and the Pattern of Trade." *American Economic Review* 70: 950–959.

Krugman, P. R. 1981. "Intraindustry Specialization and the Gains from Trade." *Journal of Political Economy* 89: 959–973.

Krugman, P. R. 1982. "The New Theories of International Trade and the Multinational Corporation", in D. Audretsch and C. Kindleberger, eds., *The Multinational Corporation in the 1980's*, Cambridge: MIT Press.

Krugman, P. R. 1984a. "Growth, Trade, and Income Distribution under Increasing Returns." Mimeo.

Krugman, P. R. 1984b. "Import Protection as Export Promotion: International Competition in the Presence of Oligopolies and Economies of Scale." In H. Kierzkowski (ed.), *Monopolistic Competition and International Trade*. Oxford: Oxford University Press.

Krugman, P. R. 1984c. "The US Response to Foreign Industrial Targeting." *Brookings Papers on Economic Activity* 1984: 1, 77–131.

Krugman, P. R. (ed.). 1986. *Strategic Trade Policy and the New International Economics*. Cambridge: MIT Press.

Krugman, P. R. 1989 "Industrial Organization and International Trade." In R. Schmalensee and R. Willig (eds.), *Handbook of Industrial Organization*. Amsterdam: North-Holland.

Kubarych, R. M. 1978. "Foreign Exchange Markets in the United States." Federal Reserve Bank of New York.

Lancaster, K. 1979. *Variety, Equity and Efficiency*. New York: Columbia University Press.

Lancaster, K. 1980. "Intra-industry Trade under Perfect Monopolistic Competition." *Journal of International Economics* 10: 151–175.

Lenin, V. I. 1939. *Imperialism, the Highest Stage of Capitalism*. New York: International Publishers.

Lewis, W. A. 1977. *The Evolution of the International Economic Order*. Princeton: Princeton University Press.

Linder, S. B. 1961. *An Essay on Trade and Transformation*. New York: Wiley.

Loertscher, R., and F. Wolter. 1980. "Determinants of Intra-industry Trade: Among Countries and Across Industries." *Weltwirtschaftliches Archiv* 8: 280–293.

Lucas, R. 1985. "On the Mechanics of Economic Development." Marshall Lecture.

Matthews, R. C. O. 1949. "Reciprocal Demand and Increasing Returns." *Review of Economic Studies* 37: 149–158.

McKenzie, L. 1953. "Specialization and Efficiency in World Production." *Oxford Economic Papers*, 5.

McKinnon, R. I. 1969. "Private and Official International Money: The Case for the Dollar." *Princeton Essays in International Finance*, 74.

Melvin, J. 1969. "Increasing Returns to Scale as a Determinant of Trade." *Canadian Journal of Economics* 2, 3: 389–402.

Menger, K. 1892. "On the Origins of Money." *Economic Journal* (June), 2: 239–255.

Mundell, R. 1957. "International Trade and Factor Mobility." *American Economic Review* 47: 321–335.

Murphy, K., A. Shleifer, and R. Vishny. 1988. "Industrialization and the Big Push." Mimeo. Graduate School of Business, University of Chicago.

Myrdal, G. 1957. *Economic Theory and Under-developed Regions*. London: Duckworth.

Negishi, T. 1969. "Marshallian External Economies and Gains from Trade between Similar countries." *Review of Economic Studies* 36: 131–135.

Negishi, T. 1972. *General Equilibrium Theory and International Trade*. Amsterdam: North-Holland.

Niehans, J. 1969. "Money in a Static Theory of Optimal Payment Arrangements." *Journal of Money, Credit and Banking* (November), 1: 796–826.

Nordhaus, W. 1969. *Invention, Growth, and Welfare: A Theoretical Treatment of technological Change*. Cambridge: MIT Press.

Ohlin, B. 1933. *Interregional and International Trade*. Cambridge: Harvard University Press.

Panagariya, A. 1981. "Variable Returns to Scale in Production and Patterns of Specialization." *American Economic Review* 71: 221–230.

Posner, M. V. 1961. "International Trade and Technical Change." *Oxford Economic Papers* 13: 323–341.

Rodrik, D. 1987. "Imperfect Competition and Trade Policy in Developing Countries." Mimeo. Harvard University.

Romer, P, 1986a. "Increasing Returns and Long-Run Growth." *Journal of Political Economy* 94: 1002–1038.

Romer, P. 1986b. "Increasing Returns, Specialization, and External Economies: Growth as Described by Allyn Young." Mimeo.

Roosa, R. V., and F. Hirsch. 1966. "Reserves, Reserve Currencies and Vehicle Currencies: An Argument." *Princeton Essays in International Finance*, 54.

Rotemberg, J., and G. Saloner. 1986. "Quotas and the Stability of Implicit Collusion." Mimeo. MIT.

Rousslang, D. J., and J. W. Suomela. 1985. "Calculating the Consumer and Net Welfare Costs of Import Relief." US International Trade Commission Staff Research Study No. 15.

Schumpeter, J. 1942. *Capitalism, Socialism and Democracy*. New York.

Seade, J. 1980. "On the Effects of Entry." *Econometrica* 48: 479–489.

Segerstrom, P., T. Anant, and E. Dinopoulos. 1987. "A Schumpeterian Model of the Product Life Cycle." Mimeo.

Shleifer, A. 1986. "Implementation Cycles." *Journal of Political Economy* 94: 1163–1190.

Smithies, A. 1942. "An Economic Analysis of the Basing-Point System." *American Economic Review* 32: 705–726.

Spence, A. M. 1976. "Product Selection, Fixed Costs, and Monopolistic Competition." *Review of Economic Studies* 43: 217–236.

Spence, A. M. 1981. "The Learning Curve and Competition." *Bell Journal of Economics* 12: 49–70.

Sutcliffe, B. 1972. "Imperialism and Industrialization in the Third World", in: B. Sutcliffe and R. Owen (eds.), *Studies in the Theory of Imperialism*. London: Longman.

Swoboda, A. 1968. "The Eurodollar Market: An Interpretation." *Princeton Essays in International Finance*, 64.

Swoboda, A. 1969. "Vehicle Currencies and the Foreign Exchange Market: The Case of the Dollar." In R. Z. Alliber (ed.), *The International Market for Foreign Exchange*. New York: Praeger.

Van Wijnbergen, S. 1984. "The Dutch Disease: A Disease After All." *Economic Journal* 94: 41–55.

Venables, A. J. 1985a. "Trade and Trade Policy with Imperfect Competition: The Case of Identical Products and Free Entry." *Journal of International Economics* 19: 1–19.

Venables, A. J. 1985b. "Trade and Trade Policy with Differentiated Products: A Chamberlinian-Ricardian Model." Mimeo. Sussex.

Venables, A. J., and A. Smith. 1986. "Trade and Industrial Policy under Imperfect Competition." *Economic Policy* 3: 621–672.

Vernon, R. 1966. "International Investment and International Trade in the Product Cycle." *Quarterly Journal of Economics* (May), 80: 190–207.

Wallerstein, I. 1974. *The Modern World-System*. New York: Academic Press.

Wilson, C. 1980. "On the General Structure of Ricardian Models with a Continuum of Goods." *Econometrica* (November), 48.

Yeager, L. B. 1976. *International Monetary Relations: Theory, History and Policy*. New York: Harper & Row.

Young, A. 1928. "Increasing Returns and Economic Progress." *Economic Journal* 38: 527–542.

Index